# Transforming Professional in Education

Focusing on teaching and learning in educational institutions, *Transforming Professional Practice in Education* explores the value of enhancing dialogue to improve both professional relationships and practices. Offering a critique of the present state of education, this book focuses on the belief that education should be about being and becoming human, and how everyone implicated in education learns through dialogue with others, and that humans are relational beings who develop and flourish within reciprocal relationships.

The authors offer an alternative to reductive and systems-driven procedures by building a case for psychologically robust educational methods. They provide an authoritative and theoretically well-grounded rationale for psychological approaches to professional practice to promote debate about the purposes of education. Rich with practical examples, the chapters discuss the risks of professional isolation, ethics vs morals in education, the nature of relationships in education, and interventions that would ground these ideas in practice.

This book is important reading for clinical, educational, and other applied psychologists. It is also of value to those within educational institutions, such as SENDCos, and those responsible for the safety of children and young people, who are seeking to develop their understanding of how dialogue enhances professional encounters, and who are looking for alternative ways of engaging with education, which improve mental health and wellbeing.

**Simon Gibbs** is Professor Emeritus of Inclusive Educational Psychology and Philosophy at the University of Newcastle.

**David Leat** is a professor of Curriculum Innovation at the University of Newcastle.

**Wilma Barrow** is a senior lecturer in Educational Psychology at the University of Newcastle.

# Transforming Professional Practice in Education

Psychology, Dialogue, and the Practice of Becoming Human

**Simon Gibbs, David Leat, and Wilma Barrow**

Routledge
Taylor & Francis Group

LONDON AND NEW YORK

Cover image: 'Dialogue' by Yulduskhon

First published 2023
by Routledge
4 Park Square, Milton Park, Abingdon, Oxon OX14 4RN

and by Routledge
605 Third Avenue, New York, NY 10158

*Routledge is an imprint of the Taylor & Francis Group, an informa business*

*British Library Cataloguing-in-Publication Data*
A catalogue record for this book is available from the British Library

*Library of Congress Cataloging-in-Publication Data*
Names: Gibbs, Simon, 1948– author. | Leat, David, author. | Barrow, Wilma, author.
Title: Transforming professional practice in education : psychology, dialogue and the
practice of becoming human / Simon Gibbs, David Leat, Wilma Barrow.
Description: Abingdon, Oxon ; New York, NY : Routledge, 2023. |
Includes bibliographical references and index. |
Identifiers: LCCN 2022028101 (print) | LCCN 2022028102 (ebook) |
ISBN 9780367360917 (paperback) | ISBN 9780367360900 (hardback) |
ISBN 9780429343766 (ebook)
Subjects: LCSH: Teaching–Psychological aspects. |
Teachers–Professional relationships. | Teacher-student relationships. |
Communication in education.
Classification: LCC LB1027 .G53 2023 (print) |
LCC LB1027 (ebook) | DDC 371.102–dc23/eng/20220720
LC record available at https://lccn.loc.gov/2022028101
LC ebook record available at https://lccn.loc.gov/2022028102

ISBN: 9780367360900 (hbk)
ISBN: 9780367360917 (pbk)
ISBN: 9780429343766 (ebk)

DOI: 10.4324/9780429343766

Typeset in Bembo
by Newgen Publishing UK

# Contents

# Introduction

We have written this in a world in crisis. The future of humanity as a species is threatened. While politicians, economists, and entrepreneurs continue to fail to avert global disasters, we wonder if there is a better role for education and educators. It seems to us that the state of education and what it does *for* and *to* those involved in it, and what it *could* do for the future is of crucial importance for the future of civilisation. In the following chapters, we hope to encourage all those involved in education to pause, stop what they have been doing, reflect on the nature and purpose of education, and discuss amongst themselves how it may be possible and appropriate to contribute to a purpose that might be of greater value to society at large. We will, by drawing attention to what is perhaps too often taken for granted – the place for and effect of interpersonal relationships and dialogue in educational settings – consider what psychological ideas and understandings can bring to education and the work of educators. Although relationships can be taken for granted, we fear that there are times (and places) in education at present when the importance of good relationships is denied and supplanted by a culture of performativity and a concern for academic attainments, as if they alone mattered (Ball, 2003; Lyotard, 1984). Cumulatively, we seek to challenge this dominant narrative here by promoting debate and reform of the central purposes of education. However, this entails other issues, and foremost for us is the fundamental need to challenge the hegemony of the individualistic ontology (how we view ourselves) that still dominates much of science (including psychology) and philosophy, in favour of a relational ontology. In the words of Nel Noddings (1990, p. 124):

> The basic nature of relation is to create new, exciting, more complex and wonderful entities. In mathematics, for example, we create rational numbers from a relation of integers, complex numbers out of a relation of reals, etc. What emerges from the relation is something qualitatively different from the elements that entered it. When we define human beings as relations, then, we see that – strictly speaking – we are not monadic; what we do for "others" we do, in part at least, for ourselves because "we" are products of relation, not mere constituent parts.

DOI: 10.4324/9780429343766-1

While we don't intend or want to prescribe or presume what the outcome of a public debate about the role and purposes of education in schools might be, we do have some thoughts about what might be deemed important characteristics of schools and practices therein. We aren't great believers in chaos and understand that many will say "please leave education alone, we don't need any more changes." Of course we recognise that in helping young people develop there is a need for them – and their teachers – to know they are safe; individually and collectively cared for. We suggest, therefore, that schools need to be well organised and led, and part of a collective shared network and ethos. We agree with others that the current environment for education is unhelpful (see, for instance, Brighouse & Waters, 2022 for a recent overview). There is, as is increasingly obvious, nothing to be gained by anyone if schools are, as they are, in market-oriented competition with each other (Jha, 2020; Parding, McGrath-Champ, & Stacey, 2017; Zancajo, 2020). However, in and amongst schools that are part of a network (such as a local authority or, perhaps a multi-academy trust) we would hope that collaboration, cooperation and reciprocity would be deeply embedded at all levels as suggested by Duffy and Gallagher (2014). This should, we think, help to mitigate the negative and corrosive effects of power and competition that demeans and derogates "others" who are, according to some metric, less successful. The collective ethos we envision would provide an environment in which all (young people, parents, staff, and other professionals) would feel able to celebrate individual and collective creative endeavours, to engage with each other to examine and be accountable to each other for their experiences and inquiries.

In what follows therefore, we present ideas about how people in education can work together professionally and democratically[1]. What we want to say is grounded in our own diverse experiences of working in education, and although at times what we say may seem rather theoretical, or even idealistic, it all arises from our growing concern that humanity and "good education" (Biesta, 2015) are in peril. Our central intention is to set out why educational dialogues amongst people talking and working together are crucial but also, as we will explain later, how important and valuable is the creation of "psychological space" within dialogues in which new ideas can emerge. Accordingly, in our exploration of human relationships we will base what we seek to discuss with reference to psychological theories and evidence. Because of the inherent complexities of psychological theories and evidence (and, we freely admit, some of the provisionality of it), this also requires us to offer a meta-perspective on the application of psychology. We will attempt to do this by considering a philosophical critique of the ways in which psychology may be applied educationally.

Before going any further, a note is in order regarding our own personal epistemological and methodological positions that may be traced in our personal histories that will emerge as recurring themes throughout the book. In our separate backgrounds we have in the past gained qualifications in chemistry, education, geography, mathematics and psychology. At the time (some several decades have passed) work in these fields was heavily influenced by the paradigms of "natural" science with all the certainties and positivity of those disciplines. Now that we are students of social sciences we can recognise that what we are also interested in are the "Sciences of the Artificial" that were outlined by Herb Simon (1996). In his book Simon proposed that rather than, as natural scientists do (in say, the fields of chemistry or geology), seek understanding of how natural objects and phenomena (earthquakes, heat, and water, for example) behave and interact, we scientists of the artificial are interested in the phenomena that emerge at the interface of systems (be they objects, organisms, or organisations). Simon (p. 52) offered a simple parable to illustrate his notion:

> An ant, viewed as a behaving system, is quite simple. The apparent complexity of its behaviour over time is largely a reflection of the complexity of the environment in which it finds itself.

Unlike the objectified, individualised ant in Simon's parable (we admit that, at least for the sake of argument, here we may only view the ant as a relatively unselfconscious organism interacting in an ad hoc manner with its environment), we suggest we might take a view of ourselves, human beings, as being imaginative and conscious of and, hopefully, respectful of others' autonomy and self-determination. Thus, reflecting on the diversity of our human environment and some of the systems in which we play a part, we will suggest that we could "redesign" how we consciously and thoughtfully respond to and learn from at least one component or aspect of our environment (education). As we will discuss in Chapter 7, a strategic change in education could mediate our understanding of and ability to change how we interact with the complexity of other less tangible and apparently insurmountable systems (such as global disease, poverty, or warming) that directly or indirectly affect what we do with each other in our social – and material – worlds. We don't naively propose a direct, simple causal link between what could happen in our schools and mitigation of global poverty; there are more immediately pressing serious "local" issues (such as the effects of socio-economic poverty, housing, marital disputes, and child abuse) that have to be addressed by staff in schools. But we do hope – and believe – that the central concerns of our thesis, how we learn to co-exist with others and what that might entail for educationalists, does have a bearing on local and, therefore, ultimately global societies.

In a commentary on Simon's work, and in particular his view of the "Architecture of Complexity," Philip Agre (2003) perceived a tension (unacknowledged by Simon himself) between the apparently static nature of hierarchical systems (as seen in many organisations), and the notions of dynamic self-organising systems (evident in neoliberal market economies) developed by general systems theorists (such as Contractor, 1999; Morgan, 1998; Senge, 2006). We are with Agre (2003, pp. 422–3) in accepting that the phenomena of hierarchy and self-organization are not mutually exclusive… The self-organization model teaches the value of the ground-work of rules to facilitate self-ordering, and the hierarchy model teaches the value of structures that simplify cognition and life in general.

After all, notions of both hierarchy and self-organisation seem to be features of the socio-economic and political world that effect schools and education as we experience them. Internally schools remain in very many respects hierarch-ical and, therefore, organisationally "static" despite being, externally, part of a neo-liberal free-market enterprise culture. For schools, therefore, the tension between the traditional internal hierarchy of management and the notional "freedom" granted by government to compete for staff, students and reputation must, in our view, serve as a distraction from any attempt to revitalise "educa-tion" as a humanising process. We address these issues in several places in the book, but especially in Chapters 2 and 3.

Although we will not routinely use Simon's parable as a background the-oretical framework throughout the book, we will leave the simple image of the ant's behaviour in response to its environmental encounters as a meta-phor for readers to consider and envisage what might be entailed in incremen-tally, iteratively, moving from the response of an individual to the immediate environment, to the environments for meetings of two professionals, to school classrooms and, ultimately, society at large. We will then return to the parable in the synthesis that we present in our final chapter and reconsider how we may, in light of suggestions made in the intervening chapters, be more creative in how we could behave in the environment of education as it is, as well as how it might be.

It is our contention that how we view our relationships (our philosophical beliefs about ourselves and others) has a profound effect upon how we use our professional skills and how we interact and intervene with each other in the environments that we inhabit. These musings will have a significant influ-ence on how the "helper" and "the helped," the teacher and her students, are positioned in relation to each other and within the systems which bring them together. The study of human interactions and relationships is core to psych-ology and also, we argue here, crucial to "good education." But the issues we are concerned about are of relevance beyond psychology; we don't think we are being too bold in claiming the issues we are concerned about are critical for the future of societies around the world. How we understand human *being* and *becoming*, and more particularly how we position ourselves in relation to other humans, has a significant bearing on our approach to human systems and relationships beyond the arena of the helping professions; they relate to what happens in schools and classrooms and what young people grow up believing, and how they, in turn, construct society – that is their, and indeed our, world. Because this theme is so important and central to what we are trying to say, we offer no apology for being somewhat repetitive, but we do apologise if we are not always able to say things simply or clearly enough.

Providing a relational rationale for psychological approaches to education and how we work with each other in ways that are oriented to support the development of humanity, human systems, and relationships seems to us to be a potentially vital contribution to debates about the role and function of education in the current and future political, economic, and social contexts. Over the last decade the impact of austerity and a culture of performativity has distracted many from understanding our responsibilities for each other as human beings. As we write, the world-wide effects of COVID-19 have put a spotlight on our strengths and weaknesses. Our focus on relationality, therefore, attempts to raise issues – and questions – that require us to consider more widely questions about the meaning, purpose, and effects of our work. These are not only psychological, but as critical social issues of huge importance in communities across the world today and, for the role of educationalists, for the future of democratic societies.

As we will argue in Chapter 1 (*"The state we're in"*) we cannot function as isolates. We are not alone in the world but are located in, and affected by, the reciprocal human and physical systems that form our environment. Here, and throughout the book, we will emphasise the critical role of interpersonal dialogues and respect for each other's humanity. However, we need also to be alert to factors that threaten our sense of both autonomy and mutuality. Thus, with reference to features of education in schools today we will, for instance, examine how certain groups are disproportionately misrepresented and mistreated; how teachers' creativity and efficacy have been stifled; how self-interest demeans us; how education as a human process has been corrupted and distorted.

We can see that professional isolation is already problematic for many teachers in schools (Gibbs & Miller, 2014, p. 157; A. Miller, 1996) and data show us that increasing numbers of teachers are suffering both physical and mental ill-health at least partly as a result of their isolation. We hope that what we say here will encourage collaborative work, bringing teachers together to help each other learn and help to reduce the risk of professional isolation. We presume that our readers want to understand more about the nature of human relationships and how the effects of these may challenge – or support – ourselves and others. Importantly for us, while we take for granted that professional practice in education should be *transformative,* we also recognise that the potential power of human relationships in education has over the past decade or two been handicapped, in the UK at least, by governmental policies (educational and economic). In what we say here and elsewhere in the book we seek to offer a necessary and practical challenge to such policies.

We will spend some time in Chapter 1 re-examining the nature of personal identities, how these are interdependent with our social identities and how "Others" are construed. In doing so we will draw on the work of social psychologists such as Reicher (2004) and Turner (2010). Philosophically our approach here (and throughout) is underpinned in particular by reference to the work of Appiah (2007a, 2007b), Levinas (1987, 1985), and Parfit (1984). Following Parfit (1984) we suggest that the pursuit of self-interests is ultimately socially and personally self-defeating. This forms the philosophical basis for our exploration of how one may best achieve what is better for all through reciprocating dialogic inter-relationships with others.

In the following chapter (*"On being and becoming human"*), starting with an examination of what it may mean to be human in the 21st century we will begin to explore alternative ways of actualising educational processes, ways that are humanising, formative, and educational; about ways of becoming a human being. With Biesta and others, however, we accept that there can be no pre-ordained definition of "humanity." None-the-less, but with that caveat in mind, we set a premise for our work with reference to the work of John Macmurray who saw a central purpose for education in "learning to be human" (Macmurray, 1958/2012). We consider that this has value in and beyond education and is of direct relevance to the range of contexts within which educators and other professionals work. In considering the nature of relationships in education we will, inevitably, therefore, come to examine the role and function of educational leadership and management: how can we help each other deal with complexity with humility and sensitivity; and what questions arise from such considerations?

In Chapter 3 (*"Building educational alternatives"*) we continue to build on the preceding chapters by thinking about how people learn, how organisations and communities support learning, and what it means to be a learner. Here we will also examine how learning becomes a practical project and how it is important to continuously revitalise and validate curiosity and inquiry as essential characteristics of any educational enterprise.

Borrowing a word from another paradigm of humankind (but not necessarily buying the conventional meaning of the word in that paradigm) we will also look at what constitutes organisational *"health"* and, in considering the *mental health* of teachers and young people, ask "How can schools support and enhance the *well-being* of those engaged in education; how can schools preserve psychological space for learning; what scaffolding does this entail; and what therapeutic responses to emotionality may be offered?"

In considering the interpersonal professional relationships of teachers and other professionals, in Chapter 3 we draw attention to political choices about the purposes of the school curriculum and how such choices shape relationships between teachers, and between teachers and students. These curricular decisions have strong consequences for the development of teachers' identities and agency, and inevitably reflect structures, ethos, and leadership which, in turn, guide and constrain professional practice. The chapter outlines conditions, through examples, where psychological space has been created in which professionals can develop relationality and dialogue.

All of the above require attention to *"Morals and ethics in educational practice"* (Chapter 4). Here, following Appiah (2007b, p. xiii) we will distinguish between the principles about how we should treat others (*morals*) and our convictions about which kind of lives are good or bad for a person to lead (*ethics*), but also recognising with Appiah (2007b, p. 278) that ethics may subsume morality and that "*It might be best to lead a life in which you treat others as they should be treated.*" As professional practitioners we know that these philosophical deliberations have practical and psychological counterparts embedded in the complexities of professional encounters and understand that difficulties can arise in negotiating the interpersonal and professional territory of moral and ethical conundrums. In this chapter, therefore, we will also examine some of the ways in which moral and ethical questions are practically implicated in professional dialogues. These considerations provide a critical philosophical and professional stance for what we say elsewhere in the book about how we may ethically and responsibly relate with others dialogically whilst maintaining ethical individuality and a sense of autonomy. By examining general notions of "self" and "identity," how "identities" may be formed and the practical and professional implications of the ways in which we conceptualise identity, we will then consider the scope of individual identity and autonomy, and how identity is both socially constructed and social. In passing, we suggest that by failing to recognise identities as being at least partially contingent on context we risk becoming illegal arbitrators over moral and ethical integrity.

Chapter 5 ("*Dialogue and awareness of the space between*") is at the heart of what we would like readers to consider. Understanding the nature and effects of embedding dialogic processes as the *sine qua non* of professional practice for educators and applied psychologists (and, we suggest, other professionals) is, we think, crucial for effective and ethical professional practice. Pivotal writers in this field include Hermans (2013), Marková (2003), and Sampson (2008). Drawing on sources such as these, in this chapter we will examine how dialogic processes inclusively validate others and underpin the essence of interpersonal and multi-voiced existence. These are the means by which we know we are not alone, and they are also the means by which we retain the critical and self-critical perspectives that lie at the heart of transformative processes (Van der Riet, 2008). The concept of interdependent voices rests upon assumptions which view self, not as a single entity, but as self-in-relation to others in an interdependent reciprocal relationship. This philosophical position of dialogic ontology underpins the contention of Arnett and Arneson (1999, p. 297) that "*we need those who know that it is not just 'me' but 'us' – self and other – that make the intentional connection of life meaningful.*" This ontological principle lies at the heart of our understanding of democratic relationship.

Previous approaches to the helping relationship have claimed a democratic basis. Rogers' Person Centred Therapy for example, optimistically (and, for its time, radically) emphasised that the authority of the individual, rather than the therapist, would provide the basis of a more democratic professional culture (Rogers, 1995a, 1995b). For Rogers, the authority and empowerment of the individual self was key to therapeutic, educational, and even societal transformation (Holdstock, 1993). The focus on the individual self has, however, been subject to critique. Some have claimed that this conceptualisation of the self leads to a loss of focus on the other and even risks narcissism (Brazier, 1993). The chapter will, therefore, consider the implications of adopting person centred and other psychological approaches based on individualistic models particularly for professional practices that lay claim to be transformative.

The theoretical and empirical findings of preceding chapters form the foundations for what we discuss in the penultimate chapter ("*Consultation and intervention for and with others*"). Here again we provide some thoughts on practical matters. As we will discuss in this chapter, providing a psychological environment in which participants feel they can safely examine and reflect on their concerns and practices may not always be what is requested but, when provided, is found to be most helpful. However, in this chapter we also need to look at what may have become a dangerously hackneyed term: "intervention." Here we will critically dissect what that term might mean and the subsequent anticipations and expectations of others. This leads us to revisit the need to hold safe the space between people so that dialogue, exploration, and transformation can take place without prejudice. We will also propose that coaching and supervision (to be distinguished from consultation) should be important activities for teachers by providing "safe spaces" within which teachers can reflect and learn from and about their professional practice in discussion with their peers and leaders.

Our focus on the non-judgemental "space between" leads us to a view which neither positions a visiting professional (such as an educational or school psychologist) as the dominant "last word" (Arnett & Arneson, 1999) nor merely a person-centred helper. In both those instances the space between is squeezed out. In the first, by the professional's monologic stance and in the second by the subjectivity of the other. We will develop what has been said in the previous chapter on the significance of dialogic relations in the process of transformation and discuss these in relation to professional practices. We will set out what such practices might look like when the space between is prioritised, but we will also examine the limits of such approaches and consider the implications for the ways in which we might use consultation and supervision: To what extent are our approaches attending to the space between and are we listening to the other, or are we merely listening for the words which will confirm our interpretation? What does this have to say about the psychology we apply and how we apply it? By referencing earlier discussion about the individualistic emphasis dominating western psychology, we will consider questions about who or what is being transformed and the extent to which the processes involved can be thought to be democratic or even human. In doing so we will attempt to ground the argument in some specific practice examples and contexts.

In our final chapter ("*Synthesis*") we will, with final reference to Herb Simon's parable, with the words "human beings" substituted for "ant":

> Human beings, viewed as behaving systems, are quite simple. The apparent complexity of our behaviour over time is largely a reflection of the complexity of the environment in which we find ourselves.
>
> (Simon, 1996, p. 53)

return to our starting point and the place of education in the interface of social, economic, and global systems. Here we will summarise and synthesise the understandings and resources that educationalists and psychologists may bring to dialogic conversations with others as fellow professionals operating at the interface of competing systems. An aim is to provide further space and distance in which to reflect on the places in which we find ourselves. We recognise that those we work with may also be amongst those who have found themselves confused, concerned or, in extremis, distressed by their experiences (and without doubt these may sometimes be the same people). Our focus here is, as it has been throughout, on the application of psychology in primarily professional and educational contexts but, wherever, with the highest possible regard for the human beings who in seeking support in consultation may discover ways to be more inclusive and enhance the quality of education for all. While we also understand that in times of stress and dehumanisation the instinctual urge for self-preservation may be valid, we reiterate that the pursuit of self-interest may not be of the utmost importance or ultimately in anyone's own best interests (as articulated by Parfit, 1984); rather, we agree with Appiah (2007a), Hayden (2017), Todd (2015), and others that a more cosmopolitan outlook, though itself problematic, may be of greater value.

In conclusion, we offer some suggestions for the positioning of psychology and psychologists as being concerned for the educational processes implicated in the development of democratic being that could be, but aren't always, central to "good education." In doing so we hope to anticipate criticism that will arise with our adoption of a paradoxical position: on the one hand espousing the paramount importance of dialogic space in which future possibilities can be explored; on the other offering a stance for professional practitioners in which "critical friends" for others may hold expertise in mind without expressing the explicit authority that can easily compromise their potential for transformative agency. We hope that in doing so we may help promote psychological theories and educational practices capable of encompassing without demur the tensions between mutuality and difference, and individuality and communion; to effect the difference that may make a difference (Arnardóttir, 2014; Bateson, 1979; Haack, 2010).

None of what follows in this book should be seen as a set of strictly objective truths or rules. What follows are our ideas; the product of discussions we (the authors) have had while writing the book. The book is, therefore, a novel product that has emerged in the synergy of those discussions. During these discussions our individual ideas about what we wanted to say in the book have changed. Our ideas changed as we listened to, thought about, and responded to each other's suggestions (and the suggestions of the reviewers and editors who read our initial proposal), as well as the way people have dealt with (or been otherwise affected by) the ongoing pandemic and global crises. We might hope, therefore, that this book could be seen as a provisional boundary object (see Chapter 5).

We hope, in turn, to engage you, our readers, with what follows, to prompt you to think about your selves and relationships with others, and, in particular, to think about your professional relationships with those you work with closely as well as others that you may meet. We do not want to dictate what you think or do as a result of your reading. What we have written are some provisional thoughts for you to consider. But we hope that in reading this book you will think about possibilities for change. We cannot predict what these might be for you, but if you engage with the book as part of the internal dialogues that you have with yourself – and perhaps with others as well – you may find that you discover different ways of being and how you relate with others. Above all we hope the book will promote discussion about what the central purposes of education could be.

## Note

1 We should emphasise here that we recognise that "democracy" and "democratic processes" and other related terms are not at all unambiguous or unproblematic. In the sphere of politics (not our realm of expertise) it is very obvious that democracy is a contested term (see, for instance, Dahl (2020) and Duncan (1983) for detailed discussion of some of the many practical problems inherent in realising the ideal), but for us simpletons it is still important to hold onto our naïve beliefs as bulwarks against the alternatives of tyranny.

# 1 The state we're in

How we are not alone and some consequences of relationships

## Introduction

In a book about education, it may seem to be a strange thing to emphasise, but as we have said in the title for this chapter, *we are not alone* – though many may, at times, feel very lonely. The planet is getting crowded and for many the concepts of participatory citizenship and liberty are distant illusions. At the time of writing, the population of the world is reckoned to be just over 7.7 billion and growing, with over 66 million in the UK. While it is probably still just possible for people to be physically alone and self-sufficient, most of us (in the western world, at least) are, like it or not, dependent on others for food, services, support, and hospitality (Todd, 2015). However, many will, paradoxically, feel lonely having no immediate, regular, or frequent contact with anyone else. Such loneliness and psychological isolation became especially apparent during the COVID-19 pandemic. But, as has also been apparent throughout the pandemic, as the world's population continues to grow, in the face of the almost inevitable scrabbling for precious resources the survival of the species will depend on people who can talk, help, and work with each other rather. Selfish isolation and hoarding of resources (that contribute to social *injustice*) are both morally and ethically insupportable if, as we surely should, as Rawls (1999) emphasised, respect the lives of others. Meanwhile, many of those who feel isolated will also feel vulnerable and concerned for their mental health that, as we know, is more likely to deteriorate without meaningful human contact and communication. Education can be a focal point for the development of relationships, but its classroom and staffroom settings may also be places in which people can feel quite separate and lonely. Without access to education, its physical settings and its social functions, children may become isolated. We have during the COVID-19 pandemic witnessed the devastating effects of school closures on the mental health of many teachers, children, and young people so that, as a result, there was a significant rise in referrals to Mental Health Services. We cannot deny the sense of isolation and vulnerability that sadly many people experience. We hope that our philosophical and psychological stance (our ontology), based in a view that we come into "being" in relationships with others, and that relationships are transformative, may help to revitalise education and avert further harm.

DOI: 10.4324/9780429343766-2

In what follows, in order to better understand what can transform or otherwise affect the quality (and *equality*) of relationships, their power and relevance for education, we will examine, for example, some of the effects of the UK government's policies on educational processes, teachers, parents, and young people. We will set out some ideas about what for us should lie at the heart of education: what makes us human beings who respect and learn from each other – our capacity and need for relationships – and what sometimes, unfortunately, separates us from each other. We will also look at how and why we form exclusive groups as well as some of the consequences of grouping people in educational settings. In the other chapters of the book, we will consider ideas about how we may make more effective bridges with each other and what can help us work together, educationally. But we will start here by looking at the context for education, with a focus on what this is like in some parts of the UK now, strongly suspecting this may also be the situation elsewhere.

## The context of education

A history of education in the UK suggests that for at least 600 years formal education in schools was almost exclusively the prerogative of the sons of the wealthy. It was not until the early twentieth century that the education of all children (including girls) was legally required (Gibbs, 2021). Income and wealth have been and continue to be major determinants of social well-being and the outcomes (outputs?) of education (Pickett & Wilkinson, 2009). While wealthy parents may often choose to "buy" education with the premise that by doing so they are providing their children with a "better" education than the state can provide (Green, Parsons, Sullivan, & Wiggins, 2017), a significant proportion of the population are living and growing up in what is officially recognised as poverty and unable to afford any alternative. The poverty line in the UK is defined as a household income below 60% of the median income. For a lone parent with two children currently this amounts to about £200 a week – for the family. At the time of writing around 4.1 million children (30% of all children) in the UK were growing up in poverty. However recent events (such as the fuel/crisis) have placed increasingly intolerable pressure on household budgets with resulting calls for an expansion of free school meals. Given the persistent structural inequalities in our society, the distribution of these children and their families is uneven across ethnic or structural groups. For example, 47% of children in lone-parent families are in poverty; 45% of children in black and minority ethnic groups are in poverty (CPAG, 2019). Since the size of a family's income is highly likely to be a significant factor in the well-being of children and parents, the present and future impact of income inequality cannot be overlooked. The long-term prospects for academic performance, employment, and health across the whole population are generally worse the more unequal the income and wealth of the population (Dorling & Tomlinson, 2016; Pickett & Wilkinson, 2009, 2015). Inevitably, those with the least wealth and smallest incomes suffer the most. Sadly, it is now evident that the UK has the greatest income inequality in comparison with the four largest

Western European countries (Dorling, 2015, 2018). It has been estimated that the richest 30% of household own over 70% of all the UK wealth, whereas the poorest 30% of households hold just 2% of the nation's wealth (ONS, 2019).

Just as the number of children and young people growing up in poverty has been growing, the total number of pupils in schools in England has also been rising steadily, from 8.06m in 2010, to 8.89m in 2020 (an increase of 10.2%) (DfE, 2020c). This increase in pupil numbers has not been matched by a con-comitant increase in the number of teachers in schools. While the total number (full-time equivalent) of teachers in state funded schools rose from 441,355 in 2010 to 453,813 in 2020, this was an increase of only 2.8% (DfE, 2020b). However, not only has the number of teachers not kept pace with the number of children and young people in schools, there is growing evidence that the morale and well-being of teachers are in jeopardy (Borman & Dowling, 2008; DfE, 2019c; Gibbs, 2018a; Kidger et al., 2016; Skinner, Leavey, & Rothi, 2021). If teachers are not well, and if there are fewer of them working with increasing numbers of pupils, more of whom are growing up in deprived circumstances, should we not be worried?

Two other factors need to be noted in establishing the context for our discussions: the fall in local accountability for educational provision and the increasing number of "academies" that are owned and administered by non-governmental (commercial) organisations, and the rate of exclusion of young people from the mainstream of education. The data show that in England at least 37% of primary and 78% of secondary schools had (been) converted to academies (DfE, 2021b). These now provide education for over 47% of all eli-gible children and young people. In relation to the "academisation" of schools it is interesting to look at the rate of exclusion of children and young people from schools. The data show that there has been a year-on-year increase in the total number of pupils being excluded from schools. 5740 children and young people were permanently excluded from schools in England in 2009–10; 7894 in 2018–19 (a 38% rise) (DfE, 2011, 2019a, 2020a; NAO, 2019). The data avail-able from the Department for Education also indicate that whereas in 2009–10 just over 10% of all permanent exclusions were from academies, by 2018–19, perhaps in line with the growth in the number of academies, this had risen to 69% of all permanent exclusions (a total number of 5416 children and young people (Claytor, 2021). While these data are indicative of the rate of exclusion by schools, we also wonder about the extent to which schools are rejected by children and young people who do not feel safe or welcomed in such schools. There may be many reasons why children do not attend schools regularly or at all. The available data is too general to do more than provide a base for specu-lation but, prior to the onset of COVID and school closures, in the autumn of 2019 the overall absence rate (including authorised and unauthorised absences across all phases and types of settings) had increased from 4.3 % in 2018 to 4.9 %[1] (DfE, 2019b).

One might wonder what these statistics tell us about the effects of educa-tional systems for us as human beings, and to what extent are our educational systems fit for purpose. The picture we have of the context and functions of primary and secondary school education suggests that educational attainments, narrowly confined to performance in core academic subjects, are prized by government above all else. The number of children and young people who are unable to make progress in their academic attainments or have a different view of the purpose and meaning of education seem to be matters of lesser importance. One of our concerns is that too little is done to support the development of *all* young people or to help them learn how to respect and work with the great diversity of humankind; there is too little emphasis on learning about relationships and how to simply *be with* others. Instead, socio-economic factors and the educational curriculum maintain structural inequalities and privilege those in certain social and cultural groups over others. (We note in passing that, e.g. a study (Williams, Papadopoulou, & Booth, 2012) reported that more than 40% of prisoners had been permanently excluded from school and a briefing from the Prison Reform Trust (2019) indicated that more than 60% of those entering prison were assessed as having a reading age equivalent of 11 years or lower. The sequelae of parental imprisonment that for children include being at increased risk of exhibiting antisocial behaviour or mental health problems, have also been reported and, though not conclusive, do not bode well for the next generation (Källström, Hellfeldt, & Nylander, 2019; Murray, Farrington, Sekol, & Olsen, 2009).)

Thus, in an age when teachers and schools are judged almost exclusively in terms of the academic progress of their pupils, teachers who think there might be more to the notion of education than just raising the academic attainments of their pupils, have begun to ask: "What is the point of this?" Lacking convincing arguments to provide an acceptable professional purpose and beleaguered by administrative tasks (not to mention the threat of an inspection) teachers have begun to wonder if this is what they want to – or can – do for the rest of their professional lives. Significant numbers of teachers are now leaving the profession of teaching in the UK within just a few years of their initial training (DfE, 2019c, 2020b). An illustration of some teachers' bewilderment in the face of the performative regime they endure can be found in a recent study of teachers' well-being. One teacher told researchers:

> I think it's *[the curriculum that's]* heavily bureaucratic and I think there's a great deal of pressure on people to perform to targets and there seems to be a loss of spontaneity that teachers used to have, and I think that, sadly, it's gone. So, it's all conforming to syllabus and rigour of that syllabus rather than responding to the children and pupils that you've got in your care. It's talk about statistics rather than the children.
>
> (Skinner et al., 2021, p. 8)

We suspect such confusion and loss of autonomy may be amongst the factors that lie behind the loss of teachers to the profession. But having invested oneself in the profession and then to begin doubting if it was the right choice to make may also provoke other personal questions, questions like: what makes "me" the person "I" am; what anchors me, my "self"; what's my purpose in life? To begin to address these questions we will now ask two more. "What does it take to be human?" and "How we view and treat each other as 'human' beings?"

## Who are we (philosophically, psychologically speaking)?

Most of us, probably instinctively, hold to some notion that "I" must be the same person that "I" was yesterday, just a little bit older. The notion of our "self" is persistent (and, some will say, illusory) and as revealed by philosophical enquiry profoundly complex and puzzling (see, for instance, Janaway, 1989, pp. 291–316). This can provoke questions such as 'What makes "me" the person "I" am; what anchors me, my "self"; what's my purpose in life?" Pragmatically we probably also think that the "I" that has so far been recognised, has been – is and always will be – recognised as a *person* (with whom it is possible to have a relationship), is not an "object." Although we may, sometimes, feel we are merely a cog in the wheels of an organisation, treated more as something to be manipulated, somebody that merely has a role and a task to complete, we still cling to the idea that we are each a human being, a person who has autonomy and agency. (But if I was always recognised as the same person, would I always be the same "thing"? Does an objectified "thing" have greater long-term consistency (more stable identity) than a "person"?)

Instinct and self-consciousness tell us that we think. As Descartes (1637/ 1968) famously concluded, "*I think, therefore I am.*" As individuals we are, therefore, aware that self-consciousness, thinking, is not only possible and allowed, but that the recurring patterns of what we each think and remember thinking, gives us each a sense of continuity as a unique identifiable individual human being. Thinking alone does not, however, allow us to deduce that other thinkers exist as separate entities (Berkeley, 2009; Parfit, 1984, p. 225). We "know" that other people, other human beings, exist because we can and do interact with them, face-to-face in real time. As self-conscious human beings we not only have our own private internal conversations with ourselves (in which we generate hypotheses about who or what we engage with), we also interact with other human beings. It has been suggested that what characterises the mental processes of human beings is that they are "*doings*" that are "*conversational*" (Brinkmann, 2016, p. 3). It is, we hope, self-evidently clear that people, human beings, matter to us, each other. Simply being with others or engaging in conversations with them can help us to develop our ideas and test our hypotheses (some of which may also provide some clues about how we are seen by other people) but can also help to generate new ideas about ourselves, other "selves" and the social world we inhabit. Perhaps to counter feelings that could threaten or challenge beliefs that we have formed about ourselves, in our engagement in conversation with others we also seek affirmation of our worth – for ourselves and for others – as we have done from the beginning of our conscious existence. So, in order not to be alone we join with others in clubs, groups, societies, and places of work. But, in our view, to do that, to join with others effectively, we need to add to Brinkmann's suggested distinguishing characteristics the idea of "*sensitive curiosity*"; curiosity – and wonder – that may, for instance, be shown non-verbally with a glance or eye-contact, or in thoughtful questions enquiring, for instance, about someone's well-being.

Along the way, in discussion with friends, colleagues, and partners, we may find ourselves agreeing about a topic or an issue that engages us. We will find ourselves bonding with those we agree with and those we like – and those who affirm their liking for us; we may also find ourselves avoiding some people, perhaps wondering what they are thinking; possibly not wondering or motivated to discover how we might get to know them better. Informal processes like these can help shape our perceived identities: who we think we are and who others might think we are. In such ways we gain a sense of where we "belong," or where we find the best "fit" for ourselves (Walton & Brady, 2017). However, we probably also recognise that our "identities" vary with the social context, and that we sometimes offer a presentation of ourselves that, in our consciousness at least, varies between home and work (Berndt & Perry, 1986; Hogg, 2016).

Our "identity" can, therefore, seem to be somewhat "fluid." Who we are depends on the circumstances; where and with whom we think we best "belong." A body of psychological research now evidences that how we function (what we do, what we believe we can do, and how others relate to us) often differs (possibly quite significantly) between settings (Brown, 2015; DiGiovanna, 2015; Hogg & Terry, 2000; Sachs, 2001; Turner, 2010). On this basis, we suggest our identity, our understanding of ourselves as human beings, is a product of our interaction with others; where "I" becomes part of a "we"; as Kenneth Gergen (1991, p. 157) put it:

> It is not individual "I"'s who create relationships, but relationships that create the sense of "I"… "I" am just an I by virtue of playing a particular part in a relationship.

And, as John Macmurray (1957/1991, p. 12) stressed:

> Against the assumption that the Self is an isolated individual, I have set the view that the Self is a <u>person</u>, and that personal existence is <u>constituted</u> by the relation of persons.
>
> (Emphasis in the original)

But what is a "*person*," a "*human*" being; and how can we recognise what we want to become? This question continues to fascinate and stimulate philosophers, psychologists, sociologists, and educationalists. But, being pragmatic, we feel a need to offer something more tangible than an intriguing philosophical enquiry since in this book we will continually refer to the processes implicit in helping each other *become* human and like many others consider this should be fundamental to the endeavours of education. The best that we can do for now, however, is to offer some thoughts on how we might know whether, or not, we are conversing with another human. (We will return to the problems that arise if we try to define what is the ideal of humanity in the next chapter.)

We talk to our pets (cats, dogs, horses, hamsters, *et cetera*) and though we may have a sense, a feeling, that they understand what we are saying because of what they consequently do, we don't get a response that reliably tells us they actually *understand* what we mean by the words we use. We can nowadays also get a response from a machine ("Hey *Alexa* play some music by Bach"; but no need for a courteous "please"). But although we usually get a correct response, we *know* that it is just a machine that has been programmed to recognise and respond to certain words; we also understand that the machine won't (yet?) be able to intuit how we are feeling and play the right piece of Bach to match our mood. In the early days of computing Alan Turing (1950) suggested that we would know we were talking to a machine so long as we could distinguish the typed responses of the machine from those of another human. Somehow, we still know that "Alexa" or "Siri" are both essentially unsentimental, unimaginative machines. In his most recent novel "*Klara and the Sun*," Kazuo Ishiguro imagined a near future in which robots (machines) are programmed to intuit and express both curiosity and feelings. But the process of "*imagining*" still, today, feels like a uniquely human ability. We don't know what our dog might imagine even if we can suggest to ourselves that the behaviour of a sleeping dog (twitching its paws, eye-flickering) is a sign of "dreaming." Even if a dog could type, would it pass the "Turing test"? While we may sense or imagine that an animal is suffering (we can see that it has a broken leg; we can hear it howl) but do we know *how* it suffers? Perhaps we can truly "sympathise" with fellow humans but only "empathise" with other animals (because although we can possibly imagine how an animal may feel, we cannot imagine that we share, take on, those feelings compassionately?) As self-conscious beings we are aware of a notion of our self who can then likewise imagine what (and how) a fellow self may feel about their experience.

But even the notion of one's "self" as the key to what makes us consciously human is problematic. This is not merely a philosophical or metaphysical issue that is detached from physical realities or our everyday experience of trying to be a human being. In fact, there seems to be no material, physical evidence of any specific neurological process or body that is identifiable as the "self"; and a substantial body of research suggests that our sense of "self," our identity, changes (is changed) according to circumstances. The notion that we each have a fixed self that may be identified by one's self and others is, therefore, probably best considered illusory or even unhelpful (see, for instance DiGiovanna, 2015; Hermans, 2013; Legrand & Ruby, 2009; Parfit, 1984; Reicher, 2004).

Contrary to the wisdom of western culture, this is not, however, a unique view. In Buddhist philosophy, for instance, the doctrine of "Annatta" holds that the "self" is a distraction from the process of seeking greater understanding of our relatedness to others (Giles, 1993; Gülerce, 2014; Markus & Kitayama,

1991). In an era when many scientists remain committed to pinning down the neurological or biological bases of psychological and metaphysical phenomena (the everyday material of human experience), it is, therefore, important and, perhaps, helpful to recognise here that we do not have to be objectified in that – or any – way. Our sense of being or *becoming* is more fluid and optimistic than that. Crucially, none of this has emerged as fact (or even just as a notion) of its own volition. It has emerged from the interaction of people: scientists, philosophers and others working together, formally and informally. In sum these ideas have emerged from collaborative human relationships.

Thus, the coming together of people, fellow human beings, is at the heart of who we are and how we may be creative. For many this becomes an ethical and moral responsibility. Emmanuel Levinas, whose experiences as a Jew during WWII shaped his philosophical beliefs, held that our primary duty lay in our ethical and reciprocal duty to be related with others:

> The irreducible and ultimate experience of relationship appears to me to be… not in synthesis, but in the face to face of humans, in sociality, in its moral signification. But it must be understood that morality comes not as a secondary layer, above an abstract reflection… morality has an independent and preliminary range. First philosophy is an ethics.
>
> (Levinas & Nemo, 1985, p. 87)

The profound implication of this lies then in the unique experience we have of our selves in each and every encounter that we have with others. We believe this is critically important for educationalists since, unless we recognise the centrality of reciprocal relationships, there is a risk that initiatives and interventions (such as those advocated by Claxton & Lucas, 2016 for instance) will continue to individualise – not socialise – learning. This, therefore, points to the moral and ethical responsibilities we have as members of a democratic society (to be discussed in Chapter 4). In our view (and that of Levinas and others) we can only exist as ethical beings if we consciously exist with others. If, however, instead of treating each encounter as unique, we perceive encounters as threatening and treat the other, another *person*, as an objective "some*thing*," we dehumanise the encounter and reduce others to objects who may be easily disposed of – as occurs in the processes of segregation, murder, and genocide. In the process, reciprocally, of course, we too become objectified, dehumanised, by others. If, alternatively, we do recognise our responsibility to others and our selves in our unique encounters, we may remain ethically, morally, respectful of others. Each encounter with an-other provides the opportunity for care, curiosity, wonder, and responsibility. But, as we will discuss in the next section, as people who are morally aware this also requires us to hold in balance our individual sense of free-will and self-determination, as well as how we live our lives with sympathetic regard for others. As Levinas said, morality and justice derive from the ethics of individual encounters and, to repeat ourselves, of relationships:

How is there justice? I can answer that it is in the fact of the presence of someone next to the Other, from whence comes justice. Justice… must always be held in check by the initial interpersonal relation.

(Levinas, 1985, pp. 89–90)

Of course, with modesty and in light of our own reflections on the reality of everyday encounters, we may, more hopefully, come to understand that our behaviours affect others that we are with, who, in turn, reciprocally affect our selves. Sometimes we behave "well" and sometimes, regrettably, less so. Since reciprocity of behaviours is central to much of what we have to say in this book – it is crucial for our understanding of relationships – we will now look at how we may experience and learn about reciprocity in our lives. But, we also acknowledge the warnings of Sharon Todd (2015) and others that an overly idealistic view of education can fail to help young people deal with the world as it is – a world in which humanity and inhumanity may be found face-to-face. As Todd (2015, p. 12) has noted:

education can never be an innocent purveyor of humanistic goods … it is an institutionalised practice that is fraught with ambiguity, living in the aporetic space that opens in the encounter between the human and the inhuman.

## The growth of reciprocity

The first experience (but not necessarily the first memory) we have of reciprocal behaviours is at the moment of birth. It is in our relationship with our parents, initially and most significantly in the relationship with our birth mother, that our early behaviours are shaped. In the ensuing inter-relationship with our carers, as infants we learn about communication and emotionality (Newson, 1979; Trevarthen & Aitken, 2001). The primary care-giver's instinctive human task is to be responsive and to ensure that the infant is nurtured and secure, that exploration and learning are safe, but also to experience the joy of being with others (Trevarthen, 2009, 2015). This physical and psychological environment, that will, in due course, include our first memorable experiences of inter-personal interaction, has profound and lasting effects that will reverberate throughout our lives. Even though, for a few, this may be a very brief relationship (ending with the death of or separation from the birth mother), for most of us it is inevitably amongst the most significant formative and safest experiences of our lives, and generally the first experience of love and being cared for. (Sadly, however, for some, love and parental care seem to end there.)

The bonding process, initially with our birth mother, later with other members of the family and carers, forms the beginnings of our experience of interpersonal communication. Thus, we develop reciprocity in the continual dialogue with the primary care-giver, in our attachment with that person, and in the developing experience of inter-subjectivity (Bowlby, 1978; Fogel, de Koeyer, Bellagamba, & Bell, 2002; Trevarthen, 1979, 1998). In these earliest interpersonal experiences, we can learn about belonging, turn-taking, dialogue, sharing and the mutual construction of intentions, meanings, and mutual understanding – and the joy of being with another (Papousek, 1995; Trevarthen, 2009). Here we not only learn about the prevailing social and cultural conventions – and social morality (what behaviours are acceptable, and which are not), we learn something about what it is possible to do but also how we might, with some help, achieve what had hitherto seemed impossible.

Skilful parents instinctively "scaffold" interactions with their child, talking about what they see, intervening at just the right moment (not too early, nor too late; providing just the right amount of help, just the right suggestion) to enable the child to solve the problem and to learn that solving problems is possible (Vygotsky, 1978; Wood, 1998). But in this process the duet of parent/carer and child also learn that they are separate beings, are an-other for each other: that (and how) one "self" is different from an-other. As adults we have become accustomed to our separateness, one from another. We take that for granted; probably, too rarely, we also consciously recognise the paradoxical similarity we have with each other in this respect. But most of us will somehow remain able to engage productively and respectfully in discussions with others. Many of us become very skilled in being able to take turns in discussion, to allow space for another to put their point of view – to which we listen and on which we will reflect. As we will discuss later in the book (particularly in Chapter 5), it is precisely in developing self-conscious understanding and respect for our mutual similarity in being different one from another that provides the basis of interpersonal dialogue in the space between us (Bauman, 1993; Hrdy, 2011). We doubt it is possible to make sense of the world on our own; we can only make sense of the world through our interactions and relations with others. If we become deprived of such helpful inter-relationships, as can happen, for instance, at work (or at home) – and sadly, somewhat ironically, in schools – the experience of separation from others, isolation, can be psychologically harmful. In general, good relationships help buffer us against adversity; in the world of education they will be indispensable for humanising students' learning and teachers' professional well-being (García-Moya, Brooks, & Moreno, 2020; Spilt, Koomen, & Thijs, 2011).

Helping each other make sense of our experiencing of the world is a socialising and affirming process. We are more likely to be able to conduct the necessary reflection on experience if we feel safe to do so and in doing so also gain a greater sense of security. To be able to join with others in a dialogue and discuss what is happening can make a great difference to how we feel about ourselves and what we can do. As we will discuss later (in particular in Chapters 5 and 6), creating the space in which partners in a dialogue may feel safe and secure can be very beneficial. This can be true of professional consultation, for teachers in their classrooms and for psychologists in training (Gayle, Cortez, & Preiss, 2013; Gibbs et al., 2016; Stengel & Weems, 2010). So too, just as a child with our primary care-givers we learn through dialogue to make sense of each other, learn each other's language, learn about each other's differences, we can as adults relearn to become more than instinctively skilful; we can become consciously adept at helping each other to reflect and learn in the space of face-to-face meetings and dialogues. This is what this book is about.

Critically, as Ivana Marková (2016, p. 1) has said:

> The main presupposition of dialogical perspectives is that the mind of the Self and the minds of Others are interdependent in and through sense-making and sense-creating of social realities…

Also, in the parent–child relationship and later in the dynamics of wider family settings and, later still, in groups (clubs, societies, professions) that we join, we also encounter and learn something about our ability to control and to be controlled; to create and to be created. We learn (hopefully in the context of also learning the prevailing social morals) and continue to learn the extent of our free will, our sense of agency and autonomy.

Before we talk about what happens to us in groups, we will consider some of the psychological and philosophical aspects of our sense of agency and autonomy: To what extent may we think we have individual power in our relations with others; how is respect for others assured?

## Agency and autonomy

As is implied in much of what we have already said, some of us will, from time to time, entertain a belief that we are autonomously free to do as we wish and that to deny that "right" is problematic or even undemocratic. (We will return to discuss some ideas about democracy and education later in the book.) However, more thoughtfully, we may also recognise that while we are where we are, and who we are, because of the choices we have made in the past, the choices about what we could do right now are, first, ethically and morally constrained by resources and legal strictures that were set in the past. Second, while personal autonomy may be a political ideal, in a democratic and ethical society we are not wholly autonomous; we are indebted to others and can ethically only act in relation to our understanding of others' beliefs and intentions. Clearly, therefore, as we have discussed above, we would also hope that if we are to engage ethically with others our sense of autonomy will be bounded by our sense of mutual respect and social interdependence. As has been said "*Autonomy and agency are not antithetical to relatedness*" (Kagitcibasi, 2005, p. 404). Further, Derek Parfit showed we should not presume that autonomous pure self-interest is necessarily in anyone's best interest (our own self-interest included), concluding that:

> Even if I never do what, of the acts that are possible for me, will be worse for me, it may be worse for me if I am purely self-interested. It may be better for me if I have some other disposition.
>
> (Parfit, 1984, p. 5)

Drawing on the work of Kant, Kwame Anthony Appiah has also argued that as ethically authentic autonomous agents we should treat others respectfully, recognising our mutual interdependence, as identically self-determining.

> To regard others as ends in themselves – to recognise their human dignity – is to regard them in this way, too. The standpoint of agency is connected, in the most direct possible way, to our concern to live intelligible lives in community with other people... This practical interest requires us to be able to articulate our own behaviour in relation to theirs, and this we do through our understanding of them as having beliefs and intentions – in short, as reasoning – and also as having passions and prejudices: in short, as always potentially unreasonable.
>
> (Appiah, 2007b, p. 58 et passim)

Accordingly, we should, in principle (and this is at the heart of the classic liberal dilemma) respect others for their own beliefs in free will and autonomy. But although we cannot legislate against tyrannical autonomy and inhumanity (although, as we have seen, it is in practice terribly possible to allow tyranny to grow and dominate), as educationalists we can strive to ensure educational and social processes are grounded in ethical, moral, and democratic processes that are indivisible from mutual respect and regard for others' bounded autonomy. Since education is a self-determining reflexive function of a community, in addition to thinking about our sense of personal autonomy, self-determination and its limitations, we also need to understand and respect what happens to communities, when people, as they do, get into (or are put into) groups. Understanding some of the aspects of intra- and inter-group attitudes and behaviours contributes to deeper understanding of how we may be locally affected by diversity and address some of the significant features (such as the categorisation, setting or streaming of children) of education in schools today. We suggest that gaining greater understanding of what happens in and between notional groups (ethnic, socio-economic, political, religious) could also help mitigate (but not justify) inter-ethnic, inter-necine, tensions. Because of its importance the following section is, therefore, quite long and deserves careful attention.

## Human behaviours in and between groups

In this section we will discuss some of the evidence of what happens to our feelings about both ourselves and others when we join – or are put into – a group; how some groups may give us comfort while others apparently hinder us. Groups that we join can help affirm what we think about ourselves but also how we see ourselves as different from people in another group. To do this we will refer to the experimental studies of groups by Henri Tajfel and his colleagues (Tajfel, 1981, 2010). Later we will go on to discuss how we may come to fear, demean, and derogate "Others" who are perceived to be alien and inferior simply because they are in another group. In the chapters that follow we will also address a major theme of the book: how we can, in dialogue with others, relearn trust, overcome fear of others, and be more open to contact, dialogue, and ethical relations with others.

As a philosopher concerned about the state of education and the diversity of human kind, Martha Nussbaum (2016) asked how we may educate more people who are able to live respectfully and reciprocally with others? (These are questions that concern us as well.) Nussbaum suggested the developmental origins of the tensions between compassionate concern and the need to dominate both lie in early infancy when infants can in rapid succession experience the bliss of completeness (full of mother's milk) and the *"agonising awareness of helplessness"* (not being able to feed ourselves). The infant's expression of helplessness, seeking comfort and bliss can, we may surely recognise, dominate parents and, as Nussbaum suggested, unless they are careful, turn them, the parents, into slaves. On the other hand, the infant who experiences parental compassionate concern and assurance of safety will gradually come to express gratitude and love for those who support her needs. Nussbaum's ideas provide some clues about how certain patterns of behaviour may be acquired. And, as Nussbaum recognised, the dyad of a parent and child is the smallest and one of the most powerful groups we will ever encounter. As we develop in this dyad, this duet, we unconsciously learn about what belonging to a group means and what group membership does for us. We also learn about the difference between "us" (the in-group) and "others."

As we've noted, most of us do not seek to be alone. That we want to "belong" is a strong motivation for being with others in a group. Without the attachments that are formed in a group, the sense of belonging that is entailed, without the affirmation of our identifiable and unique being-ness, our physical and mental well-being is at risk (Baumeister & Leary, 1995). The benefits of group cohesion and collaborative behaviours have been evident throughout the history of humankind, from our earliest days as hunter-gatherers, through the development of agrarian cultures to modern urban dwellers. Although it may be argued that in this latest (modern?) iteration of tribal life we can, thanks to modern technology, live a life of sorts without much face-to-face human contact (and far too many have had experience of this during the COVID pandemic). As we have already indicated, a solitary life is unlikely to be a good or fulfilling life. Isolation is an intrinsically alien and fearful experience for human beings. In most cultures and beliefs, it seems we naturally seek the safety and security of others or, at least, an-other. Almost certainly we do not, naturally, want to be alone or afraid. We may fear contact with others, but we do not want to be left alone. As we will discuss in the next chapter, fear is the most powerful emotion we experience; we fear the loss of relationships and ultimate extinction. Fear feeds envy, hatred, and disgust that together corrode trust, hope, and democracy (Nussbaum, 2018). The security of trustworthy and stable relationships can immunise us from fear of extinction. For democracy to survive and prosper, the process of education, therefore, needs a human rather than technical purpose that helps us learn how to be human, to trust and care for each other (Biesta, 2016; Macmurray, 1958/2012).

There are two complementary and positive aspects of groups. They can provide security and they can give us a commonality of identity and purpose. When we choose to join a group (such as a running club, a profession, or a school, for instance) we will probably hope to feel "at home" and to feel "wanted." We like to have a sense of belonging; that we are joining people with whom we share interests, whose company we enjoy or with whom we can cooperate in joint and creative activities. Putting it more formally, we may feel our sense of who we are, our personal identity, is validated and affirmed but also that our uniqueness, our autonomy will be respected (Brewer, 1991). We are probably very unlikely to willingly join a group in which we will feel diminished or derogated. However, being in a group we may also be wary of other groups (and not all groups are necessarily well-defined). In groups we want to join we will hope to recognise in our colleagues shared interests and attributes; there we will discover how alike we are, but also be respected for our difference. However, in so far as we have chosen which groups to join, which groups we identify with, we believe we will still have some sense of individual agency and autonomy; and, as we will see we may come to feel that in some groups we can do more and different things that we would do alone.

Along the way, once we have joined a group, we may start to recognise the obverse: how we are seen by others in another group, club, or profession. Sometimes we may get a sense of what it means to be seen as being a member of team X. Supporters of a football team have been known to voice strong feelings about the supporters of the opposing team, for instance. In extreme situations, for example across racial or ethnic groups (the caste system in India is another example), we will also come to also understand what it means to be positioned, by others, as a member of an-other group with no, or little, sense of agency, self-determination, of choosing to be in that group. This has been, and still is, the experience of others (such as Jews, Roma, communists, homosexuals in the extermination camps of WWII; the Bosnian Muslims in Srebrenica in 1995; Rohingya in Myanmar, 2021) construed and treated as aliens, as passive, inferior beings. For an example of recent practices in the UK, and how UK citizens of Asian heritage (and thus casually (obscenely) categorised as "different") have been humiliated when they re-enter the country after visiting friends and relatives abroad (see Blackwood, Hopkins, & Reicher, 2013).

However, we do not need to physically locate "others" in a different space for them to become "others" perceived to be essentially different, strange, perhaps even unlikeable. The work of Tajfel (1981, 2010) and his experimental studies demonstrated some of what happens when people are put into groups and how they consequently perceive and behave toward others. Tajfel's evidence of what happens to the behaviour of individuals when they are placed in groups can, we suggest, help us understand some of the behaviours of, for instance, young people who are, without negotiation classified and put into groups: those who are excluded from school, or placed in "low ability" groups with the "SEN" children (as we have heard some children to be labelled).

Tajfel was determined to gain some understanding of the roots of how people could behave toward others with such extreme prejudice that they might want to eliminate members of another group (as exemplified by the behaviour of Nazis toward Jews and others in the extermination camps of WWII). Tajfel first showed that when presented with *objects* that were described (categorised) as being in one or other of two groups (e.g. sets of lines in one group clearly longer than the lines in another group), people would consistently judge the difference between examples of each of the two groups as being greater than they were in fact. Thus, he concluded, given the chance, human perception and cognition will tend to magnify the actual, "real" difference (if any) between groups. With this evidence of human frailty and unconsciously biased perception, Tajfel then turned his attention to what happens when *people* are put into groups. He randomly assigned volunteers to one or other of two groups. Each group had a specific but essentially abstract and irrelevant identity (based in each participant's expressed preference for a painting by one of two previously unknown abstract painters). In these experiments, having been assigned to a group, each participant had no knowledge of who else was in the same group or in the other. They were simply told which of the two groups they were in. In a range of tasks participants were then asked to assign notional rewards to members of their own or the other group. (It is important to remember that each participant had no idea who was in one group or the other.) The results were consistently clear: participants favoured the members of their "in-group" at the expense of members of the other group. But not only did members of the in-group favour other members of their in-group, they also did what they could to maximise the difference between members of their group and others in the same way that in his earlier experiments people had magnified the difference between groups of objects. Tajfel's interpretation of this phenomenon was that:

> individuals have to provide [themselves with] social meaning through social identity to the intergroup situation… and this need is fulfilled through the creation of intergroup differences [even] when such differences do not in fact exist.
>
> (Tajfel, 1981, p. 276)

Cumulatively these experiments confirmed that prejudicial behaviour toward others has its roots not in the essence of any notional personality or racial types but "simply" in the process of passively *being identified* as a member of a particular group and of actively identifying *with* that group. It is relatively easy to see how this might help us understand the inter-group behaviour of members of notional groups such as supporters of Manchester City or Liverpool football clubs, members of "Extinction Rebellion" or "Climate Change Deniers."

Members of any one of these groups don't have to know or understand the views, beliefs, or behaviours of the contrasting group, it is sufficient to know that they are not in "their" group for "the others" ("them") to be in the wrong; to be the opposition and to have any perceived differences to be accentuated. More subtly, in light of these ideas, consider, for instance, what other children may think of their peers who are placed in a "unit" or a special class because their behaviour is thought to be too difficult, or their learning to be significantly slower; but also think what the children in such a unit, separated from others, might (vice-versa) think about those who have placed them there. We might also consider the attitudes and beliefs of teachers in a school that was, without any opportunity for discussion or dialogue with the inspectors deemed to be "unsatisfactory" (see Gibbs (2018a) for a fuller treatment of this issue).

Further work in this field has shown that membership of a group confers a "social identity" on members that in turn contributes to group members' beliefs about and behaviour towards others. The effects of social identification on behaviour toward others was, for instance, demonstrated in experimental studies of the behaviour of supporters of a particular football team (Levine, Prosser, Evans, & Reicher, 2005).

For these experiments the researchers recruited self-identifying supporters of the Manchester United football team. On arrival at the university where the research was taking place each participant was escorted from reception to another building where, they were told, the main experiment was to take place. Along the way across campus each participant encountered an injured stranger. There were three variations to this scenario. In one version the stranger was wearing a Manchester United shirt. In the other two variations the stranger was wearing either a Liverpool FC shirt or an unbranded sports shirt. When the stranger was identified as a Manchester United supporter almost all participants (also, remember, self-declared Manchester United supporters) offered to help the stranger. However, when the injured supporter was wearing either of the different shirts significantly fewer participants offered to help. In a second experiment instead of highlighting the importance of allegiance to the local team the experimenters emphasised for each participant that they were part of a study to discover what football supporters in general got out of their love of "the beautiful game." They were then exposed to the same type of incident and under similar conditions to those of the first experiment. However, in this experiment the majority of fans went to help an injured football supporter irrespective of which team shirt the stranger was wearing. This time, however, they were less likely to go to the aid of someone wearing a plain shirt, someone not clearly a football supporter. Taken together the findings of these two studies indicate that our capacity for empathy and altruism may be determined by the extent to which we identify with others. In the first experiment it was the recognition of commonality in a well-defined group that appears to have determined whether or not the injured stranger was helped, whereas in the second experiment intergroup rivalry was subsumed in a more inclusive identification with football fans in general. While it seems that we humans as individuals are socially oriented, and achieve meaning, identity, and purpose by aligning ourselves with others, the group(s) that are most salient and inclusive are not necessarily pre-ordained nor immune to external influence. In whatever way groups are defined and construed, in aligning ourselves with others as fellow members of the "in-group," we may still maximise the importance of our own in-group, exaggerate the difference between us and others, and derogate members of another group.

This seems to us to be important information since, as we have already indicated, formal grouping of people in educational systems is commonplace – sometimes for administrative convenience, sometimes to explicitly encourage intergroup competition. It is, therefore, important to take account of the possible effects of grouping and being grouped. The systems of educational provision in the UK (and elsewhere in the world) include various and persistent forms of grouping – of pupils and teachers. In many schools, children and young people are separated and grouped by age, gender, ability, types of need, sometimes with little or no opportunity for informal contact between members of different groups. Teachers will also inevitably find themselves in a range of groups: in types of schools (primary, secondary, or special), in subject specialities, or in promoted posts or as leaders. Increasingly schools are, by "virtue" of their ranking viewed almost exclusively in terms of exam results and academic successes. It would not be surprising to discover intergroup feelings similar to those revealed by Tajfel and colleagues amongst staff in neighbouring schools, particularly if, as now, there is an element of inter-school competition in the ranking of schools that is probably even more potentially corrosive if there are socio-economical differences in the communities served by neighbouring schools. For some teachers, perhaps especially school leaders and managers, they may feel particularly lonely, vulnerable and, perhaps, suspicious of what others are doing or saying. (For some thoughts on some of these issues, see Brighouse, 2015). We will return to consider the consequences of these groupings within education in a later section of this chapter after a brief discussion of how "others" may be created and rated.

## Others and Othering

Philosophically and psychologically speaking "Others" are what we are not; what we cannot fully comprehend. Thus, they may serve as the psychological repository of what we find uncomfortable. The capitalised "Other" signifies many subtly nuanced notions of this "repository" in different schools of thought. For instance, the French psychoanalyst Jacques Lacan saw the Other as "'the treasury of signifiers' with which there can be no automatic or harmonious fit" (Hook, 2008, p. 55), the signifier of all that we do not understand or could know. The American philosopher Alphonso Lingis (1994) saw the "Other" as an "intruder" who disrupts the otherwise self-oriented nature of our being. John Dewey presented a vision of an Other as the irrational "*Old Adam, the unregenerate element in human nature... [that] shows itself wherever the method obtains of attaining results by the use of force instead of the* [human development] *of communication and enlightenment"* (Dewey, 1954, pp. 154–5).

However, as Tajfel has shown empirically, when we create or join a group we also create and construe "others" – those *not* in the "in-group." Sometimes these "others" are the product of our fears; sometimes categorising others leads us to demean and derogate them, treating them with suspicion, magnifying the perceived differences, generating hatred or disgust at their presence. In subsequent chapters we will look at how we can, psychologically, hold each other in trusting reciprocal relationships in which fears and anxieties may be examined; ideally (though possibly hard to fully achieve in the confusing world we inhabit) to be replaced with trust and respect. But before we can do that, we need to understand how others, members of another perceived group can be imagined and, seemingly almost instinctively, derogated. Self-preservation seems to be a powerful instinct and our fear of the unknown can blind us to what might be our own and others' best interests. As we've already noted, Parfit (1984, p. 5) showed that it was not necessarily in our personal far-reaching "best" interests to pursue our own self-interest: "*It may be better for me if I have some other disposition.*"

Our society is still dealing with the casualties of dominant groups who have created (for their own selfish purposes) subordinated "*serviceable* others" (Sampson, 2008, p. 4): people of colour, women, those with differing sexual orientations, people with different views, characteristics, or abilities. We do it too easily. We do it to advantage ourselves, to disadvantage others, but in doing so ultimately demean both ourselves and others. In our view as educationalists and psychologists, the language (the terminology) that pervades parts of education casually demonstrates and perpetuates the categorisation, "essentialising" and "othering" of children, young people, and teachers (for instance talking of the "SEN children," or "failing teachers," as if they were members of a different species). This is, for us, one of the fundamental problems that need to be addressed in education now: the practice of casual labelling, "othering" and demeaning of others.

If we accept that we only exist, in a human sense, in relation one with another, we must also accept we have reciprocal responsibility for each other. If we want to be respected for our difference, we must also respect the difference of others. As Zygmunt Bauman said:

> One needs to honour the otherness in the other, the strangeness in the stranger… that it is in being different that makes us resemble each other and that I cannot respect my own difference but by respecting the difference of the other.
>
> (Bauman, 1993, pp. 235–6)

We draw attention to this because, sadly, we do not always act consistently carefully or rationally. We may not always be clear or certain about our core values. We may – or may not – hold that our actions are morally determined without regard for their consequences. But, without thinking (or thinking too fast) we sometimes jump to conclusions that lead to unethical behaviour that causes harm for others (Kahneman, 2011). Getting the wrong answers in a test of economics (for instance) may be bad enough but getting the ethically "wrong" (disrespectful) answer might be fatal in certain circumstances. We can – and do – use the power to dislocate the lives of others, sometimes because we think, selfishly, that we cannot cope with matters as they are, and think (too fast) that matters as they could be, will be better for our (selfish) selves. With this is mind we'll return to our consideration of some of the consequences of grouping and othering in education.

## Groups in education, not all of which are intentionally educational

Groups in educational settings in the UK come in a range of shapes and sizes, few of which, we suggest, are fit for purpose if our purposing of education is to help young people learn how to collaborate with each other and become more inclusive of diversity. We have outlined above how putting people into groups can adversely affect their behaviour toward others. We suggest here that the categorisation and grouping of children (and teachers) is unlikely to be associated with "good" education. One of our chief purposes in writing this book is to promote dialogue between people as a means of developing educational processes that are yet more inclusive. We see many of the instances of grouping in educational systems and settings as being artificial, not inclusive.

One example of what we see as an artificial and essentially arbitrary categorisation and grouping of children may be found in the continuing use of the "11+" test in a number of local authorities. Of the 343 educational authorities in England at present, 37 (11%) still use a one-off test (of spurious validity or integrity (Allen & Bartley, 2017; Jerrim & Sims, 2019) of children at the age of 11 to determine which type of secondary school and what sort of education the children should have thereafter. Sadly, this provides perhaps one of the most powerful lessons for the young people in these authorities – that their future educational opportunities and outcome are determined by others. In those parts of the country where the 11+ persists, at the age of 11 children are classified, grouped, and segregated. Those who fail this "one-off" test are deemed not suitable to attend one of the 163 "grammar schools" that still exist – as remnants of the middle-ages. There remains vigorous debate about the supposed merits of selection of the most able despite no strong evidence that such selection provides any significant advantages (Glaesser & Cooper, 2012; Gorard & Siddiqui, 2018). But there are several other ways that young people are grouped and segregated within education. Although the issues involved are complex and the "needs" to be addressed may be conflicting, it can sometimes seem that children are "othered" by being unilaterally deemed unfit (or unworthy) of education in a mainstream school and consequently placed in a "special" school. Some young people are excluded from school for a fixed period and an increasing number are permanently excluded from mainstream and special schools because of the perceived nature and unacceptability of *their* behaviour.

As we have already noted data from the DfE show that around 0.1% of all children and young people are permanently excluded from schools every year. The number (and proportion) of children from certain notional demographic sections of the population are significantly over-represented amongst those excluded. For instance: boys are consistently about three times more likely to be excluded than girls; pupils of "Black Caribbean" heritage are three times more likely to be excluded than their peers; children from poor families (therefore eligible for free school meals) are around four times more likely to be excluded than those not eligible for free school meals. At the same time the number of children excluded from mainstream education because of their "special" educational needs warranting placement in a special school, rose from 101,528 children in 2015/16 to 125,498 in 2019/20. (It also worth noting that children with recognised special educational needs are also six times more likely to be permanently excluded from any school than pupils without any identified special needs.)

These data provide some evidence of the ways in which children can be categorised, grouped, treated, and excluded from important aspects of education. We suggest that it is partly a consequence of the *fact* that children are grouped that they are treated differently. As Carolyn Shields pointed out:

> Educational practices that ignore inequalities, either by essentializing difference or attempting to ignore it, are manifestations of firmly rooted and pervasive attitudes that may best be described as pathologizing the lived experience of students.
>
> (Shields, 2004, p. 112)

There is evidence that people who are in some way seen as problematic and are then treated as though they are in their *essence* different, also become negatively stereotyped (e.g. children who are perceived to have difficulty with aspects of the curriculum). Studies have shown that when children are categorised and labelled in specific, quasi-medical ways teachers' beliefs about the nature of the children's difficulties change so that these are seen as though the underlying difficulties are more likely to be fixed and, therefore, less susceptible to intervention – technically more "essentialised" (Gibbs et al., 2020; Gibbs & Elliott, 2015).

But teachers and the schools they work in are also at risk of being "othered." As an outcome of the current formal school inspection protocols in the UK, schools and their teachers are classified and grouped in one of four categories (Ofsted, 2019). This can mean that the staff in a school are found to be working in an "Outstanding" school or, less happily, in a school that "Requires improvement" or is thought to be "Inadequate." In any event, they will be in a group of professionals that has been inspected and judged by members of another group;

a group that can arrive and inspect the school with very little warning, and with whom little if any meaningful dialogue can be had; a group that may be seen as more powerful than the teachers in a school. Clearly, as may be easily imagined, such judgements can have powerful effects on what teachers believe about their competence and the competence of others (including the inspectors).

Teachers working in a school that has been classified as "Requiring improvement" or "Inadequate" can expect to be re-inspected at some point in the near future and at very short notice. It then becomes more likely that the teachers in such schools are constantly on their guard for fear of the next inspection and an adverse outcome. In an especially harsh example of this regime, a school that had been deemed to require improvement was re-inspected eight times in 18 months, and during one particularly intense phase, five times in nine months. Staff of the school said they felt as though they were being inspected all the time "*in order to 'train' themselves and pupils into expected modes of behaviour*" or, in other words, to perform to order but not necessarily contingent on the pupils' needs (Ball, 2003, 2015; Courtney, 2016; Perryman, 2006). Under such conditions it would be understandable if teachers' autonomy and creativity would be stifled and "learned helpless" acquired (Gibbs, 2018a; Seligman, 1972).

It is arguable that under a regime in which teachers' performance is crudely measured and objectified, and teachers held accountable for the progress of their students, their capacity for creativity is reduced and fear for their professional status is increased. We think that this can jeopardise inclusive education, diminishing teachers' beliefs in teaching that is contingent on the needs and learning of individual children. It is also notable that in Academies where high academic performance is regarded as the top priority and students are required to conform to tightly prescribed standards of behaviour there is little tolerance of non-conformity and poor academic attainment, resulting in the exclusion of large numbers of children and young people. Thus, a significant proportion of all young people are "othered" and educated outside of the mainstream. We were recently given a simple illustration of how this can happen when a trainee educational psychologists told us a primary school teacher they were working with had pleaded that an "under achieving" boy in their class should be placed elsewhere so that the teacher might be sure to earn their performance related pay that was linked to the aggregated achievement of the whole class.

Such a regime of "performativity" and of being constantly on edge waiting for another Ofsted inspection has been likened to one of the more bizarre inventions of utilitarianism in the eighteenth century. The philosopher Jeremy Bentham (Bentham, 1791) proposed that prisons could be designed to be more "effective" (meaning that prisoners would more rapidly learn to conform and behave "acceptably") by ensuring that prisoners could be continuously observed by a single guard. Bentham called his design the "panopticon" and proposed that if prisoners could always be seen, without knowing exactly when they were being watched, they would be more likely to behave well. (Although

Bentham did not live to see his design in practice and his design was never fully realised, it is thought that the design of Pentonville Prison in London (built in 1832) was based on Bentham's ideas.)

However, as we now know from psychological experiments conducted in the 1960s and 70s, when "subjects" in an experiment sense they can exercise no control over their situation other than be passive and conform (as would prisoners in Bentham's panopticon) they often acquire a state of passivity and "learned helplessness," in fear of what might happen next (Haney, Banks, & Zimbardo, 1972; Haslam & Reicher, 2012; Milgram, 1973; Seligman, 1972). In circumstances such as these people can start to believe that they have little option but to accept their powerlessness. In consequence they then develop signs of depression or mental illness (Mikulincer, 2013; Overmier, 2002). It is no surprise, therefore, to learn that teachers (feeling threatened by Ofsted observations and judgements) are at relatively high risk of mental ill-health and, as a result, early retirement (Brown, Gilmour, & Macdonald, 2006; McLean, Abry, Taylor, Jimenez, & Granger, 2017; Stansfeld, Rasul, Head, & Singleton, 2011). When teachers are unwell how can their pupils thrive? It is our hope that this present book will help establish means of supporting staff in schools and confirming a positive possible alternative purpose for education.

Much of what we have outlined above, that forms the context for the regime of "performativity" for teachers and the development of children and young people, might be regarded as "unhealthy." Not only is the well-being of teachers threatened but the quality of children's education and their well-being at risk (Frowe, 2001; Harding et al., 2019; Keddie, 2016). It is in this context that in the following chapters we will discuss ways that teachers, other professionals, parents, and carers can work together to transform and revitalise educational practice.

## Conclusion

As we have seen in the preceding pages interaction with others, human interaction, is what shapes us as a human society – perhaps in that respect, very little different from many other animal species. But if, as we will discuss later, democratic societies are to remain viable, we argue we need to be able to continue to interact and learn from and about each other; we need to be wary of the boundaried conformity and potentially stigmatising effects of being (placed) in groups, of the effects of othering – and of being othered, essentialised, dehumanised. On those grounds we reiterate the proposal that education should have the aim of helping us learn how to become human and learn to live within the diversity of others (Macmurray, 1958/2012). We suggest, therefore, that we will only become truly human by engaging with others in interactions that are both curious and mutually respectful. In the words of Sharon Todd (2015, p. 10) "it is only in _facing_ humanity [and its potential for inhumanity] *that we can more adequately conceive of advocating an educational responsibility for dealing with injustice.*" In order to do this, as we will elaborate in the following chapters, we need in all aspects of our lives to "*create space for the impulse toward openness and hold in check the temptation to shut doors*" (Hansen, 2016, p. 122). Teaching in schools can seem a lonely occupation. We believe it does not have to be so. Teachers themselves can form communities of learners (Clark et al., 2017; Leat, Lofthouse, & Taverner, 2006) and open doors for each other and their students. Likewise, educational psychologists and other professionals can help staff in schools discover new perspectives and possibilities (Gibbs & Miller, 2014; Gibbs & Papps, 2017). In the following chapters we will discuss some of these possibilities and the role for dialogic interactions.

## Note

1 The absence rate is the total number of sessions missed due to overall absence for all pupils as a percentage of the total number of possible sessions for all pupils, where overall absence is the sum of authorised and unauthorised absence and one session is equal to half a day.

# 2   On being and becoming human
## Relationships in professional settings

## Introduction

In this chapter we want to suggest that a necessary challenge for humankind, and one that is central to what we think about education, is how we may together seek to *become* more human (we don't suggest there is or can be a defined end-state of *being* the perfect human or, as Adrienne Rich (1995, p. 5), quoting Rosa Luxemburg, suggested could be taught). We see this as a humble but valid response to the strife that continues to afflict the peoples of the world, including the very real current threats of pandemics, climate change, and poverty. We suggest that if humankind is to survive it may only survive if we can learn how to become more socially aware, collaborative, and able to listen to each other with respect for our differences. It seems to us that if we are to achieve that we should start by thinking about how children and young people can be helped to grow up as global citizens, learning to face humanity (Todd, 2015). That then calls into question what might be entailed for education and educationalists in the process of becoming human. It is part of our contention that in many parts of the world, and certainly in schools in the UK at present, it is has become very hard for teachers to give much thought, never mind practical activity, to the necessary humanising processes of education.

Teachers in schools are given (and have to some extent accepted) responsibility for a significant part of the development of children and young people. It seems important, therefore, to consider what might be involved in a role for teachers seeking to enable young people to become members of the social world, for now and for the future. Such considerations inevitably also involve critically examining factors that impinge on how their roles are created and can be enacted. To do justice to what may seem an ill-defined task we'll look at the work of psychologists and philosophers of education who have tried to articulate what might be implicated in "becoming human."

In the previous chapter we set out some of the current environment for education and teachers in the UK. We also looked at some of the outcomes of education for teachers and young people. In our more pessimistic moments, the context for education often seems to be a rather bleak and hostile environment in which notions of humanity appear either invisible or at best low down

DOI: 10.4324/9780429343766-3

the list of the priorities for teachers. While we know there are outstanding examples where this is not true, much of education, thinking for instance of the perennial debate and successive governments' dictats about how best to assess the achievements of children and young people (exams, teacher assessment, course work?), appears redolent of the dogmatism of a Dickensian world,[1] with a curriculum that might have been suitable at some point in the distant past but does very little to prepare young people for life in the 21st century (Claxton, 2014). In such a context it is hardly surprising that so many young people appear disenfranchised or excluded from meaningful education (what is education for?), or that a worrying number of teachers leave the profession each year. We will say more about the curriculum in the next chapter. To get to the heart of the issues as we see them, in this chapter we'll look first at the broad global context before focusing on the specifics of what may be involved in developing the climate and topology of education in schools.

## Social, global context

The sterility of a world that consisted of just plain hard facts is hard to imagine. It would entail the absence of any "inner life," in which consciousness coloured by emotions and our sympathetic responses to the plurality and differences of others would be largely absent. As Arendt (1958/1998, pp. 7–8; see also Skeie, 2002) said

> Plurality is the condition of human action because we are all the same, that is human, in such a way that nobody is ever the same as anyone else who ever lived, lives or will live.

We live in a social world; a world in which our existence and survival are both dependent on and resonate with others. But, we wonder, how does education as it is currently prescribed, help young people learn how to be with others and help start to solve some of the issues experienced in local neighbourhoods as well thinking more creatively about some of the problems facing us globally?

Despite the apparently mundane components and commitments of our day-to-day lives, our worlds are, in fact, full of fascinating paradoxes and challenges. Although we recognise that we need others, we persist in forming, joining, and being included by societies and subgroups that both endorse our sense of belonging and safety, while simultaneously, and inevitably, excluding us from others. Thus, we become inclusively exclusive. We are not always good at accepting and enabling others, and not always successful at explicitly valuing their different characteristics. Accordingly, we often seem to find it difficult, if not impossible, to talk with others that we don't know well – or at all. Our sense of humanity is often challenged by the presence of others. Societal schisms can be as hard to bridge as it can be to understand the position and views of "others." We give to charity but also often seem otherwise inherently selfish and self-interested. Despite our self-interest (or maybe because of it), we persist with the risky business of generating new beginnings, giving birth to raw, new people, each of whom in their infancy and development has the potential for initiatives that will interrupt our desire for a sense of stability and will, at least temporarily, usurp our, apparently unique, sense of consciousness and autonomy. Currently and, we think, perversely, education in the UK seems to do little to prepare young people for parenthood and participation in society.

Ours is, in principle, a democratic society; but democracy is hard to define in theory and in practice (Dahl, 2020; Duncan, 1983). It seems that when faced with the challenges of society as it is and the democratic choices that are offered, many people express helplessness, feeling, for instance, that whoever they vote for little will change, and expressing disgust at those who are elected (Bouko & Garcia, 2020; Pattie, Hartman, & Johnston, 2019; Remer-Bollow, Bernhagen, & Rose, 2019). Those seeking election also often appear to articulate a notion of how society should be but then in practice find it hard to critically analyse or recognise the range of consequences for others, many of which may be iniquitous. It seems increasingly obvious that in this way a model of society that benefits self-centred purposes is privileged. Meanwhile, the COVID pandemic has shown how at times of heightened public anxiety patterns of racist discrimination and inequity are exacerbated (Elias, Ben, Mansouri, & Paradies, 2021). Too often we fail to challenge media representation of racist discourses (Smith, 2020). While we seem willing, if not eager, to destroy our environment, we say we do not want that to happen, again. These are challenging times, and these form the context for education now. It against this backdrop, therefore, that, we suggest, young people might gain more from an educational curriculum that prepares them for the challenges ahead.

## Progress to date?

During the course of the development of our current civilisations much has been achieved in material matters. In just the past 100 years or so we have achieved feats of science and engineering at both micro- and macro-levels that would have completely baffled our grandparents. We now have sophisticated systems of transport and electronic communication that were inconceivable 100 or even just 50 years ago. Such is the power and speed of communication now that while our neighbours might seem to be next door, they may be just as easily on the other side of the world.

Likewise, there is now a much greater understanding of how we function biologically and what medical interventions can achieve. We can cure diseases that felled our forebears. Medico-legal interventions can be used to sustain life even when life may seem unendurable. But, thanks to the work of Kurt Gödel and others, we have also learned that truth cannot be proved, and that we can't know everything about everything at any stage in the future (Raattkainen, 2005; Smullyan, 2017).

While psychological studies have shown us something about how we learn and how, by word and deed, how we may influence and affect each other in our conversations (we will discuss this in more detail in Chapter 6), the evidence of continuing international strife and widespread global poverty suggests that we could benefit from learning more about how we might better know and understand each other locally and internationally (Grych & Swan, 2012; Michael, 2014). We wonder, therefore, if we could learn how to be better citizens of the world, with some understanding of what it might take to be a cosmopolitan (Appiah, 2007a; Todd, 2015). Being pragmatic, we suggest that a good place to start, where it is, perhaps, relatively easy and possible to make a difference, is in schools. Here, by starting at the local level in work with those who care for and help to socialise the citizens of the future it should be possible to undertake work that would make a difference to human life and social interactions, thinking about what would enable us to become humans who get on with each other with greater respect and understanding.

As Hannah Arendt said in delineating the human condition, whatever we

> "Do or know or experience can make sense only to the extent it can be spoken about" *[and that so far as we]* "live and move in this world, … can experience meaningfulness only because *[we]* can talk with and make sense to each other …"
>
> (Arendt, 1958/1998, p. 4)

The clear moral and ethical implications of this are that we have a responsibility to try to make sense of and for each other while also recognising our differences (Bauman, 1993; Todd, 2015). This happens in conversations, in the processes implicit in dialogue with others that enable us to think about what we are doing with each other within the manifest plurality of the world. But the plurality of society includes the range of the infinite variety of "humanity" – some of whom will seem to others as less human.

Thus, with respect to the need for educational settings and processes that could help us become human, we also wonder if more consideration might (with due respect to works of John Dewey and Gert Biesta) be given to the practicalities of a system of education that better supports human becoming. It is clear to us that too much attention has been given to a restricted notion of "knowledge" and how "attainment" can be measured. Too little attention is being given to learning about who we are and what we could be doing with each other in mutually respectful and helpful ways; how we can learn from and with each other. Although we may locally despair when children fight with each other and disrupt lessons, helping children learn how to work and play together, how to face the diversity of human kind, helping them learn about social behaviours does not seem to have a high priority in the curriculum (see Powell and Gibbs (2018) for an example of how this has been done). (Neither, let us note, is there space to learn about how to be a "good enough" parent.) As we discuss in the next chapter, academic achievements, aping the curriculum of the medieval grammar schools, remain the day-to-day priorities, the "gold standard" for most schools, teachers, and parents. Rather than think what students' disruptive behaviour (for instance) might be saying about the nature of the curriculum and its salience for disenfranchised young people, there appears to be an overwhelming temptation to blame the students for *their* failure to conform to what is being imposed on them. The voices of dissent are suppressed. Current educational policies seem bereft of anything but technical solutions to marginally relevant problems such as training teachers in how to control their classes and how to raise children's levels of academic attainment. Currently this seems, for instance, writ large in the UK government's proposals to revise the curriculum for initial teacher education, with a return to prescribed "training" in the use of specific classroom techniques (DfE, 2021a). As John Macmurray perceptively said more than half a century ago:

> Here, I believe, is the greatest threat to education in our society. We are becoming more and more technically minded: gradually we are falling victims to the illusion that all problems can be solved by proper organisation: that when we fail it is because we are doing the job in the wrong way, and that all that is needed is the "know-how." To think thus in education is to pervert education. It is not an engineering job. It is personal and human.
> (Macmurray, 1958/2012, p. 674)

To pose two practical questions: Does education help people develop the knowledge, understanding, and skills entailed in having conversations with strangers; conversations that reach across boundaries and barriers to talk with others about things we don't yet understand? What else do we need to do to become better citizens of and for the world?

## Education, schools, and relationships: the philosophical foundations

So far have we sunk since Macmurray gave his talk in 1958 that one might be forgiven for thinking the only way was up. (But, of course, paraphrasing Hegel, what we learn from history is that we don't.) The ethos of performativity and the commodification of teachers – "*a technical workforce to be managed and controlled rather than a profession to be respected*" (Tomlinson, 2001, p. 36) – now seems so deeply engrained that an alternative perspective seems almost heretical.

However, challenging voices may still be heard. As has been said, we

> come into our own by helping other beings (human and otherwise) to come into their own along with us *[and]* we can only <u>be</u> anything by continuing to <u>learn</u> to become it, then this means that for us, to put it boldly, to be is to learn… we can only "be" anything by continuing to become it.
> (Thomson, 2016, pp. 846–9; emphasis in the original.)

In other words, to become human we need to continue to become by being learners. To think about this, we may need to think about how schools are conceptualised and organised.

## School organisation as the basis for learning

Schools as organisations and settings for education have structures (physical and psychological) that are created and, for a while at least, are sustained by leadership and resources; leaders who are in a reciprocal relationship with their staff and able to support them in believing that they can do what they need to do by enhancing their sense of professional purpose and well-being; to be members of "learning organisations" (Levin & Riffel, 2019; Senge, 2006). Education is a potentially powerful social force. A question to be asked, however, is about what we might ask school staff to do? Are we expecting them to model past, present, or possible future ideals about social structures and processes? It doesn't seem to us that any such expectations have been explicitly stated or debated and we wonder, therefore, if they might need to be.

The primary resources of any school are the staff and the quality of professional relationships within both the staff group and the leadership of the school. It's important to note the obvious, that not all resources for education and learning are necessarily material. The crucial resources of a school's staff that are embedded in their professional inter-relationships can be reciprocal and self- reinforcing and critical to the well-being of the staff and pupils (Eldor & Shoshani, 2016; Price, 2011; Reay, 1998). School leaders (who are another important resource; we neglect their well-being at considerable cost) can, likewise, support intra-staff relationships and an organisational culture that explicitly considers "*what kinds of lives are good or bad for a person to lead*" (Appiah, 2007b).

These are "complex" times. For school leaders the complexity of educational organisations and the behaviours of those (staff and students) who inhabit them, are compounded by several factors. These include the competing and fluid priorities of forces that are both internal to the school (staff and curricular requirements) and the externally imposed environment for education (government policies; school inspection regimes). Successfully negotiating and navigating a course of action in the interface of these factors takes skill and stamina. (For some thoughts on these issues see Davies, Milton, Connolly, & Barrance, 2018; Gibbs, 2018a; MacBeath, 2009; Shields, 2004; Towers, 2022).

Given some of the features of education that we outlined in Chapter 1, amidst concerns about staff recruitment and retention, and the possible outcomes of school inspections, the qualities and successes of school leadership are crucial issues. As many have discussed, central to these concerns should be the determination to ensure the well-being and professional orientation of all staff, without which failure is likely (Gibbs, 2018a; Huang, Yin, & Lv, 2019; Kwon et al., 2020; Pagán-Castaño, Sánchez-García, Garrigos-Simon, & Guijarro-García, 2021). But it is apparent that very many school leaders feel isolated and under enormous pressure to determine success solely on the basis of the academic performance and progress of their pupils (Courtney, 2015; Harris, 2004; Nicolaidou & Ainscow, 2005; Reback, Rockoff, & Schwartz, 2014). Teachers, like everyone else, we think, need to feel they are respected and valued as skilful practitioners, as well as supported in *becoming* autonomous creative practitioners who can create an environment in which others may also become human. When, in an organisation the professional orientation of staff and leaders converge on agreed and shared aims, the success of that organisation (according to its own parameters) will be more assured. In slightly more detail, it seems that through discussion and dialogue amongst and between leaders and staff, engagement with the processes involved in developing congruence of shared perceptions and understanding of leadership, commitment, and the organisation's operational systems can be major determinants of their organisation's success. Conversely, ambiguities in mutual perceptions or a lack of certainty about respective roles and tasks are likely to be detrimental to an organisation's functioning (Benlian, 2014). This implies that if intra-staff relationships in schools, as well as the more specific relationship staff have with their leaders, involve an active sense of "partnership" and mutual respect, a shared engagement in learning can be fostered (Campbell, 2016; Thomas, Martin, Epitropaki, Guillaume, & Lee, 2013; Valcea, Hamdani, Buckley, & Novicevic, 2011). But just as the well-being of the main body of staff is important, so too is the well-being, enthusiasm, creativity, and motivation of school leaders. It is only through an endorsement of learning as a continuing and open-ended creative process for all (leaders, staff, and students), we suggest, will more students experience "good education" and be enabled to lead "good" lives now and in the future.

Studies of leadership have posited a range of models ranging from "*transactional*" via "*transformational*" to "*discursive*" (Bass, 1990; Clifton, 2012; Van Hooser, 2013). It seems probable that the currency of any one of these models will be dependent on the prevailing economic and political climate, the nature of the "business," and the ontological orientation of the leader(s). None are guaranteed success in all circumstances. Current thinking in some of the settings for education seems to favour an eclectic balance of transactional, transformative, and distributed models. However, in some sectors (for instance, in the UK in some "academies") a more directive, authoritative transactional model can be found, a model that seems to explicitly demand considerable similarity across the external expectations, imposed ethos, behaviour policies and teaching (pedagogic) practices, with no space for acceptance of diversity. One Academy Trust, for instance, included the following in its statement of "Curriculum Intent":

> We want our students to learn the "grammar" of each subject respecting the traditions and importance of subject disciplines. We provide a clear narrative of what we teach, why we teach it and how it is taught and assessed so that we know if it is understood. Knowledge and skills are inextricably linked and the performance of skills is enhanced by what we know and understand. We believe the acquisition of knowledge empowers our students and appreciate that if children don't remember what we have taught them, then even the richest curriculum is pointless. Knowledge is powerful when it is remembered.
>
> (Retrieved from www.outwood.com/
> curriculum-overview 17/01/2020)

We remain unconvinced that such regimes could ultimately be associated with "good education" and processes that sustain the aim of becoming human. Indeed, there are those (Biesta, 2009, 2015a, for instance) for whom such an approach would be anathema. We think a more democratic transformational or distributed model of leadership would be more appropriate, a model that explicitly emphasises the importance of enhancing staff commitment to change since change is inevitable (Geijsel, Sleegers, Leithwood, & Jantzi, 2003; Leithwood & Sun, 2012). We should, however, also note that although distributed approaches to leadership, helping to shape and share understandings, may be incorporated as part of transformational practice, some commentators have suggested that this style of leadership may not in fact be as democratic as it sounds, appearing as a form of prescriptive hierarchical delegation of authority rather than democracy in practice (Bass, 1985, 1990; Bolden, 2011; Harris & DeFlaminis, 2016).

While in practical, bureaucratic terms the leadership of a school is where the buck stops, it is not just in an ideal world where the extent and quality of reciprocal leader–staff relationships (the mutual respect for autonomy and individual differences) are the major factors in determining the nature and quality of learning for all. The quality and trust embedded in highly ethical and thoughtful professional – and dialogic – relationships will also be crucial factors in determining the stability of the organisation. (By stability we do not, of course, mean static or conservative.) The interaction of leaders and followers, through professional dialogues, allows for the development and sharing of everyone's understanding of their contexts and possible practices. As Sorin Valcea et al. (2011) and others have suggested, while it is traditional (and accepted) that leaders who are concerned for the long term success of their organisation should have a responsibility to help develop the competence of their staff, it is also clear that staff/"followers" have a pivotal role in the development of their leaders through the exhibition of behaviours that validate leaders' beliefs that they can do what is necessary to inspire, enable, and sustain staff creativity (Carroll & Levy, 2010; DeRue & Ashford, 2010; Valcea et al., 2011). With this in mind we wonder if the dichotomy of leader-follower is accurate; whether, within a school staff group (that is *all* staff, including the notional leaders) that is truly respectful of perceived individual differences and mutually motivated to create and sustain the opportunities for all to be learners, it might be more respectful (and democratic) to consider the erstwhile "leader" as simply "*first among equals*"? (A notion that has received some attention elsewhere (Holmberg & Akerblom, 2008; Peetz, 2015).) But, perhaps that is too idealistic, for, as Bogotch suggested, in the interests of achieving greater social justice and sustaining communities of learners, it may be more important for leaders to be able to provide a meta-perspective, being pragmatic, reconciling competing perspectives, supporting creativity, diversity, and holding the community together continuously and recursively (Bogotch, 2002, p. 146). But, in order to achieve greater social justice, especially now in the face of history and the remaining persistent structural inequalities,

one of the central interventions of *[transformative]* educational leaders must
be the facilitation of moral dialogue *[in order to]* provide opportunities for
all children to learn in school communities that are socially just and deeply
democratic.

(Shields, 2004, p. 110)

This implies attention to the benefits of effective communication; communication that is clear, respectful, and reciprocal, continuously building a dialogue
that includes opportunities for everyone to participate meaningfully. As we will
discuss in more detail in Chapter 5, dialogue can provide the space for the
development of shared meanings and purposes. Without communication that is
voluntary, dialogic, and appreciative of the inevitability of diverse perspectives,
there may be no growth of mutual understanding or commonality of purposes.
It has been suggested that dialogue may itself be *"the site of human becoming"*
(Stewart, Zediker, & Black, 2004). Dialogic perspectives also seem inherent
for some accounts of "transformational" processes (including leadership), since
clearly both dialogue and transformation imply effective communication and
appreciative discourses (see Mitra, 2013; Powley, Fry, Barrett, & Bright, 2004).

For us, education should, above all, implicate transformation and transformative practices that are not fixated on transformation to a well-defined outcome
or product but are focussed on the process of becoming what may be (see
Simon, 1996, pp. 185–91, "Designing without final goals"). Further, an educational setting that privileges learning for all implies a need for all (staff and
students) to accept they are becoming learners, learning to learn. As Gert Biesta
has emphasised, however, education cannot (should not) be guaranteed as a safe
process with clearly defined and measurable aims and objectives. In fact, Biesta
has suggested, because the end point of becoming human is unmeasurable, it *has*
to be "risky" (Biesta, 2013). One of the hardest tasks for school staff, as all may
attest, is to manage their response to risk. At one level education and schools
as organisations have become increasingly risk averse through the adoption
of risk assessments and strategies intended to avoid circumstances in which
physical or psychological harm to the health and safety of staff and students
could occur. But for Biesta the necessary "riskiness" of education lies not in
"safeguarding" procedures, but in what is entailed in the inevitably undefinable
objective of becoming human and what this means for every individual to discover along the way. If we are to pursue this aim for education, we, teachers and
educationalists, have to contain anxiety and remain accepting of the diversity of
humankind and outcomes. There are, therefore, no easy outcomes; the conceptualisation of education (our notion of the purpose of education) is, and has to
be, deeply challenging. But surely, if staff are to engage in the risky enterprise of
education, they must feel safe in doing so? Thus, the challenge posed by Biesta
may, for some, feel too unsafe, too risky. We wonder, therefore, if it is necessarily
pragmatically safer to provide opportunities for children and teachers to participate in "non-teleological dialogue," dealing more with the reality of "what is"
not what might be (Kennedy, 1999), in which *"the views of the* [participants] *are*

*held in tension and allowed to spark off each other in ways which lead to creativity and transformation*" (Barrow, 2010, p. 65).

Biesta's objection to safety, to an idea that education can be defined as producing a specific outcome is based in his objection to humanism. For Biesta (and others such as Foucault, 2002; Todd, 2003, 2015), this is a profoundly problematic creed since it requires a definition of what is the ideal for humanity. If that (a specific ideal of humanity) is specified, any other possible notion of humanity is consequently *de facto* non-ideal and inferior. Positing one idealised form of humanity (be it, e.g. Sunni or Shia Muslim, Aryan or Jew, Catholic or Protestant, Deist or Agnostic, white or black) and derogating all "others," is the key raw ingredient for racism, intercultural hatred, and genocidal annihilation of others. For Biesta the idealisation of one version of humanity is, therefore, fundamentally anathema to educational inclusion (Biesta, 2016). As Rahul Mitra has also indicated, leaders who seek to transform, to be more inclusive, have to accept that the process can be "messy," involving inspiration, motivation, and stimulation, but also the complexity and challenge of dialogue, since

> Dialogue stems from ontological difference and privileges conflict as productive of social reality, rather than seeking common ground between self and other.
>
> (Mitra, 2013, p. 400)

Acknowledging this, Mitra provided the grounds for dialogue in leadership and the "trans-formational" processes that are the central theme of this book. Thus, crucially for our purposes, Mitra proposed that leadership should consist in

> ongoing structures of action/re-action, so that even as authority is constituted by existing power relations, it is emergent and constantly contested through dialogic encounters.
>
> (Mitra, 2013, p. 411)

We suggest that schools in which democratic and dialogic processes, involving the creativity of *becoming* (and acceptance of the risk of failure), are most evident amongst staff and students, could be where there exists the greatest mutual respect for differences and ethical autonomy (Appiah, 2007b; Gibbs, 2018a). By this we mean (and agree with Biesta) that none of the participants in education (leaders, teachers, students) should be regarded as "objects" produced as outputs of education but should be able to see themselves as active *participants* who own and accept responsibility for ethical (morally acceptable) interaction with each other in co-creating the processes and outcomes of learning. As Todd (2015, p. 20), drawing on the work of Levinas has suggested:

> the respect, dignity, and freedom which have become signifiers of humanity are not bred from within, but from the relation to the disturbing and provocative event of being confronted by another … allows into education the

difficult prospect of responding to others as an actual <u>practice</u> of justice – however incomplete such practices might be – without deferring it to some future that will one day arrive.

In turn Biesta (2013) has been at particular pains to posit that education be seen as a process of creativity, with the emphasis less on a static state of achievable *"being"* and more (much more) on a process of *"becoming"* in which *learning* is in an integral component. In settings where such processes and beliefs prosper and endure, we argue it is more likely that there can be shared beliefs including, critically, that it is possible, permissible, and necessary for all to learn (Leat et al., 2006). From a psychological perspective one of the key concepts here relates to the individual and collective beliefs of all staff. For us an important notion is that of teachers' "efficacy beliefs": the idea that when teachers believe they are learning what they *can do* what is necessary to achieve better outcomes, such as, for instance, to be educationally inclusive, they are more likely to achieve that aim (Bandura, 1997; Brownell & Pajares, 1999; Caprara, Barbaranelli, Steca, & Malone, 2006; Gibbs & Powell, 2012).

The benefits of enhancing and sustaining teachers' beliefs in their efficacy are clear. There is evidence that teachers with higher levels of belief in relevant self-efficacy are more likely to be successful classroom practitioners (providing a good environment for learning), have positive attitudes to socio-cultural diversity and inclusive practices, show greater tolerance and effectiveness with "problematic" young people, and have a greater sense of personal achievement and are less likely to experience "burnout" (Aldridge & Fraser, 2016; Brouwers & Tomic, 2000; Savolainen, Engelbrecht, Nel, & Malinen, 2012; Shoji et al., 2016). It is the relationship, the synergy of individual and collective beliefs, and the effects of the staff's collective efficacy beliefs that are most salient for the present account. Thus, when teachers as a group share a strong belief in their collective efficacy, it seems that individual members of the group will themselves feel more likely to believe that they too will be successful (see Gibbs & Powell, 2012; Goddard & Goddard, 2001; Viel-Ruma, Houchins, Jolivette, & Benson, 2010). Although there is still a relative paucity of empirical research to provide insight about how teachers' efficacy beliefs may be created and/or sustained there is some evidence that aspects of transformational leadership can support the development of an organisation culture in which collaborative dialogic relationships value and sustain teachers' collective efficacy beliefs (Ninković & Knežević Florić, 2016; Schein, 2003).

## Broadening the perspective again

Having indicated some of the evidence of what may be achieved – and some of the inherent challenges – we will now locate our thoughts about the transformation of human and professional relations in a broader, yet more idealised perspective, that of cosmopolitanism to help provide the context for the local challenge, to reform education, in relation to the global challenge for humanity.

Although an ideal, cosmopolitanism may provide an overarching philosophical perspective that all people, irrespective of geography or political associations may regard themselves to be citizens of a single community, sharing an interest in mutual well-being and survival. This does not, as Sharon Todd has suggested, mean we have to disrespect pluralism; rather, cosmopolitanism can entail an aspiration as a way of life to understand that "*it is the imperfectability of humanity which binds us together*" (Todd, 2015, p. 48). It seems to us that in the world as it is now, with a burgeoning population that is outstripping the available resources, there is, more than ever, great merit in holding this notion as an aim. With such an aim in sight we might be more able to pursue the development of dialogue across boundaries and to share solutions – rather than fight over scarce provisions, territories, or rigid beliefs. As a principle, cosmopolitanism calls on us to think what we might owe to others, to strangers; what would we be prepared to do to act out our ethical responsibilities? As with all ideals, perhaps, it is not without its dilemmas.

Singer (1972, p. 231) set out the local case:

> If I am walking past a shallow pond and see a child drowning in it, I ought to wade in and pull the child out. This will mean getting my clothes muddy, but this is insignificant, while the death of the child would presumably be a very bad thing.

We already have some internationally recognised structures that exemplify aspects of cosmopolitanism that have been achieved in practice. Thus, the principle that individuals should not be subject to the vagaries of the laws of any one state but are protected by internationally agreed law is at the centre of the International Criminal Court. The idea that we all share a duty of care for others in need and an obligation to reduce others' suffering irrespective of nationality is enshrined in the work of the International Red Cross and International Red Crescent Societies, as well as in the more spontaneous responses to calls for charity to address incidents of famine, flood, earthquake, or homelessness. The reunification of Germany in 1990, some might argue, provided a model of how two related but disconnected jurisdictions could be brought together to develop commonality of resources, legislation, economic, and social welfare systems. That this has been at least moderately successful suggests what might be possible across nations whilst resisting demands within some individual states for greater self-centred autonomy and economic freedom. It is obvious that we have a long way to go to realise the ideal of harmonious world citizenship, but in what follows here, without losing sight of the central purpose of this book we'll go some way toward exploring how the ideal of cosmopolitanism could form the basis for the growth of intergroup understanding through education and work in individual settings to ultimately mitigate the causes and effects of international disputes.

As will have been evident from the studies of football supporters that we looked at in Chapter 1, much depends on the personal salience of the frame of reference and context. If you tell people to look out for others in their local club, they will do just that, but possibly no more. If, however, you ask them to look out for anyone who is a football supporter the remit of responsible care becomes bigger and potentially global. The task for educational cosmopolitans is to go beyond the world of football.

We can all, if we so wish, show allegiance to more than one team, one sport, or other forms of joint activity. Allegiances may be nested. It is possible, at least in principle to have an allegiance to the local team as well as caring for all football supporters, not just the "home" team. Passionate support does not have to lead to xenophobic hatred of the other side; it can simultaneously celebrate and respect the differences. We have already discussed some of the dangers that can arise from group membership and identification and nationalism is certainly not immune from these dangers. (For a broader discussion of nationalism, see, e.g. Greenfield, 2012). What we are suggesting, therefore, is that education could help young people recognise their allegiance to young people around the world (as perhaps those who are part of "Extinction Rebellion" feel). Accordingly, to achieve this aim we would need schools to have a broader perspective than merely striving to demonstrate pupils' attainment within a curriculum dedicated to the learning of siloed subject content.

In embarking on our defence of cosmopolitanism and to disarm claims for privileging patriotic, self-serving allegiances before caring for others in the world, we are reminded of an anecdote from first aid training: "*Switch off the electricity at the mains before attempting to rescue someone who has been electrocuted.*" Before giving aid, make sure it is safe to do so. Currently this issue is alive in the debate about global immunisation against COVID-19. Do we help immunise everyone in the world when we could keep the vaccine here and protect all UK citizens?

Appiah (2007a, p. 161) expressed the general principle here neatly (and more positively) as "*If you are the person in the best position to prevent something really awful, and it won't cost you much to do so, do it.*" Appiah's words foreshadow Biesta (2015b, p. 86) who, discussing what he had gained from his reading of Levinas, wrote about:

> when it **matters** that I am unique, that I am I and no one else... in those situations in which I cannot be replaced by someone else, that is, where it matters that **I** am there...

But Appiah's view was not an endorsement of pure self-interest (and certainly not self-aggrandisement) but a note of cautious pragmatism so that any attempt to help is not doomed to failure but may be repeated in the future. There's also more than a hint of being wary of repeating the fantasies of Mrs Jellyby (a character in Dickens' novel "Bleak House") who focussed only on schemes of aid in far off places while neglecting her own kin.[2] But the general point that we have made several times so far remains: psychologically we cease to exist without others and imperil ourselves and others if we are selective about who we respect and value; it simply matters that we are there for others. Rather than posturing, as Mrs Jellyby does as the potential saviour of others in far off places (but simultaneously neglecting her own children who live in squalor), most of us will need to be grounded in the reality of relationships and interactions much nearer to home. A cosmopolitan's dilemma is, therefore, about one's instinctive partiality, the impulse to care for one's nearest (and dearest) before caring for others, elsewhere, who also matter.

To disregard one's kin, as Mrs Jellyby does, is to expose the inadequacy of one's purported love for others. Reconciling the two is not easy. A possible solution to at least part of the dilemma is, however, available in Peter Singer's concept of the "principle of equal consideration of interests."The core of what Singer (1993) proposed was that in considering the consequences of our actions we should give equal importance to the similar interests of all who may be affected by what we propose to do: "*an interest is an interest, whoever's interest it may be*" (Singer, 1993, p. 21). Thus, according to Singer, if we were to do something with regard to the particular interests of "Joan" and "Gemma," and that as a result of the proposed action Joan would lose more than Gemma might gain, then it would be better not to act. Evoking Singer's principle as part of an examination of education as it is frequently – and, in the UK, currently – instantiated, we might ask if it is ethical to maintain educational opportunities that significantly enhance the life-long interests of some whilst clearly perpetuating the socio-economic disadvantages of many?

However, as Appiah (2007a, p. 165) has suggested,

> Any plausible answer to the question of what we owe to others will have to take account of many values; no sensible story of our obligations to strangers can ignore the diversity of the things that matter in human life.

Acceptance of difference, moving toward a more cosmopolitan perspective is, in the field of education and elsewhere, one of the greatest prizes and one of the greatest challenges. But as Todd (2015) emphasised, we must not be too idealistic. The ideal of cosmopolitanism is just that: an ideal that may be visualised in different ways. For Todd (p. 38) it involves:

> returning to the other as the fulcrum for the communicative aspects of democracy *[in order to]* radicalize the potential for democratic practices to take alternative forms... because without facing difference and alterity, there is no possibility for communication, for dialogue, for discourse.

## Conclusion: setting aside self-interest

All of the above, the hope to develop greater respect and concern for peoples irrespective of race, colour, gender, or capabilities, requires a willingness to set aside pure self-interest. It is not, we suggest, trivial but important to be reminded that

In human societies there will always be differences of views and interests. But the reality of today is that we are all interdependent and have to co-exist on this small planet. Therefore, the only sensible and intelligent way of resolving differences and clashes of interests, whether between individuals or nations, is through dialogue.

(Dalai Lama, 2000, p. 169)

But it is not easy, nor necessarily always possible to ignore self-interest, for several reasons. As we have already suggested, if one is serious about helping others – thus, being willing and able to do it not just once – it is probably wiser to ensure that one will be in a position to be able to do so again by making sure one is safe, grounded, in the first place. Although it is surely obvious that there is a strong biological, evolutionary instinct for self-preservation that is, very plausibly, necessary for basic survival, it is also evident that there is a strong cultural prejudice (at least in most Western cultures) towards self-interest that, in turn, affects our expressed beliefs and actions (Campbell, 1986; Gardner & Ryan, 2020; Miller, 1999). Studies of the relationship between self-interest and "other orientation" (or altruism), for instance, have shown that people's apparent self-interest may be strongly influenced by the prevailing norms of public opinion/pressure. Thus, when there is a strong tradition of self-interested (selfish) activity, people privately holding to a different ethic or moral view can feel constrained to conform (for fear of appearing different) and also act in self-interested ways (Meglino & Korsgaard, 2004; Miller, 1999). Thus, in-group pressure to conform prevails, again. But, if we are purely, *only*, limited to pursuing our self-interest we will not, cannot, care for the needs or interests of others. In order to develop education with an ethical focus we will need to move away from the current and persistent mediaeval-style curriculum in schools. While the aim of education remains to be for self-serving individual achievements it will be hard to sustain and develop concerns for others in education and more broadly in society.

The general, personal consequences of pursuing self-interest were thoroughly examined in a series of thought experiments by Parfit, whose philosophical exploration of self-interest started with the key question of what we each "*have most reason to do*" (Parfit, 1984, p. 17). Parfit showed that it followed rationally that if we only pursue our own selfish self-interest, we not only jeopardise our own well-being but the welfare of others as well. A corollary, almost existential, question that Parfit posed, in considering individual autonomy and self-interest, was how does someone achieve "*the outcomes that would be best for himself, and that would make his life go, for him, as well as possible*" (Parfit, 1984, p. 3). Parfit (p. 28) again argued that purely self-interested aims may be self-defeating, and that it becomes logically and morally

> [*more*] rational to do what one knows will best achieve what, after ideal deliberation, one most wants or values, even when one knows this is against one's own self-interest.

It is notable that many eastern philosophical traditions hold complementary views about the "self" (see, for instance, Fulton, 2008; Gergen, 2009; Gülerce, 2014; Sampson, 2008) that are at odds with the essentially individualistic, selfish emphasis found in much western psychology – as well as the prevailing political dogma and ensuing economic and educational policies. Parfit found that his own conclusion had parallels with the Buddhist tradition, in that his liberation from a sense of self in which he had felt imprisoned in a

> glass tunnel, through which I was moving faster... and at the end of which there was darkness...*[was such that]* when I changed my view, the walls of my glass tunnel disappeared. I now live in the open air... I am less concerned about the rest of my own life, and more concerned about the lives of others.
>
> (Parfit, 1984, p. 281)

But we must also note that self-interest and fear remain close neighbours (though not necessarily allies). Instinctual self-preservation is evoked when we come under threat, when we are afraid for ourselves and those dearest to us. The fear of extinction is a primary emotion and, as Martha Nussbaum (2018, p. 60) has said

> We are vulnerable, and our lives are prone to fear. Even in times of happiness and success, fear nibbles around the edges of concern and reciprocity, turning us away from others and toward a narcissistic preoccupation with ourselves. Fear is monarchical, and democratic reciprocity a hard-won achievement.

Earlier in the same work Nussbaum proposed fear as the primary emotion and, by implication, therefore, the biggest threat to democracy and cosmopolitanism:

> [I]t is because of infection by fear that the three other emotions *[anger, hatred and disgust]* turn toxic and threaten democracy. Yes, sure, people strike back out of a sense of unfairness. But what is that exactly? Where does it come from? Why do people feel this way, and under what conditions does blame become politically toxic? These are the sorts of questions that we need to ask about each emotion, and I believe that they all lead back to fear and life-insecurity.
>
> (Nussbaum, 2018, p. 9)

Thus, if we are to become more careful and respectful toward others, more cosmopolitan, we become less self-interested and more able to reach out to others ethically; more willing to appreciate what we value in and about others, our share in difference. With ethical concern for others comes greater consciousness of how we behave with and toward them. In turn this seems to entail that we, ourselves, become less afraid of fear, fear that has erstwhile been located in others or the "Other." Becoming less fearful we may feel safe with others, in the company of strangers. Ultimately:

> To be a person is to be in communication with the Other. The knowledge of the Other is the absolute presupposition of all knowledge, and as such is necessarily indemonstrable.
>
> (Macmurray, 1961, p. 77)

To achieve this, as professionals we may create "safe" spaces for ourselves and others, space in which we can communicate confidently and safely; if we can be with others, not avoid or confront them, but talk with them (not "at" or "about" them). Being able to be with and talk with others, including strangers, is close to the heart of truly respectful reciprocity and involves being able to attend to and support others with no fear for our own selves. As we as educationalists engage with others, attending to how we relate to what we each do with each other, democratic, cosmopolitan, practices emerge, as John Dewey observed (in an age when gender neutrality was not a fact of life for many):

> A democracy is more than a form of government; it is primarily a mode of associated living of conjoint communicated experience. The extension in space of the number of individuals who participate in an interest so that each has to refer his own action to that of others, and to consider the action of others to give point and direction to his own is equivalent to the breaking down of those barriers of class, race, and national territory which kept men from perceiving the full import of their activity.
>
> (Dewey, 1916/2011, p. 50)

What happens in schools in terms of professional relationships and interactions is a microcosm of what happens elsewhere, in this country and across the world. At the heart of what we want to communicate here is the idea that a truly appreciative dialogic and democratic approach to professional relationships in education (indeed, of course, *all* relationships) can provide "safe" spaces for authentic learning: learning about becoming human in a socially problematic world. Gaining, securing "safe spaces" for dialogue, reflection and learning is a theme that will reverberate throughout the rest of the book.

In the following chapters we will discuss how we can construct and sustain psychological environments within educational practices in which learning to become human can prosper, ethically and morally, and in which dialogic professional practices are pivotal. While it may be naive to try to change the world, we can certainly make a small start within the world of education and in our professional discussions.

# Notes

1　*"Facts alone are wanted in life. Plant nothing else, and root out everything else"* (Charles Dickens, *Hard Times*).

2

> You find me, my dears, said Mrs Jellyby, snuffing the two great office candles in tin candlesticks which made the room taste strongly of hot tallow (the fire had gone out, and there was nothing in the grate but ashes, a bundle of wood, and a poker), you find me, my dears, as usual, very busy; but that you will excuse. The African project at present employs my whole time. It involves me in correspondence with public bodies, and with private individuals anxious for the welfare of their species all over the country. I am happy to say it is advancing. We hope by this time next year to have from a hundred and fifty to two hundred healthy families cultivating coffee and educating the natives of Borrioboola-Gha, on the left bank of the Niger.
>
> (Dickens, Bleak House Chapter 4)

# 3   Building educational alternatives

## Introduction

This chapter focuses on the curriculum because it is the fulcrum for education, the interface of many systems and decisions that influence relationships and behaviour in schools (Simon, 1996) and, therefore, the well-being of teachers and young people; and yet it is barely considered in those terms. The focus widens to include the causes and consequences of particular policy and curriculum choices by government and how these reverberate through the educational system, not least in working relationships in schools between teachers and professional peers, teachers and leaders, and teachers and students. The professional identity and well-being of teachers and other professionals is substantially shaped by the curriculum, and the power structures and discourses that hold it in place. Almost inevitably "curriculum" has many definitions. It is commonly seen as the totality of educational provision for children and young people through their formal education. However, there are many elaborations, for example Bondi and Wiles (2007, p. 5):

> We see the curriculum as a desired goal or set of values that can be activated through a development process culminating in experiences for students.

The notion of a desired goal linked to values should be kept in mind, as it suggests that the curriculum is a highly political object, representing particular views of the future of society and the possibilities for its citizens (Au, 2012). Curriculum goals have profound consequences for the tenor of teacher relationships and, therefore, the curriculum changes who we are as professionals. Decisions on curriculum, pedagogy, and assessment can mean more or less (or no) opportunity for developing our humanity and capability, as they can open the door to dialogue, collaboration, social action, and reciprocity or, closing it, offer a thin pedagogical gruel. Thus, bearing in mind the views of Biesta (2013, 2015c) and Simon (1996) we suggest that what is needed to repurpose education is a curriculum design that goes beyond specifying end points and merely *delivering* narrow subject attainment.

DOI: 10.4324/9780429343766-4

Many countries have seen an emergence of teaching to the test as test results have become high stakes for both schools and their students. Underpinned by a neo-liberal view that competition improves standards in schools, exam results have become the critical metric through which to judge schools as education "providers." Schools, therefore, need to gain or retain status in the market as parents increasingly are positioned as consumers (Meier & Lemmer, 2019). Students and their parents strive for good results for entry into prestigious institutions in the next phase of their education, even though not all parents are equally placed to make market choices. However, it is not a free market, as governments feel compelled to regulate provision to greater or lesser extents, often driven by particular political ideologies. Thus, in the UK there is what is termed a "quasi market" in school education, perhaps most obviously operating in England, made very visible by the production of league tables and other comparative measures.

The term performativity, developed by Lyotard (1984) but adopted, adapted, and popularised by Ball (2003) has been applied to the technology of control by the state of public services through the use of numbers to measure performance and set targets. As late as 1988 nowhere in the UK had a National Curriculum and there was considerable freedom for teachers, singly and collectively, to design and enact curriculum within local guidelines and, to some extent according to the needs of the community. Since that date the curriculum capacity and autonomy of teachers has declined in the face of increasing government control of education (Gibbs, 2018). This control is exercised through power, exercised both directly and indirectly. The direct control, in England, is evident in school inspection and regulation regimes, which in the case of Ofsted (the Office for Standards in Education) is felt through the grading system of (1) Outstanding, (2) Good, (3) Requires Improvement, and (4) Inadequate, and the benefits and affordances that follow from good gradings such as status as providers of other educational services. More indirect, and more general control comes from the use of discursive power in the policy language that is used (Foucault, 1982). This is echoed again and again in schools, surfacing in agendas, policies, school improvement documents and meetings. This language works to inform the consciousness of professionals, as they are held to account through these terms and they begin to shape teachers' lives. The language is insinuated with power, so that teachers come to judge themselves and others through words such as standards, progress, target, value added, trajectory, and performance. This language becomes part of the technology of surveillance which is so intrusive that teachers adopt self-surveillance, as professionals evaluate themselves by the criteria used by others to judge them. There is also an increasing intensity to state control through the evolution of performance data tools that reify the importance of numbers used to quantify school and student achievement and which, ultimately, shape the way teachers and student are seen (Ozga, 2009).

## Possible models for a curriculum

In such a climate the importance of the whole person, their well-being and their readiness to become citizens leading good lives drifts into the background. Teachers' autonomy and creativity are suppressed, and little attention is given to learning to live and learn with others. There are a number of recognised models of curriculum each underpinned by particular ontological views, which lay bare very different precepts about what it means to be human and the nature of the world (Kelly, 2009). These models (termed *content, product, process*) adopt fundamental standpoints that correlate with political views, so who holds power to make curriculum decisions matters to the well-being and development of young people who go through school.

The first model is broadly known as the *content* model. This model is onto-logically conservative, accepting that there is an objective world (out there) independent of the student. Traditional subjects are revered and seen as histor-ically important ways of seeing and investigating that objective world with their distinctive epistemologies to establish truth claims and the nature of reality. It is sometimes equated with the statement about knowing "*the best that has been thought and said*" (attributed to Matthew Arnold, headteacher of Rugby School in the 19th century). Such supreme knowledge is regarded as both valuable itself but also as a form of cultural capital which unlocks access to important aspects of society's benefits and riches (Young, 2013). The model reflects strong traditions and heavily influenced the 2014 revision of the National Curriculum in England with the strong backing of Michael Gove, the then Secretary of State for Education. However, the content model is heavily critiqued on the grounds of elitism and social exclusion, as it is argued that it is the powerful who define whose knowledge is given this special status. Many minorities and disadvantaged groups argue that such models have been white-centric, and this has helped spawn the move to decolonise the curriculum. A further potential disadvantage is that there is little room for personal interpretation or for the development of critical or creative thinking. Teachers are part of the mech-anism, indeed the chain, to transmit that content and currently they now have limited bandwidth to interpret the message system – they are constrained and evaluated by means of their effectiveness for delivering (teaching) the pre-specified outcomes.

The *product* model has very different roots and intentions (Bobbitt, 1924). It has an instrumental purpose, derived from the rapidly growing US indus-trial economy in the early 20th century, when production was becoming a science in which efficiency was key. In such contexts production was broken down into sub-processes which followed one to another until the final product was assembled proficiently. The primary role of mass education was to produce workers for the new industrial economy. To achieve this, learning was broken down into manageable bits, so that learning was pre-specified and sequenced through clear behavioural objectives. Thus, this model bears the hallmark of a narrow vocationalism and centralised control, and teachers given only modest scope for creativity and professionalism. However, both the content and product models appear to be grounded in a conception of education as a somewhat mechanical exercise in which a certain body of knowledge (with or without accompanying skills) are transmitted to the next generation. They embody, therefore, a conservative or static concept of education that would be the very antithesis of Macmurray's (1958/2012) ideals.

By contrast the *process* model, or curriculum as becoming, has developmental and emancipatory intentions for the individual. In the words of McKernan (2007, p. 3):

> A curriculum to be truly educational, will lead the student to unanticipated, rather than predicted outcomes ... related to things that truly matter in life.

Learning is not pre-specified and the learner is not subservient to the economy or traditional subjects. The learner is encouraged to become the person they can be, developing their particular talents or capabilities (Biesta, 2013, 2015c; Nussbaum, 2011). Thus, this model is aligned with democratic ideals with a focus on collaboration and working with and through others, including teachers. There is a place for subjects, but it is expected that much work will be cross curricular with some attention given to societal problems and with politics definitely on the menu. This model is associated with curriculum development in the UK in the 1960s and 1970s inspired by Lawrence Stenhouse (1975). Stenhouse was of the view that there was no curriculum development without teacher development – and, we might add, this cannot be achieved without dialogic space.

These models reflect differing relationships between the student, the teacher, and the curriculum. In the content model with its focus on learning subject matter (the "best that has been thought and said"), the press is on for students to master this knowledge and prove their mastery through tests. The student is subservient to the curriculum which is fixed. The teachers' role is as conduit for that knowledge to communicate it as effectively as possible from the curriculum – as written into the curriculum as learned – and in this role they instruct, explain, monitor, test, provide feedback on performance, and summarise achievement. In this context teachers are consequentially hemmed in, positioned as the gatekeepers to knowledge with exams as the gates. While many perform their role with great humanity and skill, it is for students to prove their ability to understand and retain (at least temporarily) the factual and conceptual subject matter. In the UK and US (Hirsch, 1996) this is increasingly being referred to as cultural capital, knowledge without which disadvantaged and marginalised students are excluded from lucrative realms of employment and prestigious society. The essential metric for teachers (and schools) is whether students match up to the required standards, for indeed this is how teachers are evaluated professionally. In the product model, the aim is defined as vocational competence, fitting one's place in the economy and a conservative society (Gatto, 2002). This model heavily influenced the creation of secondary moderns and technical schools and is also reflected in the vocationally oriented schools in many continental countries. In both these contexts a more liberal and expansive education geared to progression into higher education was only available for elites and those who showed academic potential through selection examinations. In contrast, in the process model, where the focus is on human flourishing, there is the opportunity for stronger and more meaningful relationships between students and teachers and between teachers and their peers. In such circumstances there would seem to be greater opportunity for both parties to explore and evolve their identities, talents, and mutual regard.

Some of the subtlety of the impact of curriculum on students is indicated in the powerful concepts developed by Basil Bernstein in his lifelong quest to explain and challenge the relative failure of "working class" children in schools. In his early work Bernstein (1973a, 1973b) argued that middle class children found it easier to adapt to the elaborated language code found in schools because of their home background, whereas working class children found the switch to the formal language of school, from informal, everyday language of home more problematic. In further work he developed a range of interlocking concepts that sought to explain how the exercise of power through the curriculum at many levels contributed significantly to the construction of pupils' identities. Although Bernstein's ideas were not strongly empirically grounded, others have subsequently applied them, generating some sharp insights into the intricacies of how relationships in classrooms are influenced by curriculum and the lasting consequences of these relationships.

Bernstein later distinguished between vertical and horizontal discourse (Bernstein, 1999), the former being a manifestation of formal knowledge distilled through traditional forms of inquiry reflected in school subjects, such as science, mathematics, history, and design technology. The latter is everyday language and knowledge that is not bound by those subject silos but manifests itself through experience. The vertical discourse finds its form in the curriculum as the "collection code" in which subjects are taught separately with little connection between them, thus maintaining a degree of abstraction from the experience of life. The "integrated" code sees a curriculum where links are made across subjects and represented in inter-disciplinary work and stronger connections to life outside the classroom. Strong classification in the curriculum refers to siloed subjects that are kept apart in a vertical curriculum with little attention to intersections between disciplines. Weak classification refers to a more "horizontal" curriculum where the boundaries between subjects are permeable and subjects find their place through their contribution to issues or projects. The related concept of framing refers to "the degree of control teacher and pupil possess over the selection, organization, pacing and timing of the knowledge transmitted and received in the pedagogical relationship" (1973b, p. 88). Therefore, strong framing characterises a classroom in which teachers dominate often "initiating" through questions and is most likely to be substantiated in a curriculum as content model. Weak framing might occur where a process or problem centred model is being enacted. Who asks questions in a classroom is a strong marker of relationships, as at a fundamental level they reflect a relationship to the world and an epistemological stance and infer particular roles for teachers. At one extreme are teachers whose purpose is to teach mastery and recall of subject matter and at the other are teachers whose purpose is facilitate sense making and understanding from experience but, of course, skilled teachers can move between these positions. Despite views to the opposite, this does not mean that subjects have no place in the curriculum, as they are a critical means of making collective sense of the world (Rata, 2016). Bernstein predicted a movement towards a more integrated curriculum. However, he had some reservations as he feared that an integrated more progressive curriculum could be at the expense of depth. He did not anticipate the global reform movement which has seen testing and the marketisation of education come to dominate and shore up the place of subjects. It is worth noting that in Wales and Scotland the curriculum gives some attention to generic competences or capabilities, but there still remains the press for success in subject based public examinations.

## Curriculum making at different sites

To repeat – curriculum making is a strong determinant of relationships in education, between teachers and students and between teachers, their peers, and other professionals. It is increasingly recognised that curriculum making is a social practice taking place at different sites or layers (Priestley, Alvunger, Philippou, & Soini, 2021) with multiple, reciprocal interactions between the differing activities being enacted at those sites. The sites are supra or transnational (e.g. the OECD and the EU), macro (the work of national governments), meso (universities, government agencies, local authorities, think tanks), micro (school leaders and teachers), and nano (individual teachers and students). Although this may be seen as a hierarchy dominated by top-down processes there are important interactions between all sites. This chapter focuses mainly on the significance of the micro and nano sites.

### The supra layer

The importance of the supra layer in this context is reflected in the role played by the Organisation for Economic Cooperation and Development (OECD) through its international five-year testing schedule and comparison tables (PISA). These results send ripples through national education policies, particularly where a country has performed poorly or is nudging the top of the league. The most frequent consequence, especially amongst poorer performers, is to increase standardised testing, in the belief that some combination of competition and accountability will lead to an improved performance of their schools. This has resulted in the growing control of curriculum by the government in England, but the same trends are evident in other UK and European jurisdictions.

## The meso layer

The meso layer can look very different in different countries. In Scotland local authorities still play an important role, whereas in England local authorities are a shadow of their former selves, as schools have been given greater autonomy as they are converted to academies and free schools that are independent of local authority accountability. The ensuing vacuum has been filled by some large Multi-Academy Trust (MAT) chains, the Education Endowment Fund and other third sector organisations with government funding. In England much of this layer is very partisan and ideologically aligned to government policies (Ellis, Mansell, & Steadman, 2021). In many other European countries, however, there are still government agencies and local authorities which support teachers in their curriculum work.

## The micro layer

The micro layer is concerned with the activities of school leaders and their staff and, very obviously, this is the site of one of the most important boundaries, where headteachers interact with policy and messages either from direct from the government (macro layer) or indirectly, filtered by the meso layer. School leaders can mediate and dissipate the most intense effects of government policy, or they can amplify and relay them to their teaching staff. This relationship is, in turn, substantially influenced by the values and beliefs of those school leaders. Greany and Waterhouse (2016) have shown that in very few cases schools in England use the freedom they do have to construct curriculum, because of the felt constraints which overwhelm that legal freedom, and because of the accountability pressures enacted by Ofsted. School leaders need to be very driven and very confident to step away from the normative, test-driven curriculum. A slightly different picture is painted by Fuller (2019) who, whilst recognising the power of the policy discourse, found evidence of forms of resistance, which she characterised as including *game playing, mimicry,* and *sly civility*. While one might appreciate this expression of distaste by leaders it does not, for the most part, counter the unhelpful environment for teacher-peer relationships and curriculum adventure.

A high-stakes testing system generally appears to blunt the appetite of teachers to take risk with curriculum and pedagogy for fear of falling short in the tests (Frank, Zhao, & Borman, 2004; Penuel, Riel, Krause, & Frank, 2009) and may indeed lead to gaming the system (Figlio & Getzler, 2006). Andy Hargreaves and Fink (2012) pointed to the corrosive effect and resultant dissatisfaction amongst teachers when they are forced to submit to blanket standardised tests that they have no faith in. They can − and often do − respond by teaching in a very mechanical fashion devoid of energy and personal engagement. A particular danger is that teachers begin to see students as in deficit in some way, failing to come up to scratch and meet the standards expected. It can also result in some dubious methods to rate teachers' effectiveness (Good & Lavigne, 2015).

If governments press for greater focus on results with various forms of control and surveillance, freedom for manoeuvre in the curriculum is constrained. As a generalisation, performativity in England has encouraged the cult of "super heads," an idolisation of those who can navigate the pressures of accountability and manage systems to produce the results demanded in return for considerable salaries. Some receive knighthoods or other honours (Gunter & Forrester, 2009) and they are often recruited to advisory and review bodies so that their expertise is made more widely accessible and their world view more influential. However, this will often be achieved by *top-down* leadership and in which mainstream teachers are dominated by system demands and have small space for manoeuvre, collaboration, and creativity. It might be seen that this form of leadership is required by the system it operates in. Trujillo (2014) has charted the rise of this administrative efficiency paradigm over a century in the US.

By contrast, *distributed* leadership has its advocates in the cause of dissipating the worst effects of performative pressure. The sustainability of leadership and teacher well-being in Ontario, for instance, was studied by Shirley, Hargreaves, and Washington-Wangia (2020) who highlighted the importance of professional control and moral purpose. They argued that multi-disciplinary collaborative teams bring staff close together as they seek transformational outcomes for their students from diverse backgrounds. Such action needs explicit external support from government and wider society, not least to address poverty and other disadvantage and is not particularly aided by "sticking plaster" methods to address either teacher or pupil (or, indeed, both) well-being, such as meditation or mindfulness sessions. Such tactics may fuel positive, but forlorn, expectations of what can be achieved by students. Similar evidence comes from a study in Flanders, Belgium (Maele & Houtte, 2011), where it was concluded from a multi-level analysis of over 2000 secondary teachers that trust between colleagues was generated when teachers concur about the potential of their students to be taught to good effect and that leadership has a crucial role in achieving this. Overlapping features of successful support are also evident in the Netherlands (Hofman & Dijkstra, 2010), where a comparatively more successful network was teacher directed (rather than top-down), used reflection and subgroups and focused more on active learning in the classroom and the creative work of teacher communities to develop new methods and materials.

## Teacher agency and the micro layer

The concept of teacher agency illuminates our understanding of how and why teachers respond in the constrained conditions of the micro layer of curriculum making. Traditionally agency has been understood as a fixed human quality, reflecting one's ability to tackle the impediments to goals that matter to us. So, people might lack agency and be helpless in the face of adversity or enjoy agency and therefore be masters of their own destiny (see also Bandura, 1997; Ryan & Deci, 2000). Drawing upon the work of Emirbayer and Mische (1998), new understandings of ecological agency have been developed by

Biesta and Tedder (2007). So instead of agency being seen as a fixed trait, it is achieved through the opportunities provided by the working environment or ecology. Thus, the individual may be agentic in one realm of their lives, or at a time period, but with changed circumstance of another context or time, the "ecological" conditions do not allow such action. It is not that those individual qualities are irrelevant, so there may be significant differences in agency between colleagues, but agency, agentic behaviour, is now understood to be developed (as Herb Simon (1996) would have predicted) in the interaction between the individual and their context. In the words of Biesta and Tedder (2007, p. 137):

> … actors always act <u>by means</u> of their environment rather than simply in their environment [so that] the achievement of agency will always result from the interplay of individual efforts, available resources and contextual and structural factors as they come together in particular and, in a sense, always unique situations.
>
> (Emphasis in the original)

In this explanation there are three dimensions to ecological agency, the iterative deriving from past experiences, the practical-evaluative deriving from present circumstances and the projective relating to goals and ambitions for the future. Culture is identified as one major factor in understanding agency in a particular environment, represented in the ideas, values, beliefs, and indeed discourse prevailing. In British contexts, whatever else is present there will be a long shadow of exam performance. Structural issues that matter include the roles allocated, the committees and working groups, allocation of resources, the hierarchies and organisational structures. Material resources have a part to play in the shape of teaching spaces and resources, Information and Communications Technology (ICT) facilities and the quality of the building. These factors shape the degree to which individuals and groups imagine possibilities for students and interact and draw down physical, relational, and cultural support to bring them about. Coburn and Russell (2008) suggested the nature and quality of professional relationships between teachers is an important determinant of agency and efficacy in carrying out change – i.e. the social structures within which they are situated.

In a study of two Scottish high schools Priestley, Biesta, and Robinson (2013) concluded overall that there was a poverty in the discourse available to teachers through which to consider the purpose and value of the curriculum. The discourse used in these schools echoed the language of policy, with much repetition in teacher interviews of the words and phrases in policy documents. The power exercised through accountability mechanisms leveraged the importance of certain concepts, and these concepts crowd out alternative visions of school and curriculum. Of course, the longer such policy-speak dominates the stronger its hold as collective memories fade and competing ideas fall into disuse. Words and the concepts that they elaborate are vital tools in our creative powers for imagining possible futures. Sidorkin (1999) lamented the political discourse of school reform that stresses "addressing problems" and "legislative actions" and gives a premium to structural approaches – the trap, in his words, of believing that policy-making is the way to change schools. This discourse monopolises semantic space and words enmeshed in the discourse become distasteful because of the "*thick crust of permanently attached partisan connotations*" (Sidorkin, 1999, p. 4). Sidorkin positioned any policy as a monological assumption which excludes other voices. Dialogue is, therefore, important, not just as a marker of a powerful talk environment, but also a fundamental condition for loosening the shackles of policy monologue and promoting democracy.

In Priestley et al.'s (2013) study, ecological agency in one school (Hillview) was more constrained by the conditions pervading the school. The formal structures were primarily vertical with communication and accountability organised through line managers. Staff meetings were not for discussion but characterised by information given from the top. The opportunities to com-municate horizontally were limited. Timetabled meetings in faculties and departments had agendas of standard items, such as behaviour, so that the school discourse was very scripted. In the other school (Lakeside) there was more lati-tude, albeit within the general backdrop of playing by the rules. Teachers were encouraged to innovate and take risks and there were real instances of commu-nication cutting horizontally across organisational divides. Here there was more reciprocity and less operating within status defined roles. Such differences seem very likely to reflect approaches to leadership, so that within the latter case, Lakeside, leaders being far more invested in distributed leadership.

## Relational agency

A curriculum with moral purpose creates a very different set of conditions for teacher well-being and sense of professionalism. In the context of working to overcome disadvantage Anne A. Edwards (2007) argued for strong forms of agency, in which relational aspects are inspired by a sense of moral purpose, rather than institutional compliance. Her analysis was informed by a Cultural Historical Activity Theory (CHAT) which includes a strong focus on the object or motive of an activity system, such as a school. A strong moral pur-pose would focus on supporting the needs of individual children, particularly the vulnerable, but in her study of student teachers on placement in schools in England, she found that this purpose was subverted by the dominance of the lesson plan inherited from the teacher and maintaining the focus on progress towards targets. This focus, relayed from the national (macro) layer of govern-ment policy, through the meso and micro layers, including school leaders, had a profound effect on teachers' capacity to work with their peers for the real benefit of school pupils (p. 10):

> Yet the (teacher) students we tracked were becoming polished performers in the art of curriculum delivery, unable to admit to any difficulty rarely

looked for help from other teachers and avoiding any situation which took them away from their prepared plan.

Theories and empirical evidence related to ecological agency point the way for school leaders, whilst recognising that "the way" leads into gale force winds representing the overwhelming norms in schools. In a review of the role of social capital for teacher learning, Demir (2021) summarised that nearly half of the reviewed works pinpointed structural conditions for teacher interaction as a key affordance for the development of social capital. Network analysis was used in many of the studies (e.g. Fox & Wilson, 2015) that provided a picture of the importance of connections and relationships between teachers and then on beyond the school into wider resource structures. We can see social capital as a proxy measure for agency, reflecting one of the key components in the environment that permits teachers to act on their ambitions. Spillane, Hopkins, and Sweet (2015) concluded that organisational structures, such as teacher working groups, were more important in the development of social capital than individual characteristics. However, there is work to do for school leaders beyond setting up working groups and organisational roles to support teacher collaboration, there is the need to go beyond gestures and reinforce structures with resources and suitable processes. For instance, evidence from China (Li & Choi, 2014) has shown that social capital could not be mandated or somehow created from above, rather it has to be "nurtured" over time from the ground up as trust develops. In that case it seems that such a school climate was a foundation for trying new ideas in the implementation of new technology. In such circumstances being able to call for help, pick up tips, and learn from modelling by others will yield rewards.

It looks, therefore, as though teacher peer relationships, in pursuit of a meaningful curriculum informed by moral purpose can be fostered by distributed leadership and relational agency, in which collaborative talk would be a key medium. Horn and Little (2010, p. 182) provided a long list of reasons, as to why teachers just talking might be harder to achieve than one might imagine:

> Research suggests a number of possible explanations for why talk about teaching, even among teachers who are attracted to collaboration and committed to reform, may not add up to much: the difficulty of making tacit knowledge explicit (Eraut, 2000), the challenge of confronting well-established norms of privacy and non-interference (Little, 1990) or contending with disagreement and difference (Achinstein, 2002; Grossman, Wineburg, & Woolworth, 2001)), insufficient structural and social supports (Louis & Kruse, 1995), taken-for-granted language and frameworks that reify assumptions about learners and learning (Coburn, 2006; Horn, 2007), and the urgency of the immediate and multiple tasks to which teachers must attend (Kennedy, 2005; Little, 2002).

The differentiated potential for collaborative teachers to develop curriculum is evident in a critical taxonomy based on analysis of talk in American maths teachers' school meetings (Horn, Garner, Kane, & Brasel, 2016). Four categories – Conflicting Goals, Tips and Tricks, Pacing, and Logistics – made up 67% of the meetings, and were classified as monological with no teaching concepts explicitly developed. Two dialogical categories – Collective Interpretation, separate from future work (8%), and Collective Interpretation, linked to future work (24%), were suffused with greater opportunities for teacher learning about curriculum. Thus, it seems leadership which makes space for a more teacher generated, values-informed curriculum, needs to go beyond the mandating of meetings with a focus on the development of deep professional learning and provide support for meeting co-ordinators so that they know how to use micro-discourse structures which allow many voices to be heard in pursuit of the development of powerful teaching concepts.

## A case in particular (meso, micro, and nano layers)

A particularly instructive example of the interaction between curriculum and teacher relationships is given in Leat et al. (2006) who described the professional development process that accompanied the integration of Thinking Skills approaches into the mainstream curriculum in one secondary school ("Bridge View") that was part of a larger project. Leat and colleagues used research on social capital in large organisations (Burt, 1992) that described how some managers drew on personal informal networks which cut across organisational structures to establish new information flows, providing new insights into businesses. Burt coined the term "structural holes" for these networks and, in a later paper (Burt, 2004, p. 349), suggested that "*people who stand near the holes in a social structure are at higher risk of having good ideas,*" arguing that there is likely to be greater homogeneity of views (and behaviour) within groups, whereas those who "broker" ideas across groups (e.g. leaders and managers) will be more exposed to alternative ways of thinking about common problems. Thus, redolent of some of the ideas we espouse about dialogic processes, Burt suggested

> New ideas emerge from selection and synthesis across the structural holes between groups. Some fraction of those ideas are good... a good idea broadly will be understood to be one that people praise and value.
>
> (Burt, 2004, p. 350)

In Leat and colleagues' study ten teachers, from across different subjects explored the use of Thinking Skills in their lessons with the full approval of the school senior leadership and eight kept diaries of their experiences. There was an unusual degree of both formal and informal infrastructural support for the teachers in their setting. In addition to meeting in school every month there were three 24-hour residentials during the course of the project and a number of teachers attended meetings of the larger project. University research staff visited the school intermittently and two of the teachers were trained as peer coaches and each coached one other colleague. Some of the teachers were also part of other networks such as subject groups across the area or Higher

Education (HE) module cohorts and had the chance to discuss their work in these contexts. Almost inevitably there was much informal support which evolved spontaneously, as those with less experience or confidence drew upon advice from those with more. Leat and colleagues suggested that the teachers were using a structural hole in the school organisation, as this school, as with most schools, had a largely vertical structure built around subject departments with limited interaction across that structure. The fundamental glue holding the teachers from different departments together in the project was trust, as they were freed from the usual reporting and information processes.

The diaries and other evidence indicated that there was an overall pattern to the teachers' experience and responses which were captured in descriptions of six phases, which although not universally applicable to all the teachers, did suggest some commonality. Along with each phase there was evidence of the support that was pivotal in the development of individual and collective practice. The phases and the relevant support are shown in Table 1.

There was a catalytic effect of the intensity of the interaction in the structural holes and some teachers became very close collaborators. Three critical factors seemed to be at work. First, although the teachers were working closely together inside school, they were also drawing on a range of outside networks and support mechanisms. While many schools in the competitive quasi-market in the UK tend to be inward looking, here teachers were being pluralistic. A second important factor was the sense of control permitted to the group who were able to determine the pace and direction of their innovation, which therefore assumed a human scale, where the individual could explore the interaction of new classroom strategies and curriculum outcomes with their existing personal classroom ecology. This had a dialogical perspective, as one teacher commented that they were learning "*to view practice from more perspectives*" (Leat et al., 2006, p. 669).

The third factor was the intensity of relationships developed through the 24-hour residentials that started on Friday evenings after school. As well as the social connections engendered by the chance to eat and drink in an

*Table 1* Phases of experience in integrating Thinking Skills approaches into lessons and the support drawn upon to progress to next phase

| Phase | Helpful Support |
| --- | --- |
| Initiation | Creditable or trusted source of ideas |
| Novice | Practical help, ideally from inside school |
| Concerns | Internal and external support that provides advice and contextual perspective |
| Consolidation | More of the above |
| Expansion | An opportunity to influence "implicated" decisions and policies within home subject and school |
| Commitment | "A platform or a pen" – a chance to narrate one's experience and learning in order to articulate a new aspect of identity |

unpressurised setting, professional discussion was opened up by being able to watch videos of some of the group teaching in the classroom. This allowed the featured teachers to explain the context and issues of the lessons and raise questions and challenges they perceived as important. There was a deliberate stance to steer clear of judgements of efficacy or lesson observation gradings. This is not to say that there was no critical or analytical edge, but rather that the purpose was collaborative inquiry. This created some distance between such an approach and the anodyne prescription of seeking "best practice." One of the effects was to clarify the use of language related to the pedagogical approach and motivate further exploration, as in the words of one of the Maths teachers reflecting on the value of the weekend:

> I am much more sure on what TS *[Thinking Skills]* involves and aims to do, as a result more keen to teach and discuss thinking skills.

This suggests that much of the talk is likely to have fitted the group talk category "Collective Interpretation, linked to future teaching" (Horn, Garner, Kane, & Brasel, 2017).

Peer coaching training was made available through the university, taken up by three teachers, in which there was a particular focus on coaches listening and the coached teacher having significant control of the agenda. Much of the worst excesses of lesson judgement and power are dissipated when there is a high degree of trust and respect for professionalism, as expressed here:

> There is no doubt in my mind that this is the way to do it – to share ideas and resources, to try things out and narrow down on things till you get them right through coaching and discussing videos. You feel that everyone wants to learn and it is not just in a department. The coaching has been absolutely brilliant.
>
> (Leat et al., 2006 p. 666)

It is important to recognise here that such a bottom-up process of professional learning is hard to sustain in current performative contexts, where control from national government is continually being reinforced. School leaders find it hard to accommodate such grass roots innovation when there is a perpetual government imperative to be implemented. It is incredibly difficult to stand away from such norms. In Italy, Sannino (2008) has referred to the normative pressures as the dominant activity, which is always likely to shade out the non-dominant activity, however admirable and beneficial. Part of the difficulty here is that if leadership creates the space for agency, then those teachers generating ideas for change want to have some influence on decision making, which does not fit well with a very centralised education system seeking to maintain control. It is only a quasi-market system. The last phase of the cumulative experiences and support gained by the teachers in this study, *Commitment,* brings teacher identity into focus. Identity is a dynamic entity, not only do we present and conduct ourselves differently to suit the social context, but we also change over time as we, and our circumstances, change. As we have discussed elsewhere in the book, identity does not happen, we construct it, using the raw materials of our experiences, feelings, and thoughts – we story ourselves. Teachers and other professionals who are innovating, working creatively with others, generating new insights, practice, knowledge, and systems benefit from being able to narrate the experience and construct new aspects to their identity to articulate who they have become. Being able to present at a conference or professional development event, write a higher degree assignment based on personal experience, pen an article for an academic or professional journal, host visitors from other schools to showcase work – all of these provide the chance to tell the story. The problem is that this expression of independent thought and/or action may create a distance between the "self" and the institutional agendas, although this is not inevitable.

In recognition of Biesta and Tedder's (2007) elaboration of the importance of context and resource to support individual agency, it is appropriate to note that the teachers at Bridge View drew on a range of external support, not all of which is so readily accessed today. Reassurance, where others show an interest or are able to comment based on their own experience, is one of the major benefits of such discussion. There was a sense of not being alone but being part of a bigger enterprise. In addition to valuable practical advice, there was also a certain frisson to being part of a sub-culture.

The impact of a dialogical perspective on curriculum is expressed well by one of the Maths teachers in their diary:

> The new curriculum lessons have really made me think about my practice – the questions I and the pupils ask, as well as the quality and importance of discussion in my lessons. Maths has traditionally been viewed as a subject that can be learned in silence, examples on the blackboard followed by exercises, but Thinking Skills has reinforced my view that learning is also a social skill, many things can be absorbed by discussion with other pupils as well as myself. One other change that I am placing a greater emphasis on is the PROCESSES the pupils use to obtain a solution to the problem, rather than the solution itself. We now use these processes as a basis for discussion and evaluation.

One of the history teachers, who became one of three or four leading advocates of the work, was also particularly conscious of the change in her perspective and identity:

> It's really impacted on my career. At first I was just an ordinary classroom teacher not knowing much about the wider world of education and suddenly we are getting offers to go and disseminate thinking skills in LEAs and at … conferences and so on, and that's opened my eyes to see who else is involved in education … what is going on.

## The nano level: the effect of equitable curriculum and pedagogy on students

There are clear models of more democratic and reciprocal approaches to curriculum. Jo Boaler (2008), a long-term advocate of more progressive mathematics teaching provided critical evidence from California in a study of three high schools: Railside (diverse and urban), Hillside, and Greentop (less diverse and suburban). Boaler referred to Eisner's (2014) contention that the goal of school is not to do well in school but to do well in life and declared that one of the goals of school, through curriculum, should be the development of citizens (p. 167–8):

> ...who treat each other with respect, who value the contributions of others with whom they interact, irrespective of their race, class or gender, and who act with a sense of justice in considering the needs of others in society.

Boaler has a strong and declared belief in equity, but instead of the more common understandings of equal access or equal outcomes in her study she was concerned with "democratic equity," or an individual's standing in society (Anderson, 1999). Thus, she was deeply concerned with how people, in this case school students behave with each other. In this view differences in ethnicity, gender, colour, appearance, wealth, or test scores would not affect a positive disposition towards the *other*.

In the study over four years, Railside had a different approach to curriculum and pedagogy. With a mixed demographic (38% Hispanic, 23% African American, 20% White, 16% Asian, and Pacific Islander), there was plenty of scope for othering and racial stereotyping. However, mathematics was taught using an approach termed *Complex Instruction* (Cohen & Lotan, 1997) based primarily on group work but with several instructional features to overcome the common frictions that make group work unpopular with many students and teachers, particularly differences in perceived attainment, motivation, and work rate. Thus, to foster respect and responsibility, classrooms were realised as multi-dimensional, in which a range of talents would be recognised, such as asking questions, trying different ideas and promoting productive discussion and not just rapidly completing math exercises. Another teacher strategy in *Complex Instruction* was to assign competence by drawing attention to talents that might otherwise not be noticed and thus raising the status of those who might be low in the normal pecking order. In addition, a variety of roles were allocated, such as facilitator, recorder/reporter, team captain, and resource manager, thereby reinforcing the value of different contributions. Overall, the approach to relation equity, which was not part of a research intervention but chosen and refined by the mathematics teachers had three strands:

1   respect for other people's ideas, leading to positive intellectual relations;
2   commitment to the learning of others; and
3   learned methods of communication and support.

In the two comparison suburban schools (Hillside and Greentop) the students received a predominantly traditional mathematics approach. The teachers "lectured" (21% of class time) and asked whole class questions (15%), leaving students doing exercises in their books (48%) and working in groups (11%). Students presented work only very rarely (0.2%). Meanwhile at Railside, with its greater diversity, the teachers offered a more collaborative approach characterised by longer more open conceptual questions and for most of the time students worked in groups built on the foundations of *Complex Instruction*. By contrast the teachers lectured rarely (only 4% of class time) and used whole class questioning in moderation (9%). The majority of time (72%) was spent in highly collaborative groups with 9% spent in presentation of students' work and ideas.

The research team collected qualitative and quantitative data on the impact of the two approaches. The traditional teaching and the ability grouping in the two suburban schools led to some antipathies and insecurities, which are not indicative of democratic or dialogic leanings (p. 183):

> I don't want to feel like a retard. Like if someone asks me the most basic question and I can't do it. I don't want to feel dumb. And I can't stand stupid people either. Because that's one of the things that annoy me. Like stupid people. And I don't want to be a stupid person.

However, the students at Railside had very different dispositions to others in the study, indicating that they did not see learning as an individual enterprise. The students had developed a commitment to working with and through others, so that everyone succeeded (pp. 183–4):

> T:  You got everyone's perspective on it, 'cause like when you're debating it, a rule or a method you get someone else's perspective of what they think instead of just going off your own thoughts. That's why it was good with like a lot of people.
>
> C:  I liked it too. Most people opened up their ideas.

It is critical to acknowledge that these perspectives from the maths curriculum leach into and suffuse an outlook on the importance of others. Something very powerful was internalised (p. 185):

> R:  I love this school, you know? There are schools that are within a mile of us that are completely different – they're broken up into their race cliques and things like that. And at this school everyone's accepted as a person, and they're not looked at by the color of their skin.
>
> INT:  Does the math approach help that or is it a whole school influence?
>
> J:  The groups in math help to bring kids together.
>
> R:  Yeah. When you switch groups that helps you to mingle with more people than if you're just sitting in a set seating chart where you're only

exposed to the people that are sitting around you, and you don't know the people on the other side of the room. In math you have to talk, you have to voice if you don't know or voice what you're learning.

Importantly the collaborative approach was not at the cost of achievement. While the students at Railside entered high school with lower mathematics levels than the two other schools, they had significantly higher scores within two years. In addition, in later years more were taking advanced mathematics classes and, overall, they enjoyed mathematics more. The teaching at Railside also reduced differences in achievement between different ethnic groups. It seems that in some circumstances you can have your cake and eat it, but there are no shortcuts as such teaching needs commitment and the building of strong foundations through *Complex Instruction* or comparable pedagogy.

In another study of a successful project to change the mindset of mathematics teachers in the US in the direction of the progressive approach exemplified at Railside (Anderson, Boaler, & Dieckmann, 2018) one of the key factors was "space" for teachers. Not only did they have time for themselves to reflect on their teaching and attitudes towards mathematics, but they also had time to talk and discuss without pressure. They were given the scope to work out what they wanted to do and to attend to the emotions involved in recognising not only the weaknesses in their teaching but their negative experiences of mathematics, induced by feeling less than successful. Space is a very powerful concept, as it captures the significance of open dialogue.

## The nano level: struggling to get it right

It is clear that the workplace ecology experienced by teachers and mediated by senior and middle leaders in schools can make a difference to the curriculum that they are able to offer. In another example, also from the US, Lori Philbrick-Linzmeyer (2011) gave an intimate account of work on relational aspects of the curriculum in a progressive middle school in San Diego, California. As she made clear there are many schools where her work would not have been possible as she would not have had the permission and support to pursue her values, but even here her efforts were, at times, a struggle. It was a case where the teacher exhibited a high degree of individual agency, and this was nurtured by the school. The HTH website (www.hightechhigh. org/about-us/) indicates the level of support and encouragement needed for staff to work with teacher colleagues, students, and their families, not least in designing curriculum:

> We are committed to building a school culture where there is respect and cooperation among students, adults, and families. Applicants should be open to a dynamic, collaborative, teacher-driven school where teachers have the freedom to design curriculum in collaboration with directors and colleagues.

Philbrick-Linzmeyer's starting point, with democratic underpinnings, was wanting students (p. 11):

> to have choices in where, how and what they learn. I want my role in classroom management to become minimal. If a problem arises, I want there to be a process to address it, either by the students or myself.

She also wanted an environment in which students could speak freely. At a deeper level she was motivated by seeking educational and social equity. As she approached her classroom innovation as action research, she grounded her action in knowledge of students' perspective on school. The responses from her survey suggest that many students had perceptive insights into pooling one's humanity into a larger whole. The following three student contributions give a flavour:

> a community is when there's a buncha people and they all work together.

> I think a community feels like you fit in and that you get along with the people around you.

> (a community is) people who trust each other, work together and have different ideas but don't argue.

Philbrick-Linzmeyer concluded that to achieve a cohesive classroom she had to find ways for students to know and understand each other and where differences were respected. In her journal she openly admitted to doubts about her ability to steer her way through this change as her classroom control becomes problematic: "*I feel stressed, anxious, frustrated, and unsure about my expectations.*" The creation of a new classroom dynamic is an awesome undertaking and very difficult to embark upon as an individual teacher. Fortunately, she worked in a supportive school with colleagues on similar journeys and was, therefore, able to both listen and offer advice. She learned over time that there was no one "trick" or strategy to making the change but that she was trying to change the culture. In addition, she appreciated that she was not handing over authority but sharing it.

The central pillar of her work on community building was a process she called "Friday Forum." Her inspirations were John Dewey and Summerhill School. The Friday Forum was the realisation of her desire for student voice, for her pupils to be able to speak freely. The agenda was created by students posting items on a board. The forum was structured around Recognitions, Current Events, Thoughts, Discussion Items (from the board), Final Word, and Food. Various roles were fulfilled by the students: a *facilitator,* a provider of the *current event,* someone to offer a *thought* via a poem, quote or idea, and someone who would *cater* for the class.

Although this is a broadly positive account it is disarmingly honest about the challenges and stresses. Philbrick-Linzmeyer was completely unnerved at a moment well into the school year, when two of the most prominent and vocal boys in the class, between whom there has been some ongoing needle, arranged to meet after school for a physical fight. Furthermore, all the class knew about it and indeed most attended the spectacle. She was mortified that after months of Friday Forum, no one in the class informed her despite her explicit attention to community. There was a contradiction for her in that, while she was aghast at the fight, her survey showed overwhelmingly positive attitudes to Friday Forum:

> It has affected our class by making everybody more comfortable to talk to each other.
> We got to learn more about people and their opinions from having these conversations.
> It brought us closer and some further apart, but overall it's given everyone a better understanding of each other and made the classroom feel like a safe place to share.

At one point she called together a particular friendship group to challenge them about their exclusive use of the word "Steed" to refer to each other during Friday Forum. The use of the term declined to a degree but still continued leaving her to reflect:

> The process of opening various friend groups to the entire community was frustrating, however I felt strongly about our class being cohesive. It was also a struggle in determining when to step into the Forum when I saw students feeling hurt. Where was the line between student control and teacher intervention? With these conversations, I began to understand that I could work through these issues with my students instead of for them.
> 
> (p. 97)

This is a tension evident in all her work related to curriculum and there is a sense throughout the account of work in progress. Philbrick-Linzmeyer concluded that some students did not arrive at an understanding that disapproval of a topic or statement was potentially hurtful to others, despite the evident progress made. For her, developing shared values takes "*time, energy and a lot of understanding*" (p. 106). She made the point that students do not enter a new class knowing their peers and it needs work to reach the point where any one is comfortable to work with every other person. There was also the realisation that for community to develop students needed to collaborate in meaningful ways, in this case in the Project Based Learning (PBL) structured curriculum with its emphasis on the form of peer assessment known as critique (Patton & Robin, 2012).

## Conclusion

It is salutary to reflect that the social conditions and learning environment we might to seek achieve in curriculum development are mirrored by teachers' working environments needed to bring this about. More generally, research in the field of "organisational health" (for instance, Di Fabio, 2017) suggests that the climate or health of an organisation is associated with staff well-being and effectiveness. More specifically, studies of the organisational "health" of schools (e.g. Busch & Fernandez, 2019; Hoy & Woolfolk, 1993; Smith, Hoy, & Sweetland, 2001) indicate that the more positive the trust in leadership's ability to enable staff and the ensuing agentic beliefs of staff, the greater may be the achievements of students. In summary, our view is, therefore, that if agency is to be achieved through the curriculum, it must be possible for teachers to demonstrate this in their work through collaboration with their peers. In contrast, directive leadership that mandates most aspect of teachers' lives is not conducive to such ends. Instead, distributed leadership is essential, in which physical and intellectual resources, space for manoeuvre and subtle leadership encourages dialogue.

# 4  Morals and ethics in educational practice

## Introduction

In this chapter we will explore just some of the moral and ethical issues that arise for people working in education. While we can't address all these in one chapter, we wonder if, perhaps, the greatest moral issue in the field of education is the absence of "wondering"; an absence of the joys of education and discovery for its own sake? We sense that education has been for some time, so besotted with the need to demonstrate "utility" that all other possible purposes are forsaken (Biesta, 2009). The utilitarian approach to education and *learning* is, of course, not new since from the beginning of formalised education in this country it has had the aim of training people in the skills and knowledge required for work; first in the church, then management of estates, then commerce and industry and since the start of the 20th century training people to be part of a stratified workforce. As if this was a new phenomenon, Biesta (2016) indicated that in his view education had become "commodified" as an economic transaction in which the learner purchases education from a provider. While we do not think the phenomenon is new, Biesta's language is none-the-less apt for a critique of the dominant paradigm of our times. But, as we have already suggested in previous chapters, given global and local concerns a paradigm shift for education is indicated. To formulate what the purposes of education may be in a new paradigm, given the context as we see it, requires debate and debate requires ethical dialogue. Dialogue requires working with and for others.

To repeat what we have said earlier, our individual experience is based in relationships with others and, as Emmanuel Levinas (1985) and others have emphasised, we have moral and ethical obligations to others in our face-to-face interactions, our sociality. As Martha Nussbaum (2016, p. 79) has said

> We live in a world in which people face one another across gulfs of geography, language, and nationality. More than at any time in the past, we all depend on people we have never seen, and they depend on us. The problems we have to solve – economic, environmental, religious, and political – are global in their scope. They have no hope of being solved

DOI: 10.4324/9780429343766-5

unless people once distant come together and cooperate in ways they have not done before.

There is, therefore, a continuing need to doubt the supposed merits of an individualistic ontology (that still dominates the world of *"natural"* science and much of philosophy) in favour of a relational ontology that recognises the fundamental role of relationships. However, inevitably, as we engage in dialogue with others, the language we use and the issues we discuss will be affected by – or arise from – interactions with the environment and, therefore, we must, as Ivana Marková (2003) indicated, recognise the moral importance and ethical aspects of communication and dialogue.

As we have suggested, the work of educationalists may be seen to be at the interface of an environment of perceived conceptual systems such as the notion of "education" and "organisational factors." With regard to the "organisational factors," we include here examination of how educational settings such as schools, that form the most obvious environment for teachers and professional relationships, are ethically structured and morally managed – or not. Also, as Nijhof, Wilderom, and Oost (2012) have commented, professionals can experience the conflict of divided loyalties: to their profession and to their employer (an ethical issue we'll return to in Chapter 6). Thus, as both Nijhof et al. (2012) and Verhezen (2010) have indicated, there is a need for organisations (and their managers) to think about the moral integrity of the organisational culture in order to mitigate against issues that might violate or compound personal or institutional values. This requires that we also consider the notion of "ethical" leadership and whether that can be associated with dominant discourses in education policy (Ehrich, Harris, Klenowski, Smeed, & Spina, 2015; Harris, Carrington, & Ainscow, 2017). As readers will recognise, one of our central intentions is to stimulate debate about what "education" is and might become, and this, in itself, involves for us both ethical and moral considerations. Challenging the accepted state of things may appear as a moral cause to fight but it also entails careful consideration of what "good" may come of it. It has been argued that because of our reliance on each other, social and educational inclusion is *"necessary as it signals a reciprocal acknowledgment of our underlying interconnectedness"* (Tyler, 2019, p. 53) and it is, therefore, ethically responsible to challenge educational systems that fail to attempt inclusion. Just as we are responsible to each other, we are vulnerable in like measure. As Judith Butler (2004, p. 30) has commented, in our precariousness we share a *"common human vulnerability"* that in turn calls for ethical responsiveness to others. Our practical response to that is to endorse and promote ethical dialogue in education where, as Martin Buber (2002) has insisted, relationships are central and *"the relation in education is pure dialogue"* (p 98).

In this chapter we will try to tease out and examine the tensions teachers may experience in terms of moral imperatives (the principles that determine how we should treat others) and ethical beliefs, our convictions about what one needs to do to lead a "good" life (see Appiah, 2007b, for a detailed elucidation of "ethics" and "morals"). Before moving on, a simple example might help clarify this distinction. In advertising a teaching post, a school has a moral responsibility to set out clearly what the job entails in order to attract the most suitable candidates. When, eventually, a teacher accepts the contract to teach to that job description, they are accepting their moral obligation to carry out the tasks assigned to them. Their ethical responsibility then is to be as good as their can be (and that should be for them to determine) in how they work with the children in their classes. Having been through a rigorous process of advertising for and recruiting the teacher, it would, we caution, then be unethical for a member of the school leadership team (for example) to carry out any form of surveillance of teacher's work without prior discussion and dialogue. Thus, there are moral and ethical issues for both school leaders (managers) and staff to consider, and some are to do with power and control. We suggest that at the heart of the issues that need to be explored in relation to the development of dialogic processes in education (to be discussed in Chapter 5) is a self-reflexive question about the extent to which education and the work of teachers morally pre-determined and do the current "moral imperatives" for educationalists affect the ethics of autonomy for qualified professionals?

Given that for many, perhaps especially those in positions of leadership or management and their day-to-day activities, there may arise a risk of adopting an uncritical de facto assumption that a professional is merely an individual member of a well-defined group, and that by virtue of being members of that group individuals come to be regarded as having very similar (fixed) identities. To help guard against that risk it may be helpful to examine a little more carefully some of the issues related to individuality and autonomy that we discussed earlier. As may be self-evident discussion of how one's identity can be conceptualised is personal and ethical.

## Professionals, identity, and autonomy

From a sociological perspective it can be seen how changes wrought in education can, as we've implied above, force teachers into a changed role, one that may feel inimical, and at their personal level feel very much as though their social identity had been unilaterally – immorally – changed. Thus, in a study by Woods and Jeffrey (2002), of *The reconstruction of primary teachers' identities* they captured (with consent) the voices of teachers, many of who had had a child-centred view of education but were then, with the onset of the regime of performativity (more of which shortly), required to adopt a more technical, instrumental approach to teaching. So, while teachers had formerly been able to value relationships, the enforced changes were seen as an unethical assault on their values. As one teacher interviewed in this study said:

> We're not saying that the education system didn't need a review because I'm sure it did, but it has meant that children have become slots in a machine who have to come up with the right numbers and we're the ones

that have got to make them come up with the right numbers whereas before you were dealing with the whole child. You were dealing with its emotions, you were dealing with its social life, you were dealing with its grandma, you were dealing with its physical development in a much more intense and bonding relationship than you do today. You had a real effect on these people and you felt that you were actually doing something that was worthwhile and they come back and see you and you're still "Miss," you're still important to them. I was referred to as "Miss" by a twenty nine-year-old. Being that important to other human beings is a real privilege, but that joy has been dampened until I don't think it's a privilege any more.

(Woods & Jeffrey, 2002, p. 94)

While for another teacher the assault had an almost physical implication and was clearly perceived as deliberately demeaning, feeling she had to:

chop the top of my head off and show somebody what's in it. "Is it OK? You don't like what you see? Then I'll go and get another one." The assumption is that teachers are inadequate. That's why I don't like this, it stinks! It thrives on inadequacy. What does this do for teachers' self-esteem? Why do I have to have all these people checking up on me? I just want to do my job – the job I used to love, I was there till 6 o'clock every night until I had my kids. Even then I used to take work home and kids home, take kids out for netball tournaments. I loved it, because people trusted me and I felt good about things. I don't feel good about anything I do anymore.

(Woods & Jeffrey, 2002, p. 95)

Having explored some of these issues in Chapter 1, where we noted that philosophically and psychologically one's identity may be thought of in the abstract more as a rather fluid notion, a helpful reminder of this alternative, contextualised, identity comes from Gee's (1990, p. 99) summation:

The "kind of person" one is recognized as "being," at a given time and place, can change from moment to moment in the interaction, can change from context to context, and, of course, can be ambiguous or unstable … all people have multiple identities connected not to their "internal state" but to their performances in society.

In this view we are to some extent social chameleons, adapting to the circumstances and norms of the contexts we move between. In reality few people will present themselves identically at home, at work, and in social activities, as our roles, status, language, and dress tune to the environment. As well as adapting on short time scales, we also change aspects of identity over time, as life events such as leaving home, parenthood, illness, retirement, and ageing change the way we (may be able to) narrate our lives. However, such flexibility and change does not deny the existence of a "core" identity, so that one is rec-ognisable as the same person across contexts – a chameleon is still a chameleon whatever the background. Thus, we can understand how the teachers in Woods and Jeffrey's studies felt they had been personally assaulted, unethically, by what must have seemed an imposed alien morality.

Another alternative perspective can be found in "dialogic" theory (that we will return to in the next chapter) and in particular dialogical theoretical conceptualisations for I-other relations. These attempt to shed light on the self-processes triggered by performative pressures which help to mould the person we become and the person we project. Dialogic theories of the self in relation with others have the advantage of inter-relating concepts used to explore the internal landscape of the mind and the vital processes stemming from inter-action with others. According to Akkerman and Meijer (2011, p. 310):

> The theory is presented as a self-theory, but directly addresses the notion of identity, with self referring to the self-as-knower and identity referring to the self-as-known.

Dialogic theories conceptualise "I" as a voiced position in the landscape of the mind. Some "I" positions are internal and originate in the mind, and others are external, voiced by others. At moments of reflection and consideration particular voices come into internal (self-dialogue) or external dialogue with others, but which voices are enacted depends upon the environmental and internal triggers. Some will carry more valency than others and the voices may reach a resolution or remain unresolved, leaving the individual conflicted. Many will argue that in performative contexts, where power is being wielded and one's role and status and perhaps even one's job is at stake, then the external voices consonant with the institutional agenda, relayed by managers, are likely to prevail with, there is little doubt, conflicted loyalties to one's self and to one's role. Internal voices representative of core values will therefore be overwhelmed, and personal ethics and morality are called into question. Dialogic Self Theory helps to explain the contemporary understandings of identity. Thus, in different contexts different voices, both internal and external, are in play and naturally over time new voices are introduced and others fade into irrelevance or insig-nificance. In Akkerman and Meijer's (2011, p. 315) conceptualisation of teacher identity they suggested:

> … defining "teacher identity" and "someone who teaches" as an ongoing process of negotiating and interrelating multiple I-positions in such a way that a more or less coherent and consistent sense of self is maintained throughout various participations and self-investments in one's (working) life.

If, however, we fail to recognise the possibility that perceived identities may be vulnerable epiphenomena, we risk being disrespectful of others' ethical integrity and authentic selves. This is particularly sensitive with regard to issues such as those relating to racial, sexual, and gender identities.

Thus, dialogic identity conceptualisations also point up the role of narrative in constructing identity. The stories we tell about ourselves are a strong indication of identity, as storytelling is a way of maintaining some coherence in identity, explaining to ourselves and our collocutors how we are making sense of experience and our actions in the world often with specific reference to "I" positions. This may be implicit or more explicit, as when someone explains a conflict or says something like "on the one hand ... but on the other ...," laying open the importance of dialogic space in which professionals can speak freely, including their hesitations and oppositions, as these may represent very important voices.

It is one of our major contentions that the work of the professional relationships and dialogic encounters that we have with each other should be directed toward greater justice for others and for ourselves, meaning that we behave in ways that are respectful, reciprocal, and enabling for others and each other. This is clearly no easy matter, though in Levinas' words it might seem simple:

> How is there justice? I can answer that it is in the fact of the presence of someone next to the Other, from whence comes justice. Justice, exercised through institutions, which are inevitable, must always be held in check by the initial personal relation.
>
> (Levinas, 1985, pp. 89–90)

But, if in dialogic spaces "speaking freely" was truly possible, might that suggest that individuals could assume unfettered autonomy, and if so, is that, could that be, ethical?

As is implied in much of what we have said so far, most of us will, from time to time, entertain a belief that we are free to do and speak as we might wish, and that to deny us that "right" is undemocratic. However, we may also recognise that while we are where we are, and who we are, because of the choices we have made in the past, the choices about what we could do next, right now, are, firstly, constrained by resources and legal strictures that were set in the past. Second, while personal autonomy may be a political ideal, in a democratic and ethical society we cannot be wholly autonomous; we are inextricably indebted to others. Respecting that responsibility, we can, therefore, only act ethically with regard to others' beliefs and intentions as much as we can understand these. This clearly implies that if we are to engage ethically with others, our sense of autonomy will be bounded by our sense of mutual respect and social interdependence. As has been said "*Autonomy and agency are not antithetical to relatedness*" (Kagitcibasi, 2005, p. 404). Further, as Derek Parfit showed, we should not presume that autonomous pure self-interest is inevitably, necessarily in anyone's best interests (our own self-interests included), and concluded that:

Even if I never do what, of the acts that are possible for me, will be worse for me, it may be worse for me if I am purely self-interested. It may be better for me if I have some other disposition.

(Parfit, 1984, p. 5)

Drawing on the work of Kant, Kwame Anthony Appiah has also argued that as ethically authentic and autonomous agents we should treat each other respectfully, recognising our mutual interdependence, as identically self-determining:

> To regard others as ends in themselves – to recognise their human dignity – is to regard them in this way, too. The standpoint of agency is connected, in the most possible direct way, to our concern to live intelligible lives in community with other people… This practical interest requires us to be able to articulate our own behaviour in relation to theirs, and this we do through our understanding of them as having beliefs and intentions – in short, as reasoning, – and also as having passions and prejudices: in short, as always potentially unreasonable. We respond to others with gratitude and anger, praise and blame, and so forth – and we wish to hold on to and make sense of these attitudes. It's in this realm that we conceive our goals and aims, our decisions large and small, the life we want to make.
>
> (Appiah, 2007b, p. 58)

Thus, in summary, as far as we are able and willing to respect each other, thus far we may lead ethical lives.

## Managerialism, power, and control

However, as we have already noted in previous chapters, a major ethical threat in the current professional environment for teachers (amongst others) is the burgeoning phenomena of managerialism and the performative conduct of public services, in which a technology of control via targets appears to override concerns about developing human relationships. John Macmurray warned us of this, writing in the 1950s that what he saw as the greatest threat to education was that

> We are becoming more and more technically minded: gradually we are falling victims to the illusion that all problems can be solved by proper organisation: that when we fail it is because we are doing the job in the wrong way, and that all that is needed is the "know-how." To think thus in education is to pervert education. It is not an engineering job. It is personal and human.
>
> (Macmurray, 1958/2012, p. 674)

In the present century Stephen Ball (2003), in writing about the terrors of performativity and its implication for the "soul" of the teacher, also described the threat of managerialism in schools as mechanical and technological:

What do I mean by performativity? Performativity is a technology, a culture and a mode of regulation that employs judgements, comparisons and displays as means of incentive, control, attrition and change based on rewards and sanctions (both material and symbolic). The performances (of individual subjects or organizations) serve as measures of productivity or output, or displays of "quality," or "moments" of promotion or inspection.

(Ball, 2003, p. 216)

The performances that Ball referred to here are constructed as a form of moral and financial accountability, as part of increasingly political systems that seek to hold public services, and the leaders thereof, to account for the money (and role) allocated to them. This feeds into the logic of an educational marketplace in which commodified outcomes in the form of exam results are used as a proxy for quality and competition which will "drive up standards," beguiling for parents seeking the best outcomes for their individual children. (Parental complaints to schools and universities are now frequently lodged on the grounds that their child has not achieved the results that were, they thought, due to them.) This form of accountability in educational settings is experienced as oppressive and accompanied by unethical surveillance (Page, 2017a, 2017b) and increasingly relayed by schools' leaders who replicate forms of surveillance imposed by Ofsted inspection which become panoptican-like, self-surveilled by teachers themselves (Foucault, 1977, 1982; Webb, 2005). Stephen Ball (2003) argued, forcibly, that the policy technologies at play are, therefore, unethically transformative (unethical because there is no discussion of whether or not the changes are appropriate) of what it means to be a teacher, immorally reshaping their subjective experience, professional (and social) identity, creativity and autonomy, as well as their relationships with peers and students. In the process values are challenged and many teachers live with a sense of conflict (that too often becomes untenable) between what they believe in and what they find themselves forced to do, with profound ethical, moral, and practical repercussions (see also Gibbs, 2018a; Nijhof et al., 2012).

The exercise of pressure is magnified by data management systems that demand frequent input of performance data to monitor pupils' progress and, for instance, being required to use specified and strictly monitored proformas for marking and feedback for students. It is little surprise then that teachers often have to accept that they are not the teacher that they had wanted to be, feeling now more like just a cog in the machine. Wagner (1987) has referred to such issues as "knots." This pressure is most intense in those year groups taking public examinations. Whilst many schools strive to provide care and positive relationships (Noddings, 2002), there is some warping of the value placed on each individual student, as they become primarily data points in the accounting system as well as, secondarily, unique human beings. Care is still present, but it is suborned/dragooned by neoliberal agendas to sustain the pressure on students and teachers to perform and meet targets. Marginalised students are not responded to as individuals with unique contexts and relational needs

(Dadvand & Cuervo, 2020) but as needing to conform to supposed "equality" policies that treat student cohorts as homogeneous to the detriment of caring relationships. The dissonance experienced by individual teachers is evident in one extract from a teacher interviewed by Jeffrey and Woods (1998, p. 131) in England:

> You are only seen as effective as a teacher by what you manage to put into children's brains so they can regurgitate in an examination situation. Now that's not very satisfying to one's life ... My age group came into teaching on a tide of education for all ... But I don't care any more. I think that's why I haven't found my self because I do in fact care ... I don't feel that I'm working with the children, I'm working at the children and it's not a very pleasant experience.

Carr (2020) has assembled sources to argue from the standpoint of Self Determination Theory (Deci & Ryan, 1985; Ryan & Deci, 2000) that pressures associated with performativity suppress the autonomy, creativity, and curiosity of both teachers and students. Student well-being and motivation is promoted by teachers who are supportive of student autonomy but where there is pressure for particular achievement outcomes teachers become risk averse in relation to that autonomy and instead become more controlling (Pelletier, Séguin-Lévesque, & Legault, 2002; Roth, Assor, Kanat-Maymon, & Kaplan, 2007) squeezing out more motivating teaching practices (Niemiec & Ryan, 2009). These last authors have also suggested that teachers experience lower levels of energy and creativity themselves affecting their capacity to enthuse. Standards can stifle creativity; standards can be professionally unethical.

Contrary to much political reform rhetoric, the managerial turn in education should also, according to Stephen Ball (2003), probably not be seen as *de*regulation but as a process of *re*-regulation. Teachers are now not freer to practise according to their values and ideals, but they are now arguably more constrained by management procedures, norms, and discourse, and they are checked if they diverge from expectations and protocols. As Bernstein (1996, p. 169) put it "*contract replaces covenant.*" For some teachers in Ball's account (2003, p. 216), these changes evoked an emotional response and/or life-changing decisions.

One asked:

> What happened to my creativity? What happened to my professional integrity? What happened to the fun in teaching and learning? What Happened?

Another admitted that practically,

> I find myself thinking that the only way I can save my sanity, my health and my relationship with my future husband is to leave the profession. I don't

know what else I could do, having wanted to teach all my life, but I feel
I am being forced out, forced to choose between a life and teaching.

The questionable morality and ethicality of such policies comes into sharper
focus on consideration of differential effects on school students when blanket,
monological approaches to curriculum outcomes are pursued. Students who
are regarded as high achieving can be frustrated by the lockstep of regimented
teaching while those with barriers to learning become alienated and demotivated.
A study of Canadian children (Rogers & Tannock, 2018), including contrasting
samples with high and low levels of attention deficit/hyperactivity disorder
(ADHD) symptoms, that focussed on children's autonomy, relatedness, and competence, found that the "ADHD group" reported feeling less valued and cared
about by their teachers, with lower levels of competence in learning. Issues such
as these are compounded by pressures on schools to demonstrate rising levels of
attainment and progress. Under such pressure teachers and schools frequently
resort to supporting students who can achieve and neglecting or rejecting those
who cannot (Dadvand, 2020; Hedegaard-Soerensen & Grumloese, 2020; Lupton
& Hempel-Jorgensen, 2012; Teague, 2020), providing, we suggest, some of the
reasons for the rate of school exclusions we drew attention to in Chapter 1.
Such outcomes illustrate the apparently morally and ethically irreconcilable
difficulties for teachers and school leaders of striving for greater performative
accountability as well as the inclusion of a greater diversity of student needs and
capabilities (Dudley-Marling, 2020), and fall short of social justice standards as
particular groups are prevented from achieving the healthy and fulfilling lives
that are within their human capability, and thus are of highly questionable morality (Nussbaum, 2003).

## Summary: the general effects of performativity on schools and colleges

We are, therefore, suggesting that the power of performative pressures has
changed schools and teachers' beliefs about themselves and others. As a background for understanding changes in relationships between teachers and other
educational professionals that are, we think, in their consequences both immoral
and unethical, we provide a general landscape of such changes.

One hypothesis emerging from critical analyses of performative policy and
educational practice is that it strengthens power hierarchies and works against
distributed leadership and other, more democratic, educational practices. Moral,
ethical, and financial accountability for performance rests with senior leaders. It
is perhaps understandable, given the environmental pressure and constraints of
governmental policies they experience, that senior leaders be required to take
on an "entrepreneurial" mantle in order to shape "their" school and staff to
achieve the targets set for them. One might ask if these leaders are given a moral
warrant for their position and power, but also wonder if then their power is
used ethically? It seems to us that many (but not all) leaders in schools, no doubt

encouraged by the entrepreneurial climate of today's educational policies, have acquired a new aura, and as Ball (2003) indicated, assumed the mantle of a new moral imperative, embodied in the fortunes of the institution in the performative and competitive steeplechase they may – or may not – embrace, but which is hard to abjure. The words that recur in agendas, such as performance, intervention, progress, test, data entry, subject knowledge, retention/remembering, target grades, behaviour, and reporting become tools through which teachers view and act upon their professional world. These agendas are set by senior leaders and come to structure the thinking of staff that leads to "*the ideological co-optation of the moral and ethical consciousness of the teachers*" (Smyth, Dow, Hattam, Reid, & Shacklock, 2000, p. 86) with consequences for the identity of teachers as they fall into step, compliant with the new narratives of institutional life. Does this amount to an unethical diminution of teachers' professional status?

Whilst our focus is mainly on what happens in schools, we should not ignore the pervasive effects of performativity and managerialism in other sectors of education. (Of course, as we will continue to emphasise, good relationships are critical to success – almost however that may be envisaged – in any phase or sector of education.) Thus, for example, a series of complex effects of performativity on inclusion in leadership and decision-making were discernible in a study of staff in colleges of Further Education (Lumby, 2009). Although Lumby found that here too it was commonly declared that everyone was listened to, some chose to be silent – or were not heard or considered. But it also appeared to be the case that those who were perceived to be "competent" according to the rules of the particular game imposed on the college, were afforded more respect and the opportunity to speak and influence discussion. Trust was thought to be in short supply and only sparingly available to those who can deliver on targets. Otherwise, Lumby (p. 362) argued that:

> ... the predilection of many to assume lower competence amongst those with minority characteristics or who are a minority within their group, for example, women senior leaders or black leaders, emerges repeatedly in research.

In such circumstances the capacity of a school or college leadership to acknowledge and respond to the voices of those at lower levels of the pyramid may be constricted and thus ethical equity of regard compromised. Performativity as a moral burden with its incumbent pressure to measure up, induces anxiety and ultimately affects how some people construct their identities. Lumby, with a particular interest in the nature of communication as the means to establish trust and social norms, found a pattern in meetings at different levels of the colleges. In both senior leadership and meetings amongst rank and file staff there was open discussion with the opportunity for ethical dialogue. However, at middle leadership meetings that were chaired by a senior leader, the norm was for a middle leader to report to the senior level on an area of responsibility with other, lower status, contributions demeaned only to clarify or extend.

Lumby also noticed that representatives of minorities were clustered in the lower-status levels of the organisation where they had little access to decision making, and furthermore certain competences were looked for in the managerial process which, along with apparently stereotypical and unjustified assumption could work against those deemed "other." Thus, Lumby concluded:

> Competence is constructed differentially, the multiple identities of those who appear different to an unstated norm being computed, the calculation sometimes leading to assumptions of lesser competence, or competence being viewed as limited to certain specialised areas.
>
> (Lumby, 2009, p. 366)

Performance management is one of the preferred and explicitly powerful techniques of control and surveillance across many, if not most, western organisations. If one passes muster there is some leeway for professional judgement, but if one falls short of the benchmark, continued surveillance is inevitable. Either way a low trust environment pervades. Avis (2003) argued that performativity changes identities, as it changes the conditions that legitimise the living out of certain characteristics as we have seen in the Woods and Jeffrey (2002) study. Thus, as any notion of the equity of relationships is denied, eroded, or deformed, identities that can be stigmatised (such as sexuality) or regarded as low status become devalued in the conformity demanded.

Some of the greatest perceived threats to teachers' morale and well-being have been found in this culture of performativity and school inspections. As Steven Courtney (2016, p. 639) noted, in contrast to Foucault's insight that self-surveillance via the self-surveilled panopticon made control less visible, "*the operationalisation of power* [in schools subject to Ofsted inspection; performing to the test] *may be made explicit, primary even, provided that habits of compliance have become entrenched such that its objects' identities rely on their compliant state.*" In one case study, the effects of a period of near continuous inspection (five inspections in nine months; a total of eight inspections in 18 months) on the compliance of staff in a school placed in "special measures" were investigated by Jane Perryman (2006). Perryman found that as a consequence of this regime staff were showing narrowly defined conformity, compliance, and depressed morale. As Gibbs (2018, p. 56) commented "*with no chance to escape an imminent inspection, staff often experience a sense of 'learned helplessness.'*"

The silencing of critical voices, the suppression of creativity is clearly opposed to ethical and democratic practices. Accordingly, it has been argued that "*attempting to overcome moral silence in organizations will require management to move beyond a compliance-oriented organizational culture toward a culture based on integrity*" (Verhezen, 2010, p. 187).

Here, in the UK, the dominant educational competitive managerial and commercial discourse, encouraging a performative system that may be aggravated by aggressive inspections by Ofsted, Education Scotland inspectors, and other bodies, suppresses imagination and induces compliance (Webb, Vulliamy, Sarja,

Hämäläinen, & Poikonen, 2009). We are not surprised, therefore, that this has been reported to generate negative emotions such as fear, anger, disaffection, and professional attrition (Perryman, 2007). As one primary teacher inter- viewee in the study by Webb et al. (2009, p. 417) put it:

> The head is under pressure to perform, she puts pressure on us, we put pressure on the children and then everyone is just under immense pressure and stress.

And so the vicious cycle of immoral unnegotiated externally imposed pressure generates unethical treatment and positioning of others. The activity of agencies external to a school (Ofsted, for instance) that could, in principle, treat staff in schools ethically, helpfully, is not always seen in that light even when the formal outcome might be celebrated.

Following, and consequent on, two consecutive Ofsted inspections that culminated in a judgement that it was "*an effective and rapidly improving school that provides good quality of education and good value for money*" (sic), Perryman (2007, p. 187) recorded that the school had lost "a lot of experienced staff." The inspection process had, Perryman wrote, exhausted many of the staff:

> People [were] tired, people have had enough of it all, it was full-on for so long, we had months of it, the month or so of build up and then them coming in and people have just said "Right, summer, I'm just going to see it out now until summer." I'm getting impatient and losing patience and I'm tired every day.

One of those leaving, a "middle manager," said

> I was getting more upset about being here, going home and being more upset and I just thought "life is too short and no I don't need to be here," so I decided to make a change.

Thus, in addition to the morally conflicted ethos of education and the unethical treatment of so many teachers, we might add concerns about the immoral waste of human resources that follows from such attrition.

## Taking a morally and empirically warranted ethical stand

If the picture we have provided so far has seemed rather dark, we should now look where there are more positive and illuminating examples of morally and ethically valid educational practices warranting closer attention. Since, in our view, many of the concerns we have can be located at an organisational level, we will start by thinking about "ethical leadership" before looking at some examples of how teachers themselves may initiate and sustain their own ethic- ally justified practice.

## Ethical practices and leadership

Successful, ethically thoughtful, leaders of schools manage and care for competing demands (Day & Leithwood, 2007). They appear to do this by building and sustaining a vision that can be shared and adopted by staff; understanding and caring for staff, their inter-relationships and relationships between staff, students, and the communities in which they live; ensuring organisational structures and processes support collaboration, creativity, and productivity; and having oversight and management of learning for all. It might seem appropriate, we wonder, if we were to subsume such characteristics of successful leaders as belonging to the "Ethics of Care" as discussed by Ann Diller (2018) in her review of the work of Nel Noddings (1984). However, it is not clear that an "ethic of care" is sufficient to ensure justice or that "ethical decisions" are made in relation to the effects for staff caused by the decisions of leaders (Crigger, 1997; Nelson, 1992; Noddings, 1990). Trust, reciprocity, and mutual respect are additional and necessary qualities. As Noddings (1990, p. 123) noted, "*In any necessarily unequal relation, we* [should be able to] *look for a form of mutuality or reciprocity that represents the weaker party's contribution to the relation.*" The relationship between leader and staff imposes what may be a necessarily unequal relationship but that does not have to be also an unethical relationship if mutuality, reciprocity, and ethical dialogues are sustained. That reciprocal relational leadership may be possible has been considered by Guowei Jian in a recent paper (Jian, 2021). Here Jian has challenged some of the more leader-centred theories of leadership by drawing attention to a socially constructed, reciprocal, notion of empathy. Thus, he suggested, relational leaders can be both empathisers and the empathised since in this view "empathy" is constructed in two-way communication.

From a rather different empirical perspective such as that provided by Brown and Treviño (2006) in a review of evidence of perceived ethical leadership in industrial settings, not dissimilar characteristics to those enumerated above were discerned, and though more obviously located as *individualised* rather than *relational* (but such is the nature of that science), as is possible to detect at least the possibility (if not a probability) of some respect for ethical, reciprocal communication in the authors' summary since:

> ethical leaders *[were]* characterized as honest, caring, and principled individuals who make fair and balanced decisions. Ethical leaders also frequently communicate with their followers about ethics, set clear ethical standards and *[though more regrettably, in our view]* use rewards and punishments to see that those standards are followed.
>
> (Brown & Treviño, 2006, p. 597)

We recognise there are risks in comparing cultures or jurisdictions (or research paradigms). On the one hand it may be thought that to portray one as wholly more successful than another is too simplistic, relatively easily overlooking some unique and distinctive strengths in the comparator; on the other hand, it is near impossible to take account of the effects of historical events that can, for instance, provide great stability or involve considerable turmoil. However, it may be that we can learn from others. It is also in the particular case here, that our intention (to briefly compare the status and effects of educational systems in the UK and Finland) is not to suggest that wholesale adoption of the Finnish model is to be recommended – though we believe there is much to admire.

The historical contexts and cultures of these two nations are very different. The population densities and climate are different; spending on education as a percentage of GDP fluctuates, but World Bank data for 2017 (the most recent comparisons available) was 6.4% in Finland, 5.4% in the UK; the island of Britain has not been invaded or overrun by others for over 1000 years and education system have accordingly grown slowly and steadily without, (according to Gibbs (2021)) any significant major changes. In contrast to such general social stability that for English educational thinking almost amounts to stasis or even ossification, socio-politically Finland was a part of Sweden from the 13th to 19th centuries (Swedish remains one of the two official languages of the country) when it was annexed by Russia until the early 20th century. Finland was able to declare independence in December 1917 only to be almost immediately submerged and divided by civil war, the effects of which lasted for several decades (in fact still reverberate today). During WWII Finland was attacked by the Soviet Union and tactically aligned itself with Nazi Germany to fend off the soviet forces. After the war Finland regained independence though, partly because of geographical proximity, it has generally maintained economic links with Russia.

Following lengthy debate and widespread consultation in the 1960s and 1970s some radical and apparently very effective changes were made to education in Finland. (For a detailed account see Sahlberg (2015)). Pre-school education is now rare (whereas, of course in England formal education is required from the age of 5 years) but comprehensive education in Finland (private and special schools are also now rare) is compulsory between the ages of 7 and 18. In terms of international rankings of educational systems, the outcomes for Finland have been consistently good (OECD, 2020). Up to the age of 16 students are not selected, tracked, or streamed. At 16 students must choose between pursuing an academic or vocational programme.

In Finland teaching is a highly respected profession and entry to the required 5-year masters degree programmes is highly competitive (only about 10% of applicants are successful). Schools (for children and young people aged 7–18) are almost exclusively funded by the local municipality. Classes are generally small (rarely more than 20 students). The teaching workforce is fully unionised and while teachers are required to follow the national curriculum guidelines, they have considerable autonomy in choosing how to teach and what materials they wish to use.

In Finland, school inspections were abolished in the early 1990s, so that, critically for our purposes here, in Finland:

> Today, school principals, aided by their own experience as teachers, are able to help their teachers recognize strengths and areas of work that need improvement. The basic [and, we think, realistic] assumption in Finnish schools is that teachers, by default, are well-educated professionals and are doing their best in schools.
>
> (Sahlberg, 2015, p. 126)

The Finnish system seems to work well in Finland and, it must be noted that there are aspects of what has been set in place that appears to have prevented the attrition of staff well-being that has been observed elsewhere. There are, however, other examples of emerging practices much closer to home that are worth reporting. These include work on coaching for teachers that in principle can lead to teaching staff promoting and sustaining their own morally justified and ethical practice.

## Ethical teachers and relationships

"Coaching" as a form of support for teachers' professional status and practice exists on a sliding scale of power and accountability differentials which have heavy influence on the nature of the interpersonal ethical "space" and trust created and engendered.

One of the key characteristics of peer coaching (see Lofthouse, Leat, & Towler, 2010) is that it is based in equity not power. It is a professional relationship between two or more teachers or other educational professionals (see also our discussion of "consultation" in Chapter 6) who are inquiring into practice with an intention to improve that practice. Ideally that inquiry would include both means, that is practice, and ends – thus the understanding of "improvement" would be open for debate and, therefore, ethically realised and not the outcome of a "moral" imperative. Pragmatically, however, as with communities of practice (Fuller, Hodkinson, Hodkinson, & Unwin, 2005) there is a danger that such intra-school coaching relationships remain conservative and unable to challenge the "status quo" (Lofthouse & Leat, 2013). It can be helpful, therefore if there is an impetus to question, a direction to improve or a specialism held by one of the parties, or by working across more than one institution. Power is rarely completely put aside, so if one party does bring particular knowledge the imbalance may disrupt the provisional ethos of equity. Interestingly, however, it has been found that when a more junior member of staff coaches a more senior colleague, perhaps because of particular expertise or interest, the different dimensions of power (relative seniority vs expertise) may cancel each other restoring a sense of respectful equity and curiosity (Towler, Lofthouse, & Leat, 2011). However, forethought is needed in case support from senior leaders – in the form of directed time or integration into a school's development plan or by dictating pairings/ triads, the coaching focus or indeed targets – could evoke the shadow of surveillance and managerialism that might capsize staff commitment to coaching (Hargreaves & Skelton, 2012; Simkins, Coldwell, Caillau, Finlayson, & Morgan, 2006).

Lofthouse and Leat (2013) observed that because peer coaching has such a strong pedigree in terms of effectiveness in improving student outcomes, it might be hoped that with approval from teachers and advocacy for ethical professionalism coaching would be universally adopted. Ironically, whilst many schools take it up, and many teachers have said they have gained from it, few persevere; often, perversely, because of interference by school leaders. For example, Lofthouse and Leat reported an observation from a teacher who concluded that she would *"not let them near it,"* the "it" being a peer coaching system and "them" being the school senior leaders.

As we have noted above, the dominant discourse and culture in educational settings, pervaded by managerialism, surveillance, and accountability is hard to break free from. Using Activity Theory as an analytical frame, Lofthouse and Leat (2013) examined factors that illustrated why coaching does not always succeed in schools. They reported, for instance, how a senior leader in a college reflected on the tensions she encountered, as in her institution the coaching partner was expected to be both a judge of progress and to help the coachee establish her own intentions for improvement.

> With my other role as a quality observer within the college and in ITT when we go out and observe people we are making judgements about their performance, it is almost expected, so it was very easy for me to fall back into that mode and he (a coached teacher) was looking for direction from me all the time and I do think that that very much happens in the first cycle, it's not until the relationship has been established and also that the coachee is almost empowered and realises that they have the power to drive it forward.
>
> (Lofthouse & Leat, 2013, p. 14)

The degree to which teachers can feel free to explore practice in coaching, in order to bring it close to their ideals is heavily shaped by the building of trust (Cox, 2012; Lofthouse & Hall, 2014). Solomon and Flores (2001) positioned trust as a central problem in human relationships and needed to be accounted for if coaching is to be fulfilling. Without interpersonal trust, it is difficult for people to take calculated risks and to be honest about what makes them tick, what they value, what they want to achieve, and to engage in an ethical dialogue, being open to change and not defensive.

Lofthouse and Leat (2013, p. 15) uncovered in a coached teacher's words both the importance of trust and generosity in a coaching relationship and how this *"epitomises the quality of relationships that can be developed as coaches privilege trust over power and how this has a long-lasting impact"*:

I often discuss learning with this teacher and learn a lot from doing so. I am aware of how much time he invested into the exercise, willingly, because time was not easily available for coaching at that stage. At the time I felt guilty about this. He is a really supportive member of staff and innovative in his approach. It was one of the best forms of professional development because it really made me consider my teaching and the small changes I could introduce to make a difference. I felt supported with my work in the classroom in a way in which I don't really feel on the whole. It reminded me of the way things used to work in the department when there was a great spirit of sharing and we have formed a mutually supportive relationship as a result.

Trust is understood as "a psychological state comprising the intention to accept vulnerability based upon positive expectations of the intentions or behaviour of another" (Rousseau, Sitkin, Burt, & Camerer, 1998, p. 395). Where trust exists it is safer to take a reasonable risk in experimenting with practice with the expectation that you gain understanding and support from those with authority and from peers. You should suffer no harm as a result of taking that reasonable risk. (In a related domain, the supervision of trainee educational psychologists, Gibbs et al. (2016) reported that one of the factors that trainees found most important was a "safe space for authentic learning" within which they could trust their supervisor, in confidence, to enable them to explore, reflect, and learn.) Dibben, Morris, and Lean (2000) drawing on a classification from Lewicki and Bunker (1995), have described a trajectory of trust development, which starts with "on-trust" which is founded in the reputation of the party from third party sources. "Calculus-based trust" develops as each party estimates they can gain from the interaction. In many cases in school teachers, because of the accountability pressures, will take a defensive stance, hoping to protect whatever status they have. The manager will be seeking assurance that pre-determined benchmarks of performance are being achieved. The agenda is not growth or development. "Knowledge based trust" should develop as people work together and learn more about the other, becoming familiar with their knowledge resources, histories, values and attitudes, and behavioural traits. They can begin to depend on the other and therefore predict with some confidence how they will behave and respond. The final stage is "identification-based trust" whereby there is an emotional connection between parties, based on experience and personal resonance and to some extent roles become interchangeable.

But, as we reiterate, trust in relationships is central to education; central to the work of teachers, their professional inter-relationships and with their students. For education to be meaningful betrayal is unthinkable. As Martin Buber (1965, p. 116) said:

> Trust, trust in the world, because this human being exists – that is the most inward achievement of the relation in education… and the relation in education is one of pure dialogue.

## Conclusion

We are conscious that in this chapter we have not been able to address the full range of moral and ethical issues that are implicated in education and the classroom practices of teachers; indeed we have perhaps raised more questions than answers. We would argue that that is ethical since although we have views about what education might be purposed to do it seems presumptuous to impose those too forcefully here. We are anxious to promote dialogue about education. In the next chapter we will set out to explore in more detail what we mean by dialogue and dialogic processes. In the meantime, what we hope to have done here is to point out some of moral and ethical threats to education and the development of professional relationships, as well as some ideas about how these might be mitigated. We are, however, still left wondering about what is being done in the name of education and what a difference might be.

# 5 Dialogue and awareness of the space between

## Introduction

As indicated in the previous chapter many teachers are conflicted or unfulfilled by their professional work. They may hold constructs about what should constitute education and how this should be made available to all young people but also how these constructs are interlinked with their general values. These constructs come variably from their own influential educational experiences, both positive and negative, and sometimes from their adult experiences as parents, volunteers, or working with young people in some capacity. Sometimes it is about the passion for a subject, or perhaps being helped by a sympathetic adult in a time of adversity and sometimes it is from being a parent. These constructs can be relatively conservative, inspired by an effective but disciplined teacher or they can be more radical in offering more autonomy and creative space to young people. Equally they can be about the importance of caring relationships. Most people imagine their roles before they embark on their professional training, they can "see" themselves in their professional setting, living out those constructs. However, as government has increasingly been held to account for public services and the monies they consume, so government wants some accounting in a measurable form, which has led to a technology of standards and targets, which easily becomes a set of constraining orthodoxies about professional practice. With increased investment there is an expectation of improved outcomes or outputs. Our ideal practice is corralled. We are forced into applying policies which have a "common sense" or political imperative, aimed at efficiency (what works) and transparency, and our practice is forced down unwelcome tramlines, often at the expense of those treasured ideals; often disabling us from listening to and working *with* others.

In this chapter, therefore, we set out some ideas that provide the context for the use of dialogue in education. We do so in a spirit of provisionality, recognising that while we cannot be certain how these ideas may be used, we do feel it important to explore them if education and democratic societies are to prosper. There is provisionality, too, in how we discuss these ideas since, in writing this chapter, we have, as in any professional dialogue, discovered some of our own differences regarding the ideas about dialogue that we each have and

DOI: 10.4324/9780429343766-6

cannot, therefore, pretend we have arrived at an agreed definitive, homogenised, version of our ideas. We are still learning with – and from – each other.

## The issue of "space"

The concept of space is central to the discussion in two ways, firstly in the sense of the dialogical space between us as individuals and secondly as a means for distancing ourselves and professional colleagues from the straight-jacket of the systems we work in. In both cases interdependent mutual relationships are critical, as are democratic ideals. Furthermore, it is vital that as professionals we have a situational awareness such that we can explore and exploit the opportunities for dialogic practice, acting *with* colleagues and not doing *to* them.

A particular interpretation of the concept of space is central to the importance of dialogue. Space is a recurring metaphor in literature about professionals and professionalism, especially related to emotions, reflection, and learning from practice (maybe praxis too). This popularity can make one wary and indeed Crang and Thrift (2000, p. 1) fired a warning shot about the metaphorical use of space in contemporary social science:

> Space is the everywhere of modern thought. It is the flesh that flatters the bones of theory. It is an all purpose nostrum to be applied wherever things look sticky. It is an innovation which suggests that the writer is right on without having to give too much away.

So with that warning, we proceed with care. Nespor (1997) writing about schools as interconnected systems was one of the first to focus on "social spaces" reflecting cultural and political factors, and similar ideas were developed by Massey (1993), with an emphasis on spaces emerging from multiple and dynamic relationships. From that we can fathom that there is an opportunity to shape and arrange some of those intersections. Importantly space, as a metaphor, is also seen as a stand against power, as Edwards and Fowler (2007, p. 108) argued that

> the attempt to write a decentred space has been to the fore in much social theory influenced by postmodernism, post-structuralism, post-colonialism and feminism. Margins, third spaces, boundary zones and in-between spaces have been conceptualised as ways of framing alternatives to the powerful discourses and discourses of power of the centre.

Zembylas and Barker (2007) emphasised "spaces for coping" in the context of reform initiatives. They drew from Hargreaves (2004) the term *emotional geographies* to reflect the varying closeness or distance in human relationships in schools. However, we think space should be seen as more than a respite or protection from unwelcome pressures, important though that be, but also as representing conditions which promote agency. This accords with the view of agency being seen less as a personal trait, that you either lack or possess, and more as something that is achieved in the circumstances of the setting. Some settings constrain people, as we have argued, and others provide conditions that invite them to overcome the barriers to what they see as important. Such conditions will include material conditions and organisational structures but also the culture and discourse habits. This conceptualisation is termed eco-logical agency.

Another example of the use of the term *space* was provided by Edwards, Lunt, and Stamou (2010) who drew on the work of systems theory (e.g. Midgley, 1992) to focus attention on the tensions and contradictions at the boundaries of work with other professionals. Such boundaried zones are fertile sites for new practice, as one can justify the neglect of one policy by reference to another and because these sites may be "outwith" the practices of local bureaucracies which normally hobble innovation. To take advantage of opportunities practitioners can then rule bend in their own organisation, allowing new possibilities of action. This gives particular importance to "relational agency" – a capacity for working with, or bringing the best from, others who have particular know-ledge, expertise, or resources, but who align with the values being exercised. Such space may not be physical but the conditions on which it thrives, will abut the usual pressures of accountability and dominant discourse and it is important to be conscious of this potential friction. While this introduction positions the concept of space as important in organisational settings, we first need to estab-lish its significance for inter-personal communication and beyond into human functioning and sense making through dialogue.

## Space in systems

Important though dialogic space is to individuals, it has wider significance from the perspective of systems. Professionally, we are also in frequent and necessary contact with others, from other professions and organisations and this is espe-cially the case in education, with its overlaps with social services, psychological services, health, and police. In our professional meetings while there may be only a little physical space between one and another, it can often seem as if there is a huge, apparently almost unbridgeable gulf between representatives of differing organisations. Members of different professions can feel (and some-times behave) as if there is a significant difference in their professional brief and orientation to the issues under discussion. In Cultural Historical Activity Theory (CHAT, Roth & Lee, 2007) this is interpreted through the concept of the "object," the driving purpose of systems or people and object has historical origins. Systems have some defining characteristics or "nodes" – subject, rules, divisions of labour, community, and tools (in addition to object). Whilst the ongoing functioning of a system, such as a school, factory, cultural group, office, or public service generates internal contradictions which may or may not lead to resolution or change, the interaction of different systems generates more scope for contradiction as the differences between the respective nodes become apparent. The object or guiding purpose of different organisations may be at tangents, the community (stakeholders) different, the tools (e.g. for recording events and plans) distinctive to each and the rules that guide expectations, responsibilities, and behaviours at variance. Such differences can become problematic if we don't at least share an agreement that we are all enjoined participants in a similar enterprise. If, however, we can attend to and respect the different perspectives we each inevitably have, we can learn from and with each other. After all, with regard to the psychological phenomena that are the stuff of educational meetings, there are at least two sides to any and every issue; such is the complexity of human interactions.

Where individuals representing organisations are collaborating for the educational benefit of young people, there is scope for the creativity inherent in dialogue, not least if opportunities for rule bending at the boundaries are explored. Here is a hybrid space, where participants may have one metaphorical foot in home territory and the other in less familiar ground, where their expertise is uncertain and solutions are not from their everyday playbook. We are in the realm of boundary crossing. *"A boundary can be seen as a sociocultural difference leading to discontinuity in action or interaction"* (Akkerman & Bakker, 2011, p. 2). So there may be difference across the fault line, but there is also commonality in purpose for instance relating to the interests of a young person. Boundary crossing therefore assumes significance as one or more parties seeks to overcome the difference and possible contradictions. According to Akkerman and Bakker (2011, p. 134):

> the term boundary crossing was introduced to denote how professionals at work may need to "enter onto territory in which we are unfamiliar and, to some significant extent therefore unqualified" (Suchman, 1993, p. 25) and "face the challenge of negotiating and combining ingredients from different contexts to achieve hybrid situations" (Engeström, Engeström, & Kärkkäinen, 1995, p. 319).

For us the notion of "boundary crossing" developed by Akkerman and Bakker (2011) resonates with the ideas of Ronald Burt who, as we noted in Chapter 3, suggested that *"people who stand near the holes in a social structure* [the gaps between groups] *are at higher risk of having good ideas"* (Burt, 2004, p. 349), and with the ideas of Herb Simon that our behaviour is an artefact of our experience of the systems that we encounter. In Miller's (1996) study of what teachers valued about successful encounters with educational psychologists (that we will return to in the next chapter) he suggested it was possible for both parties to enter what he termed "a temporary alternative universe" in which with the support of a psychologist a teacher might feel confidently able and safe to explore their present situation and what alternative could be possible. Our view is that the notion of a "temporary alternative universe" as described by Miller matches the physical and psychological realities of what Sanne F Akkerman and Bakker (2011, p. 141) said about the "ambiguous nature" of boundaries in that these divide and connect people reflecting "*a nobody's land, belonging to neither one world nor the other...* [causing] *a sandwich effect for people that cross or stand in between sites.*" Burt (2004, pp. 349–50) similarly argued that within a group (say the staff of a school) behaviour and opinions are more likely to be homogenous than they might be between groups. In contrast, where there is brokerage across groups (e.g. between teachers and psychologists) "*people are more familiar with alternative ways of thinking and behaving, which give them more options to select from and synthesize.*" By being an observer between sites one may examine at greater leisure how the systems and practices affect one outside of "*nobody's land.*" In the company of a critical friend (as a psychologist may be) in "nobody's land" one may also then be able to envision alternative ideas and from such options select some that may be more fruitful. A meta-awareness of boundaries and holes or opportunities is highly advantageous; and, in some circumstances one person may helpfully take on the mantle of co-ordinating across organisations.

If there is a space between systems, where power is neutered and usual protocols held in abeyance, and where dialogue may flourish towards creative ends, then one needs to know where it is and what expectations may apply. As indicated by Edwards (2011) there is scope for rule bending at these boundary zones and knowing that there space is pivotal. This is a case, perhaps, of knowing how different rules or policies might be brought to bear, where different locations might offer alternative circumstances. Furthermore, there are sensitivities to be negotiated and knowing the geography of the application of rules enhances chances of creative outcomes. Back at the centre of one's organisation, one needs to return to the cultural norms and avoid provoking alarm, until circumstances for positive change emerge. There is an element of social dynamics of contexts or settings to be factored in, as may be seen in a study by Reeves and Forde (2004) of changing practice Scottish Qualification for Headship (SQH). This case study noted that participants in the course operated in two separate contexts or "activities," in the course and the school (Engeström, 1999) with each characterised by its own discourse, norms, and values. The course, therefore, provided a space in which the "usual" power dynamics were pushed back, hierarchies flattened, and peer dialogue became possible. However, course members, senior leaders (who are not yet headteachers), needed to undertake course tasks in school, thus overlapping the boundaries of the respective spaces which required the course member to negotiate permission for the SQH activity (a task) from their colleagues. In this accounting process there was a sense of defining and protecting the space to provide legitimisation. This brings attention to the importance of narration in establishing space, which in turn has implications for identity, which is increasingly understood as multi-faceted and dynamic. This Scottish account also draws attention to centrality of boundary objects (Star & Griesemer, 1989), usually artefacts or tools, which help work across boundaries as they have meaning or functionality for different activities or groups, as well as a unifying role. In this case the course task, related to school improvement, fulfils this function. In many educational settings, notes or a joint reporting/recording form will perform this role, but in some circumstances, it could be something more creative such as a video recording.

In a wide spectrum of educational settings, both those involving professionals as well as those involving professionals and young people where dialogue is a cherished goal, it is important to remember the importance of actions. As humans our communication is associated with speech, but this is embedded in a multi-modal physical world where words are amplified, skewed and elaborated by gesture, intonation, inflection, and physical actions to convey nuances, but these are embedded in and related to physical actions taking place in the setting. Tiplady (2018) paid tribute to the environment in Forest School sessions for underpinning the growth of relationships between vulnerable children with their peers and teachers – the whittling, hammocks, leaves, and string/rope all help call up a space where voices are coaxed from their hiding places and brought into the open, to be fully heard. The community of campfire, with food on sticks, opens avenues not available in more formal settings.

## Education, democracy, relationships, and transformation

While there are notable islands of innovative practice such as the above, in our view the formal topology of education appears have remained relatively untransformed for the past hundred years or so (Decuypere & Simons, 2016; Gibbs, 2021, 2022) and, with only a very few notable exceptions has, if anything, become less democratic in the past half-century (certainly we suggest this is true for teachers and for children and young people). As we have already noted, politically and conceptually, democracy is both hard to define and inherently problematic in practice (Dahl, 2020; Schmitter & Karl, 1991), and, as an ideal, a problem for educationalists, certainly those seeking to promote a more inclusive society (such as Biesta, 2016; Dewey, 1916/2011, 1937/1987). It is also perceived by many to be under threat (see, for instance, Kutz, 2000; Monbiot, 2021; Somer & McCoy, 2018), despite, but perhaps also because, democracy may be seen as offering humanity *"its best prospect for freedom and peace"* (Mandel, 2005, p. 209). However, if we turn to the interaction and inter-relationships of the professional agents who may affect what happens within educational settings, we can see there are opportunities for radical but democratic change. We suggest, therefore, that democracy and education should be in a symbiotic relation: one without the other cannot survive (Ahlstrom-Vij, 2019; Glaeser, Ponzetto, & Shleifer, 2007). So, while, as we have argued elsewhere, the autonomy of teachers may have been eroded (Strahan, Gibbs, & Reid, 2018), within inter- and intra-professional dialogues we believe autonomy and creativity may be re-established and re-created. This strategy is not, however, without risk. By reformulating the inter-connections of just certain of the key players (a teacher and a visiting psychologist, for example) and their relationships, the homeomorphism of education may be challenged in ways that might seem, to some, as politically insensitive or undemocratic.

But, if we are to continue with the presumption that education could be a necessarily *humanising* (rather than commercial) enterprise, this entails accepting that the exploration, transformation, and continuity of relationships is integral and necessary. Education also remains a *democratic* enterprise if the essence of relationships is held to be ethically respectful. As Robert Dahl said:

> Democracy, it appears, is a bit chancy. But its chances also depend on what we do ourselves. Even if we cannot count on benign historical forces to favor democracy, we are not mere victims of blind forces over which we have no control. With adequate understanding of what democracy requires and the will to meet its requirements, we can act to preserve and, what is more, to advance democratic ideas and practices.
>
> (Dahl, 2020, p. 25)

It is, of course, one of our major contentions that education and educational processes can provide the settings in which children and young people (the citizens of now and the future) discover and learn how to become democratic human beings; and that they will learn this through their relationships and interactions with others (both other young people and adults). We further propose that the adult members of school communities can, in their interactions, model dialogical relationships that respect difference and seek mutual learning.

Thus, as we conceive them, approaches based in dialogic relationships can provide genuinely educational opportunities that are not prescribed or dogmatic. While we don't, however, want to seem overly idealistic or prescriptive about dialogue, perhaps with Lefstein (see Asterhan, Howe, Lefstein, Matusov, and Reznitskaya, 2020) and Haslam, Reicher, and Platow (2020) we might agree to be pragmatic and speak of the development of possibilities that encourage inter- and intra-personal understanding so that, with reference to dialogic principles, we learn how best to support each other in specific contexts? That said, our view is, nonetheless, that there may be an ethical imperative for inter- and intra-professional dialogues in educational settings in order to promote and facilitate development and understanding. Thus, we accept that, as John Dewey wrote over a hundred years ago, for democracy and education to thrive it is the case that

> "…a society which not only changes but which has the ideal of such change as will improve it, will have different standards from one which aims simply at the perpetuation of its own customs." [*and that*] "…two elements in our criterion both point to democracy. The first signifies not only more numerous and more varied points of shared common interest, but greater reliance upon the recognition of mutual interests as a factor in social control. The second means not only freer interaction between social groups… but change in social habit – its continuous readjustment through meeting the new situations produced by varied intercourse. And these two traits are precisely what characterise the democratically constituted society."
>
> (Dewey, 1916/2011, pp. 47–9)

But of course, as may be already clear, we are not suggesting that dialogue is a one size suits all solution. It may take different forms, conversations, dialogues, that help to connect us, reminding us that we are interdependent.

## Interdependent selves and others

We have argued that the assumptions we make about who we are as humans, and particularly, about the extent to which we are independent of, or interdependent with others, are relevant to our practice. How we position ourselves and others in our work and what we mean when we claim to engage in relational practice are, for us, profound considerations.

As we've repeatedly said we are personally (psychologically and materially) not alone, and it is very hard to see how one could nowadays safely lead a wholly solitary life. We are demonstrably physically and psychologically interconnected. Our food, fuel, and much of our entertainment has its origins in others' labours and, as these may be often located in another hemisphere (almost another world?), we are also dependent on yet others who organise and form the supply chains that we now rely on. Very few people these days can lead the "Good Life" entirely dependent on their own efforts and produce. But our psychological and physical resources are, in any case, enhanced by the presence and support of others. How near or far (or, how abstract) these others may be, we are inextricably linked with them.

But while acknowledging our interconnectedness, what of our individual "selves"? As we noted in Chapter 1, the notion of a distinct "self" is a puzzle. Philosophers and psychologists continue to attempt the dissection and definition of this illusory concept. In the second half of the twentieth century the work of Carl Rogers, for instance, with its focus on core conditions such as unconditional positive regard, and the importance of an empathic understanding of the other's frame of reference was a considerable influence on practice in health care (Arnold, Kerridge, & Lipworth, 2020), social work (Murphy, Duggan, & Joseph, 2012), and education, particularly in relation to transition planning for pupils identified as having special educational needs (see, for example, Michaels & Ferrara, 2009). Critiques of person-centred approaches, however, have focussed on Rogers' individualistic approach to the human person. Arnold et al. (2020), for example, argued that in healthcare contexts, the individualistic credentials of person-centred approaches could be used to support less benign consumerist ideologies. Small, Raghavan, and Pawson (2013) researching person centred planning among ethnically diverse young people diagnosed with "intellectual disabilities," also concluded that the individualistic premise of person-centred approaches failed to take account of complex interdependencies, raising questions about the relevance of his work for a contemporary culture characterised by diverse and interacting voices. For some, Rogers' understanding of the self leads to a loss of focus on the other almost to the point of narcissism (Brazier, 1993). In addition to weakening Rogers' claims to altruism, the charge of individualism has been argued to contradict his democratic political ideal (Sampson, 1985).

In our view relational practice needs a contextualised, interconnected understanding of who we are (Gergen, 2009; McNamee & Hosking, 2012). Shifting the focus away from an individualistic to a more dialogic, relational ontology highlights the importance of attending to what transpires in the space between us (Buber, 2002; Kirschenbaum & Henderson, 1989; Sampson, 2008).

Given the significance that has been given to the ways in which we view the person for our understanding of relationality, an ontological sense of dialogue is important. The development of dialogic ontology has been heavily influenced by Bakhtin (Salgado & Clegg, 2011; Salgado & Hermans, 2005). Bakhtin's position was paradoxical, involving the coming together of opposing positions, yet maintaining the differences between them. The aim of dialogue from this perspective is not to reach a convergence of self and other in inter-subjective agreement. Thus, "dialogic space" may be seen as "a space in which different perspectives are held in tension in a way which does not lead to resolution but produces sparks of insight, learning and creativity" (Wegerif, 2007, p. 145). Dialogic ontology is based on the interplay of same-different/self-other which neither leads to fusion nor to the maintenance of difference as a "stand-off" position. Dialogic is, therefore, continuously dynamic and open. A dialogic ontology is able to account for "innovation, creativity and change" (Marková, 2003, p. 255). Grasping dialogism as ontology can have immense practical significance for how we understand relationship and interaction (Grossen, 2010; Marková, 2016) and be crucial to our interest in exploring understandings of the human person in relation to others that may underpin and transform professional practice. Failure to recognise the importance of the space between can occur when individualistic ontological assumptions are held and support views of others as external to the individual. Such assumptions dominate many areas of psychological theory and when humans are viewed as ontologically interdependent rather than as individual units of analysis, the ways in which we understand relationships and interaction shift considerably (Grossen, 2010; Marková, 2016; Sampson, 2008). However, for us, while abstraction and theory are crucial for our reflection, in practice it is important to be grounded: dialogics are more than ontological, they are founded on relationships. Dialogic ontology instead considers social reality to be in constant flux due to the ongoing negotiation of different voices in dialogue.

## The dialogue of self and other

Dialogue has aroused multi-disciplinary interest and various academic traditions have built up around the concept (Mifsud & Johnson, 2000; Renshaw, 2004). Linell (2009) suggested that dialogical is a meta-theoretical framework with the potential to integrate a range of theories that all focus on contextualised joint meaning making and recognise the perspective of the other. This takes us some way beyond Buber's dyadic focus (Markova, 2003; 2016; Linell, 2009). From this perspective the social world is composed of multiple I-other relations encompassing the dyadic I-other, and wider relations such as I-family,

I-community, my group-another group, I-organisation, I-culture, and even I-virtual community (Marková, 2016). By extending beyond the dyadic in this way, a dialogical theoretical framework offers possibilities for our understanding of the social world at the personal, interpersonal, and transpersonal (the wider social, institutional, and professional domain) levels (Grossen & Salazar Orvig, 2011).

In addition to extending Buber's idea of dialogue beyond the dyadic, this approach also moves away from his focus on mutuality in dialogue. As we have seen, dialogue does not aim to reach a "*happy unification with the other*" (Markova, 2003, p. 255). Instead, we exist in a dynamic world of multiple, competing voices – outside us and, in our inner dialogue with real or imagined others (Linell, 2009; Marková, 2016; Marková, Linell, Grossen, & Salazar Orvig, 2007). Our talk expresses the dynamic nature of the tension between these different voices. From this perspective, the self is dynamic and multi-voiced.

## The ethic of dialogue

Markova's notion of a dialogic self although emphasising our interdependence, avoids a dialectic fusion of self and other in the dialogic encounter. The distinction between dialectic and dialogic has profound implications (Wegerif, 2007). Where opposing positions are synthesised, self can subsume other in a "*totalising system of explanation and control*" (p. 35). When otherness is defeated through dialectic, there is no longer any point to dialogue, nor any mechanism for self-critique and change. The dialogic perspective does not merely celebrate the diversity of different voices available in dialogue. Rather, as Vasterling (2003) argued, there is a need for "*recognition of plurality and other … because it enables the critical function of open dialogue*" (p. 167). There is no point to communication if all we are doing is reducing the intersubjective space between us. It is in the critical space between us that we struggle with, and judge the message of the other (Markova, 2003). This carries with it ethical responsibility (Markova, 2016). It is not knowing about the other but being open to the other that is our ethical responsibility, and this requires dialogic interaddressivity (the expectation of being surprised by the other) (Matusov, 2011). Within European education diversity is often hidden or denied (Surian, 2016). We have experienced "*progressive universalization of the human condition*" (Bauman, 1995, p. 202). Biesta (2016)) argued that developing the kinds of educational communities in which there is openness to the other cannot be achieved through tools or programmes but rather there is a need for space to be provided to enable pupils (and teachers) to face the different and to find their own response. This requires an openness to the other which goes beyond celebrating difference. This is well summed up by David Kennedy (2004, p. 747) who described it this way:

> I am required both to think more for myself, since I am faced more and more with my own decisions about my truth…as well as having to think more with others, because I am more and more aware of the relativity of

my truth vis-á-vis the truths of others and the necessity of coming into some sort of coordination with those truths in order to cope collectively.

Here Kennedy was describing the experience of engaging in collaborative philosophical inquiry (CPI). Oliverio (2016) argued that in educational contexts CPI offers the potential to open space where difference can be faced within educational contexts describing it as providing a "space of borders" (p. 37). This is more than a celebratory space since, as we may see from Kennedy's description, in confronting otherness we are engaging in an evaluation of our own position (and responsibility) in the face of others. Evaluation of the other is part of our human connectedness and is part of the ethical dimension of human interconnectedness (Markova, 2016).

Such work has of necessity, therefore, incorporated a growing ethical concern for human development and social phenomena (Marková, 2016) and takes as the starting point the interdependence of one and another. For Markovà this implies an ability to imagine and evaluate how others think, to trust others and to aim to achieve a "good life" with others. As Levinas emphasised, human thought and deed, our relationships, are primarily ethical issues:

> The irreducible and ultimate experience of relationship appears to me to be… not in synthesis, but in the face to face of humans, in sociality, in its moral signification. But it must be understood that morality comes not as a secondary layer… First philosophy is an ethics.
>
> (Levinas, 1985, p. 77)

To enact this reciprocally requires acceptance that our minds, our consciousness, are interdependent: as conscious human beings we do not exist as isolated individuals, nor are we solely self-conscious. However, it is perhaps also important to stress that, at least in the professional relationships that are our focus here, we respect the differences that exist between professionals – and between adults and young people.

For Marková (2016, p. 1), however, "*the mind of the self and the minds of Others are interdependent in and through sense making and sense creating… .*" We can also see this, for example, in the work of Vygotsky (1978) who showed how children learn to solve problems and articulate (externalise) their thinking in their interactions with another – such as a parent or teacher; in studies of interpersonal attunement of children and adults (Braten, 2007; Kokkinaki, Vasdekis, Koufaki, & Trevarthen, 2017); in the synchrony of non-verbal communication and rapport in counselling (Chartrand & Lakin, 2013; Tschacher, Rees, & Ramseyer, 2014); and in interthinking (Littleton & Mercer, 2013; Pantaleo, 2007). In lay terms we can, perhaps, see synchrony in the very tightly regimented interdependence of guards on parade (trooping the colour, for instance) marching as one body, or in the way members of a top-flight football team anticipate and coordinate their movements to pass and receive the ball without ceding it to the opposition. Thinking and moving together in these latter two examples happens with very little, if any, verbal communication but self-evidently with considerable regard for the position (stance) of each other and thus seeming to conform to an "interactional epistemology" in which individuals and their environment (other guards, other members of the team) "*form irreducible onto-logical… existential, units*" (Marková, 2016, p. 91).

But for us, considering the structure and process of professional dialogues, we do not suggest that a teacher and psychologist (for instance) should form an "*irreducible ontological*" unit within which personal or professional identities should merge or disappear. We suggest there is, as Hubert Hermans and others have indicated (Hermans, 2013, 2015; Hermans, Kempen, & Van Loon, 1992; Sampson, 2008), something distinctive in the "*dialogical self*": "*the self as dialogically extended to an independent other*" (Hermans, 2013, p. 82). In this conception of the "self," the "*I-self*" flexibly relates to, is positioned by, the environment of "*others*" so that within a dialogue of one's self and other-selves each participant has an independence, by virtue of being

> partners in the "democracy" of the self… In other words, the other has an existence as an outside reality but is also as part of my extended self in which I make something of him. In this field of tension, internal and external dialogues meet with the potential to correct, influence, and develop each other.
>
> (Hermans, 2013, pp. 83–4)

## The face-to-face of dialogue

Some principles should underpin taking a dialogic approach in practice. The first of these is physical care and we should not underestimate the import-ance of providing a comfortable setting with refreshments, nor indeed by establishing an exchange of information, as appropriate, about health, family, recent excursions, and leisure interests. Dialogue is not just an exchange of words creating an interdependence of minds, it is founded also on a respect for and interest in the other, which comes partly from knowledge of that person – it is relational as one distances oneself from organisational roles and bindings. Becoming familiar with the multiple voices of the Other, and their multi-faceted identities rounds them out as human beings and offers other points of contact with them. Revealing Self is the reciprocation, but in the knowledge that this can always be misjudged. The realisation of relation agency and overt moral leadership presumes some personal resonance between professional part-ners. Another principle in the pathway to dialogical space is through the use of micro-discourse structures which invite all participants to speak and be listened to (Horn & Little, 2010), and although this can feel a little formulaic at times it creates an atmosphere and expectation that voices will be heard. Thus, it can be valuable, especially where there are more than two people, to establish and follow some protocols, such as allowing everyone to give their view or inter-pretation without interruption while also establishing periodic summarisation and opportunities for clarification.

One might expect the more creative aspects of dialogue to build on more basic information-giving and sharing. We do not generally immediately launch into higher cognitive realms in inter-thinking, but rather there is a building process (Leat & Nichols, 2000). These points mirror elements of practice in Philosophy for Children (P4C, Lipman, Sharp, & Oscanyan, 1980) which provides such an insightful introduction to dialogue for children of primary school age, and indeed is not wasted on older students. In P4C most young people learn to listen well and about the prospect of mixing one's ideas with the ideas of others to get better ideas. They learn more about the thoughts and feelings of others in their group blurring the boundaries of difference between friendship groups. However, we refer the reader back to Chapter 3 and the account of Philbrick-Linzmeyer (2011) in the US and her travails with her students – dialogue is not a magic word that transforms interaction, more often it is hard won, as one or more participants makes the effort. Nor is it a permanent state, and one might expect that one slips in and out of the dialogic space as new personal impulses and external imperatives intervene and fracture the common ground.

To help them develop and understand their curiosity and attention, we encourage our students (trainee educational psychologists) to take a "helicopter view" of themselves listening to each other in discussion of a situation of mutual interest (Carroll & Holloway, 1998; Hermans, 2013). In groups of four or five they can also help each other learn about what happens in dialogic exchanges by forming a "reflecting team," ideally sitting on either side of the axis of a dialogue between two other students (Andersen, 1987; Cox, Bañez, Hawley, & Mostade, 2003). At thoughtful moments the reflecting team may suggest a pause in the dialogue in order to offer comment of what they think they see and hear within the dialogue of their partners so far. The peer commentary can thus not only provide other alternative interpretations of what those involved in the dialogue have been discussing but can also help to validate the curiosity and sensitivities implicit in the ongoing process. In these exercises there is an obvious spatial relationship between the participants, and this serves to reflect the psychological space within which professional dialogue occurs.

## Provisional summary and concluding thoughts

There are varying conceptualisations of dialogue in academic literature (Mifsud & Johnson, 2000; Renshaw, 2004) risking definitional confusion. There is no one dialogic theory but rather a range of uses of the term dialogic. Wegerif (2007), for instance, suggested four uses of the term dialogic:

- referring to dialogue as the activity of shared inquiry;
- the view that texts are not monologic but contain multiple, competing and cooperating voices;

- an epistemological paradigm that assumes meaning to be constructed between partners in a dialogue and not to reside in the utterance itself; and
- an ontological position that views the self as interdependent and defined through relationship with others.

We subscribe to a view that dialogue may be understood as

> the communicative exchange of embedded agents standing their own ground while being open to the other's standpoint, conceptualizing meaning that emerges in discourse situated between persons while engaging a common text in their communicative event… A dialogic ethic begins with the presupposition that we enter into an ongoing human conversation that is never concluded.
>
> (Arnett, Arneson, & Bell, 2006, p. 79)

Going further, we would rather suggest that in the interests of achieving an outcome that is better for both, or at least no worse for any (perhaps evoking the principle of "equal consideration of interests" due to Peter Singer (1993) that we mentioned in Chapter 2), we may enter into what Gergen (and we) call *transformative* dialogue. As (Gergen, 2009, p. 193) put it:

> By this I mean forms of dialogue that attempt to cross the boundaries of meaning, that locate fissures in the taken-for-granted realities… that enable participants to generate a new and more promising domain of shared meaning… Softening the boundaries of meaning *[de-emphasising the importance of content or specific positions]* give ways to the development of new realities, rationalities, values, and practices.

We see this as a relationship in which the participants have respect for each other and are jointly seeking to research alternative possibilities, alternative solutions to a puzzle (or puzzles). Dialogue provides a process in which we can help each other restructure educational activities. It is a process of exploratory dialogue, not a process of dialectic argumentation. It is possible to consider exploratory dialogue as a form of *participatory research* (Aldridge, 2015; Barrow, 2010; Van der Riet, 2008).

The potential transformative power of participatory research is, as Van der Riet (2008, p. 551) has written,

> …based on three core principles. First, the participants are actively involved… second, there is co-ownership of the research process and outcome; last, any investigation of a phenomenon builds on what people know, accessing their local knowledge.

Thus, in professional dialogue that embodies the spirit of participatory research and is thus mutually respectful and jointly "owned" by the participants, there is not only an engagement and motivation to gain new understanding of an external issue (such as how to support a particular child; or to better understand dialogue as a humanising process) but also an implicit process of developing understanding of each other's position and intentions *via* the sense making and creating of interthinking by interdependent minds. This, for us, requires both trust, curiosity and a commitment to continual exploration, research, and preservation of safe spaces for thinking and acting. An explicit consciousness of the terrain in which one works is needed, knowing where there are alternative priorities, agendas, funding, or policies which open up spaces for working differently either internally or in multi-professional contexts. Policy landscapes are rarely homogeneous and there are niches or spaces for more dialogic approaches. This may require a certain political astuteness, not least in knowing what "rules" might apply in the space and how to relate the outcomes from the dialogic space with what might be termed "normal." Finally, such spaces cannot be opened and closed with flick of a switch, there are entry conditions resting on developing of relational aspects underpinned by a respect for and trust in the "other," indeed many "others." Such relationships are easily frayed by the misuse and abuse of power.

However, notwithstanding what we have said in this chapter we cannot tell (let alone dictate) how you, reader and your colleagues, may make use of these concepts and suggestions for practice. We can only hope that the outcome is democratic and leads to further exploration of alternative positions for education and educators.

# 6 Consultation and intervention for and with others

## Introduction

With a view to support the use of dialogue and consultation in educational settings and professional relationships, in this chapter we set out what we see as some of the important components of dialogic consultation and how the professional relationships we have may be used to help discuss and resolve work-related concerns. While we won't entirely avoid relevant psychological, philosophical, and educational ideas, we will provide some practical suggestions about how consultation as a form of educational intervention may be ethically warranted and instantiated. Ultimately, we hope that discussion and implementation of consultation may be of help to schools and school staff and, in doing so, support professional learning for individuals and organisations. We suggest that consultation can help orientate educational activity *toward* long-term learning and the development of inclusive practices, and *away from* precipitate solutions and social exclusion. We suggest consultation can provide the opportunity for expansive and transformative learning in a psychologically "safe" space (as discussed in the previous chapter) in which it is possible to envisage and examine alternative possibilities (for empirical warrants for this see, example Minkle, Bashir, & Sutulov, 2008; Gibbs et al., 2016).

Before discussing aspects of communication and the ethical considerations that are fundamental to psychological consultation, to help orientate readers we first provide a brief overview of some models of professional consultation in education. Since for us consultation provides a forum for learning, we then provide a brief discussion of what might be understood by "learning" and the spaces in which this may occur. One of our major motivations in writing this book has been to offer support to those whose practice in education may be compromised by external factors that derogate "good education." (We fear that may be all of us.) We hope, therefore, that in reading this chapter readers may come to conceptualise, reflect on, and revise frameworks for consultation that are ethically helpful to educational professionals (including teachers and psychologists) engaging in problem solving and professional learning.

DOI: 10.4324/9780429343766-7

## Models of professional consultation in education

For us consultation is dependent on the quality of professional relationships, the mutual respect and trust of all involved, as well as the willingness to enter dialogic discussion with others (see Chapter 5). In offering the following for consideration, once again we do not seek to be prescriptive but simply want to suggest what may need to be considered and discussed in order to provide a service that can be *"the difference that makes a difference"* (Bateson, 1979). These characteristics and an agreed understanding of the purpose of consultation provide the psychologically and philosophically warranted basis for processes in which teachers and/or parents can safeguard the time and space in which to talk openly about what concerns them – or what can be celebrated; that they can feel able to tell the story about why they are concerned and how they have got to the point of wanting to – and being able to – talk with another person. It is not always easy to acknowledge or admit to having a problem; people often don't feel naturally comfortable admitting they have not been as successful as they might have hoped. For parents to admit that they are struggling in one of life's major tasks (being a "good enough" parent) is a brave thing to do. For a teacher, whose livelihood and professional identity is tied up in being the person who can teach and will be judged by others for her effectiveness in the classroom, being seen to be successful is often the *sine qua non* of her professional life. (And (fear of) being judged for not being successful can be crippling.) So, it is quite possible that these factors and more will be part of the story to be told. Part of the role of a consultant, then, is to support and enable the story-teller (teacher, parent, young person) to relate and better understand her story. As Jerome Bruner (1987, p. 709) recognised:

> Any story one may tell about anything is better understood by considering other possible ways in which it can be said.

We suggest that enabling storytelling (finding ways of telling the story) is a key feature of consultation, coaching, and learning, and a means of providing ways to explore what may be possible; what we can do in the situation we are in, as well as developing our dynamic and multi-faceted identities as human beings.

Consultation is a process of exploring what could be different, providing the "tools" that enable someone to reflect, gain confidence and feel able to try different ways of being and doing (for elaboration of this notion, see Edwards, 2011; Engeström, 2007a). It is not an interrogation of one person by another (<u>not</u> "why did you do *that*?") that can easily erode the confidence of a parent or teacher. Being able and willing to explore what might be different entails both curiosity and, as far as possible, at least initially, a lack of attachment to any particular position. Curiosity (seeking to understand) and a determination to support the development of "collective attention" (Shteynberg, Hirsh, Bentley, & Garthoff, 2020) on problems (and their solution) are, undoubtedly, critical to successful consultation. As Cecchin (1987, p. 405) noted:

Curiosity leads to exploration and invention of alternative views and moves, and different moves and views breed curiosity. In this recursive fashion, neutrality and curiosity contextualise one another in a commitment to evolving differences, with a concomitant nonattachment to any particular position.

In the UK many educational psychologists and some psychological services have, for some time, been using consultation as the starting point for their involvement in schools. In many cases this has provided the psychologist with an opportunity to show genuine care and concern about why psychological services are being sought. Practically "consultation" has also been used as a means of managing referrals or formal requests for a psychologist's assessment of a young person. An early example of such a "consultation service" was developed in the NE of England by Joan Figg and Robin Stoker in the 1980s. Their initiative was a key part of a strategy to prevent being overwhelmed by referrals at a time when they did not have sufficient staff to respond to all more traditional formal requests for the involvement of an educational psychologist that were often, Figg and Stoker speculated, possibly a ploy by a school in difficult circumstances. Their model was based in the work of Gerard Caplan (1970) and they defined consultation as *"the interaction between the consultant and the consultee."* Critical to their model was as Figg and Stoker (1989, p. 35) proposed the idea that *"Central to the nature of the work undertaken is the practice of the consultee retaining full responsibility for any action that needs to be taken after the consultation"*; in other words for the consultant to avoid doing or saying anything that could disempower or de-skill the consultee. In structuring their model Figg and Stoker identified the psychologist as the consultant, the teacher as the consultee and the client a specific child or group of children. Following from the underlying psychological approach of Caplan's work, the focus of the interactions between the consultant and consultee was on the psychodynamic processes that exist between the consultee and members of the client group. Thus, considerable attention during the consultation was paid to the feelings that were generated (or recalled) by teachers when talking about the presenting "problem." Figg and Stoker described how they were simultaneously seeking to establish a community-based form of preventative work and, therein, *"to facilitate consultees in the more effective management of their work problems"* (p. 37). (See also Figg and Gibbs (1990) for an elaboration of the project and how the psychological service developed a form of peer supervision to support and develop the consultation service within their community.) Around the same time as Figg and Stoker were developing and promoting their model, a framework for the use of group consultation in schools similarly based in psychodynamic theories was being developed by Phil Stringer and colleagues (also coincidentally in NE England). In their model, in addition to the attention paid to interpersonal psycho-dynamic processes, Stringer and colleagues drew specifically on ideas from family therapy, arguing that there is (or at least might be) a close analogy between the way families as systems function and the systems that locate teachers amidst their colleagues and respective roles (Stringer, Stow, Hibbert, Powell, & Louw, 1992).

By way of introduction to her model of consultation (introduced as a means of regulating referrals, but also based in psycho–dynamic theories of human interaction), Patsy Wagner posed the salient question "*What is the problem to which consultation is a solution?*" Our own perception of the current situation, more than two decades since Wagner offered her answer, is that although the underlying causal mechanisms may have changed, for very many educational psychologists working in or with schools there is still very often:

> A strong *[demand for]* individual assessment and report writing *[that]* leads to progressively more children having "special educational needs"; the cost of providing for these children has spiralled; the positive or significant outcomes for the children concerned are few relative to the time, effort, and cost of the process. Broadly put, more "statementing" *[now provision of Education and Health Care Plans, (a change of label but no fundamental change in effect)]* has led to less problem-solving.
>
> (Wagner, 2000, p. 10)

As we have already suggested elsewhere in this book, it seems to us that the current environment for education creates the difficulties that many schools and school staff in the UK now experience, and the persistent and seemingly inexorable mechanisms that lead to the exclusion of children from the mainstream of education. It is, therefore, our view that there is now, more than ever, a need for processes in which applied *educational* psychologists (psychologists who practise in ways that are, in themselves, educational) can engage with other educationalists, teachers, and parents to explore what the effects of the prevailing educational environment and procedures are for children, young people, and teachers – and what alternatives are possible. We suggest that the opportunities for structured, sensitive professional dialogue embedded in a process of consultation provide the means of conducting such an examination at an important moment: the point at which meaningful education is, for some teachers and young people, breaking down.

In order to develop readers' understanding of what is entailed in proposing and instantiating professional consultation we will now turn to consideration of more of the necessary and important components of consultation, namely communication, ethics, intervention, and learning.

## Communication

In order to engage in "consultation" we need to be able to communicate. The languages of communication can include non-verbal as well as oral signals. We pay attention here to the complexity and nuancing of our oral language because it is fundamental to the process of consultation and, as Jerome Bruner said, "*language constructs what it narrates, not only semantically but also pragmatically and stylistically*" (Bruner, 1987, p. 696). Because human relationships depend, as they do, on our ability to understand each other, we rely, at least partially, on our use of language, how we say things, our intentions and how they are understood. Some of these requirements are embedded in the context of interactions (whether, for example, we are talking with a colleague at work or with a partner at home.) Here we are thinking mostly about the use of language in professional settings, settings where there may well be conventional "shorthands" that can sometimes leave unspoken the details that for those unfamiliar with the conventions can anchor meaning. We are mindful of what Charles Dickens said in David Copperfield that "*[C]onventional phrases are a sort of fireworks, easily let off, and liable to take a great variety of shapes and colours not all suggested by their original form.*" Professional conversations too can spark off and illuminate unexpected ideas.

Amongst the elements of both oral, written, and signed language, the vehicles that carry the message are the words and phrases we use – as well as the melodies that infuse them. (A useful guide to this aspect of communication is provided by Schuller et al. (2013).) While we recognise the importance of non-verbal communication (and especially signed communication), here we will attend exclusively, but briefly, to aspects of oral language to illustrate the need for attention to all aspects of communication within consultation. We don't want to labour the point but before discussing professional consultation in more detail we think it important to ensure readers have some sensitivity to the nuances of interpersonal oral communication. It is, we think, therefore helpful to be sensitive to what may be unspoken in the words that are spoken: the feelings, intentions, and motivations that can be implicated in professional concerns. As Erving Goffman wrote:

> [T]he individual must phrase his own concerns and feelings and interests in such a way as to make these maximally usable by the others as a source of appropriate involvement; and this major obligation of the individual *qua interactant* is balanced by his right to expect that others present will make some effort to stir up their sympathies and place them at his command. These two tendencies, that of the speaker to scale down his expressions and that of the listeners to scale up their interests, each in the light of the other's capacities and demands, form the bridge that people build to one another, allowing them to meet for a moment of talk in a communion of reciprocally sustained involvement. It is this spark, not the more obvious kinds of love, that lights up the world.
>
> (Goffman, 1967/2005, pp. 116–17)

As simple artefacts, words (as tokens of meaning) can seem to be as unchangeable as material facts or physical objects. After all they help ground our sense of reality, don't they? But words do not have a fixed meaning; they are as open to interpretation and change as fashions are. In childhood as we develop our skills of communication, we come to recognise that words are malleable and should not always be treated "literally"; we learn that words are not always reliably objective. It is, for instance, evident that over time there have been significant changes in both the meaning and appearance of words. Words, languages, are continuously evolving. We can see this, for example, in the way words and/or symbols are now used in text messages. (One of us was recently lectured by an enthusiastic niece about our "misunderstanding" of what certain emojis might say!) Their appearance in written form can change (*doubt* was once *dout; shew* became *show; connexion* is now *connection*). That the conventional meanings of words have shifted over time can be seen in that at one time *nice* meant "*simple*"; something that was *awful* was "*worthy of awe*"). But words can also have more than one meaning – leaving, for instance, scope for ambiguity in oral communication (*been* vs *bean; address; plane* vs *plain*). The origin of "*patient*" is in one who suffers – is that what we mean when we say "please be *patient*"? (See also Fredriksson & Eriksson, 2003). We have also become adept in the use of metaphor and simile. We see golden fields of wheat and, of course, every cloud has a silver lining. (Though not all metaphors connote such wealth). Thus, in our face-to-face conversations the subtle meanings of what we want to communicate – and what we understand in what others are saying – are created, clarified, modified, and illustrated. What we mean to say, what we are trying to say, may not be what others understand us to say or mean. Words alone do not necessarily always convey what we are trying to say. So, for instance, if we talk about a "book" others may know more or less what we mean (but be careful if you say "you've been booked"); but if someone talks about a "young person's behaviour and how he doesn't respect books," for example, we might want to seek some clarification about what this young person (how old is he?) might be doing with (or to?) books (what sort of books; books about fishing or mathematics?) In professional dialogue, as in life (when we are paying attention), we come to realise that we may have to work carefully, thoughtfully, and sensitively to better understand what someone is wanting to say, to commune-icate.

"*When communication occurs*" John Dewey wrote,

> all natural events are subject to reconsideration and revision; they are re-adapted to meet the requirements of conversation, whether it be public discourse or that preliminary discourse termed thinking. Events turn into objects, things with a meaning. They may be referred to when they do not exist, and thus be operative among things distant in space and time, through vicarious presence in a new medium.
>
> (Dewey, 1958 [1929], p. 166)

In what follows we will dwell on the idea that engaging in professional dialogue (for us the fundamental operational principle of consultation), exemplifies how, as Dewey suggested, we may be able to deal with matters that are of great immediate importance but may also be distant in time, place, or degree of abstraction. Consultation, therefore, can involve the discussion of the possible meaning or impact of events, but also of different perspectives and alternative possibilities. But just as we have been discussing the meaning of words in the abstract, we might also pay heed and be wary of what we could mean by "consultation." Thus, *Consulting* with a *consultant*, to have a *consultation,* may itself mean different things in different circumstances.

A recent search of academic literature, for example, revealed some of the potential variety in the use (conceptualisation?) of the term "consultation" that might be relevant here. For example, while *Consultation* appeared in the title of more than 23,000 journal articles, of these only 339 were also associated with *Education*; and of those only four were also associated with *Psychology*. Some of the 23,000 articles reported studies of governmental consultations on topics, setting out a government's view of what might be possible or preferred changes and asking the public for their views on the matter. Other papers provided insights into the process of psychological consultations, which typically start with no initial, preferred solution, but remain open to the exchange and development of new ideas. It is clear that there is, therefore, a range of possible meanings and functions of the term "consultation." Here we will restrict ourselves to considerations of professional consultations in which no participant is posited as dominant nor as "therapist" (Arnett & Arneson, 1999, 2014; Arnett, Arneson, & Bell, 2006).

Considering the nature and potential benefits of dialogues that constitute interpersonal, professional "consultations" we will suggest what might need to be in place in order to ensure that the "psychological environment" for professional dialogue is one in which the participants (e.g. a teacher, the parents of a child and an educational psychologist) can all feel "safe" and engaged in mutually respectful discussion. Importantly, we hope it will also be clear that we hold no brief for a hierarchy of expertise. All those involved in consultations as we see and practise them have differing areas of expertise. There may be overlap where the inter-professional "*boundaries of practice intersect*" (Edwards, 2011), but in the complementary space in between us there are also opportunities to examine ideas and to begin to see things differently and, as we will discuss later in this chapter, how we may learn from and about each other's professional expertise (Daniels et al., 2007; Leadbetter et al., 2007). To quote Julia Wood's introduction to the work of Arnett and Arneson, we seek to promote "*thoughtful dialogue*" (Arnett & Arneson, 1999, p. xi), in the service of interpersonal professional communication that is ethical and committed to mutual respect for persons in their time and place, civility, and the possibility of multiple perspectives on the topic under discussion. We understand that at times people's anxiety to make a difference, to be seen to be "effective," can lead to impatience and an urgency to find *the* solution. For us that risks closing down the space needed in which to understand and accept the emotions that may underline frustrations and uncertainty but can also hinder the development of "caring conversations" (Fredriksson & Eriksson, 2003). Since the discussions we envisage here are care-full and intended to help but are not intended to be prescriptive or directive, we need to ensure we are ethical in the use of – and intentions for – consultation.

## The ethics of consultation

In any meeting of professionals, perhaps especially those involving professionals who represent different agencies, questions can arise about respective responsibilities and the boundaries that define the role of each participant, what they "ought" to do in the meeting. (The ethics of "ought" are discussed by Arnett et al. (2006) and Fredriksson and Eriksson (2003).) But, for example, the respective responsibilities in a discussion may seem predetermined. For instance, in the UK both teacher and psychologist have prescribed roles with respect to "safeguarding" children. So, if grounds for concern about the physical or psychological safety of the child arise there are clearly delineated legal (moral) duties for the psychologist and teacher respectively. In other situations, however, for example in a discussion about how the teacher might support a child's progress in an aspect of the curriculum, the inter-relationship of freedom and responsibility is less clear-cut, more open to negotiation. The teacher, the professional raising the concern, might believe she has a responsibility to herself to explore possible ways forward with the child. But the teacher might also, very possibly, believe she has responsibility to the child as well as to her colleagues in the school and the child's parents. It might also be suggested that the teacher, having raised the concern has a responsibility to herself and the psychologist to engage fully in the exploration of what is possible, seeing the meeting as an opportunity for learning. The psychologist, in turn, may believe she has responsibility to attend first and foremost to the needs of the person seeking the consultation.

For a psychologist who has engaged to work with colleagues in a school there is likely to be a sense of professional responsibility not only to the teacher (and her colleagues in that school) and but also to ensure that they recognise that they have been supported and helped. There are different ways of doing this. As John Shotter (anticipating the work of Shteynberg et al. (2020) who discussed the importance of establishing conjoint attention and the development of "common knowledge" for learning *with* others) noted in stressing the importance of dialogue:

> As soon as I begin an interchange of looks with another person, and I sense them as looking toward me in a certain way (as they see me looking toward them in the same way too), a little ethical and political world is created between us. We each look toward each other expectantly, with anticipations, some shared some not, arising from what we have already lived in our lives so far. Indeed, to put the point more generally, in any living contact between any two or more human beings, in the meetings between us, at least two things of importance occur: (1) yet another form of life emerges between us, a collective or shared form of life with its own unique character and its own unique world, in whose terms, for the duration of our meeting, we can mean things to each other; (2) but also, within this world, we are present to each other…*[and, citing Bakhtin, emphasised*

*how distinctive this is compared to a monologic approach]* "With a monologic approach another person remains wholly and merely an <u>object</u> of consciousness, and not another consciousness."

(Shotter, 2005, pp. 104–6)

One way of appearing to support teachers and parents is to appear to be the expert who is able and willing to give prescriptive advice along the lines of "what I think you should do is..." In our view such a monologic stance not only disrespects others as having no voice or opinion, it can also disengage or disable participants from addressing their underlying anxiety and curiosity. By absolving others of their autonomy, by minimising the risks inherent in becoming a learner, this stance stifles the potential for development of a sense of "agency" and of ownership of change. It also disavows holding a safe space for experiential learning and helping others to learn and can, therefore, be considered unethical by imposing a prescription that "*omits the reality of differing standpoints*" (Arnett et al., 2006, p. 63). However, as part of genuine dialogue, it may seem quite appropriate and natural to offer an idea about something to try – not as the solution to the supposed problem – but as a form of "experimental" tool within the spirit of genuine inquiry, with a follow up question about "how did that feel" or "what happened when you tried that?" This can help support reflection as a process in which it becomes possible to distinguish and clarify the relationship between one's own attitude or disposition and the environmental factors that sustain or challenge the attitude or disposition (Dewey, 1916/2011).

Ethical issues also arise for psychologists in relation to how their application of psychology positions them and those with whom they work. These issues arise in considering possible answers to the question "Who is deemed to be the 'client'?" and "How should I (the psychologist) work with this client, if at all?" Such questions were probably not often asked explicitly in the early days of educational psychology practice in the UK, since the primary function of psychologists at that time was to determine, by means of psychological tests, what sort of education should be provided for children. In accepting such a role, the implicit primary client of psychologists was the state. The psychologists' task was to administer tests so the state could allocate children to "appropriate" forms of education. This, in due course, ensured that the state secured a stratified workforce with knowledge and skills appropriate for their future status in society. (Accounts of the history of the role and deployment of educational psychologists are provided by Arnold and Hardy (2017) and Wagner (2000)).

Since the 1980s, however, local government has had the legal responsibility to ensure that children's "special educational needs" are identified and met. Educational psychologists were then employed as agents of the local government authority with a rather different remit. Psychologists' ethical professional responsibility was, accordingly, often thought to be to the local authority and involved helping to "safeguard" the authority's scarce additional and more specialised resources. (Such additional resources (such as placement in a specialist school) as might be required if it proved impossible to support a mainstream school in working to enable a child to continue her or his progress in that local mainstream setting.) However, many psychologists also saw themselves as independent advocates for the child and, when asked, would state unequivocally what form of education, what degree of additional help might be necessary to secure a better future for the child. Psychologists were, therefore, often seemingly caught with a moral dilemma. Who best to serve? Who was their client, their employer, or the child?

In the present era of neoliberalism in which many psychological services are "traded" (see, for instance Gibbs & Papps, 2017), schools have often become viewed as psychologists' main, proximal, clients. In common with other traders in a "marketplace" in which competitors abound, psychologists, too, often feel required to have entrepreneurial and commercial skills and responsibility to ensure that schools continue to purchase their services (and the services of their employer, the Educational Psychology Service). A need to be politically alert and to interrogate the influence and reach of neoliberal governance has been suggested (Sugarman, 2015; Sugarman & Thrift, 2017; Szulevicz, 2018). Thus, for instance, in order to secure the continuity of their relationship with schools a psychologist might be faced with a dilemma about whether to decide that the safest, commercially sound, entrepreneurial "moral" option is to do more of what a school requests (such as expedite transfer of a child to another type of school) or to do the ethically "right thing" for a child – such as supporting the individual child whose best interests and the interests of the child's peers might be served by remaining with her peer group in that school.

In sum, "in whose interests are we working?" or "what interests are we protecting and/or promoting?" are amongst the ethical and moral questions to be considered in professional work. How to resolve that question is necessarily by no means easy. We think resolution becomes impossible without dialogue with "clients," whoever or however many there may be. In such discussion it will then be important to give due consideration to the interests of all who may be affected by the issues at stake. Singer (1993, p. 21) suggested that "*equal consideration of interests*" may then lead to a decision about how best to act – including the possibility that if the outcome for one party is worse than the gain for another, it might well be more ethical *not* to act.

Thus, in both the interpersonal dialogue of consultation, as well as the internal dialogue that each participant will have with themselves, there are ethical and moral issues. However, the fundamental issues reside in communication between people. As has been said of the ethics of communication:

> A dialogic communication ethic is responsive to a relational space that invites content and insight to emerge between persons. Dialogic ethic lives in creative possibilities invited between communicative partners that have neither prescriptive ambitions nor descriptive roots. A dialogic ethic both invites and prescribes – prescribing an alternative to individualism that precludes attentiveness to the other... Dialogue ethics are, additionally,

prescriptive as one understands them as communication implementers of a narrative sense of the "good." Dialogic ethics is both perspective and transcendent in that new ideas emerge "between" persons of difference.

(Arnett et al., 2006, pp. 80–1)

Thus, communication between people that is ethical accepts that there are differences in the interests and motivations of the participants and demonstrates respect for these differences, eschewing as far as possible the imposition of individual opinions, prescriptions, or directions. It is in attending to and reflecting on what emerges in the differences, the psychological spaces between people, in the interaction of communicants, that learning occurs, because "learning" is voluntary and simply the only item on the agenda, not because one is a "teacher" or an "expert." Having respect for each other in working together as professionals with different orientations is of fundamental importance. Mutual respect and due acknowledgement of this in the process of consultation is the central ethical demand. Thus:

> If we and our interlocutors are to communicate readily and easily, we rely on those with whom we are involved to sustain the sense of a collective-we between us, a shared reality that is our reality. And it is only in relation to such a shared reality that we can express to each other who we are, express the nature of our unique inner lives to each other. To an extent, we owe our very being, our identity, to it. If it collapses, then it is quite easy for us to feel unheard, or unable to express ourselves… only if you respond to me in a way sensitive to the relations between your actions and mine can we act together as a collective-we; and if I sense you as not being sensitive in that way, that is, as not being responsive to me, but as pursuing an agenda of your own, then I will feel immediately offended in an ethical way. I will feel that you lack respect not only for our affairs, but for me too.
>
> (Shotter, 2005, p. 103)

In our view what is central to ethical consultation includes matters that we have already discussed in previous chapters but bear repetition here: mutual respect (not pretending /professing to be experts who know what others should necessarily do – or not do), use of dialogue, creating and sustaining spaces in which exploration and learning can occur. To these we would also now add understanding of the limitations of language, the patience to be curious, and a moral determination to support learning. To paraphrase Paul Ricoeur (1992), we ask: what is it to do "good" for those involved in consultation in schools? We must ask this since to engage in consultation is to do something different, to interrupt, intervene, or even, perhaps necessarily, disrupt the status quo (see also Biesta, 2013).

Before saying more about consultation as a form of "intervention" (temporarily only using that term in the sense of doing something different) that will enable learning, we will attempt a dissection of "intervention" to anticipate some potential misunderstandings or unreliable expectations that could jeopardise the continuing search for the ethical "*difference that makes a difference*" (Bateson, 1979). Following this digression, we will present some ideas about what might be meant by "learning" and how that may be enabled.

## What do we mean and understand when we talk about intervening?

As we've indicated above, some models of "consultation" are problematic in that these implicate the disruptive presence of an outsider who may be seen as either an expert or as an interloper. As many teachers have said of school inspectors "*They really don't understand what it's like for us in this school.*" (For more on that issue see Ball, 2003; Courtney, 2016; Gibbs, 2018b; Perryman, 2006). Some experts being external to the school who intervene without validating or attempting to understand others' situations and feelings may tell you what you *should* do, by giving advice. That sort of model – of a prescribed intervention – is also likely to be time limited; a set of activities designed with a specific outcome in mind and for a limited duration. Thus, "intervention" might be synonymous with external "influence" (Rosenau, 1968, 1969), though for others it could be an "innovation" created by another (Cianciolo & Regehr, 2019; Davis, 2008). Such models as these can, we suggest, prevent those who are the advised – made the passive recipients of advice – gaining the skills and beliefs that come with first-hand experience and heuristic learning. Worse, sometimes being told what "you should do" can increase a sense of incompetence ("*why didn't I know that when it now seems so obvious?*"). Having someone else do it for you can also be deskilling (Eddleston & Atkinson, 2018; Wagner, 2000). Ways of working like that raise ethical questions about the right of an other, an outsider, to suggest or impose a solution on a client. Such practices call into question the extent and nature of curiosity or any attempt to gain understanding of the client's situation, the history of the case and what may have already been tried; but it also calls into question the right of an outsider to take control. Taking things further, we also suggest that a general unethical presumption of prerogative power to "intervene," to impose change, could provoke a state of "exceptionality" which, far from being a temporary and finite phenomena (Rosenau, 1968) would seem like the fiat of a dictator (Agamben, 2005). However, as we have already acknowledged in this chapter, there may be times when, for instance a child's safety is clearly at risk or if an opportunity for learning is being missed, there may be a moral responsibility to offer guidance – or to act.

We also suggest that the notion of an externally devised intervention that includes a measurable outcome of impact may be more closely associated with a positivist view of science which for us does not sit easily with the complexity and uncertainties of education as a *social* science, a science of the artificial (Simon, 1996). In evidence-based medical practice understandably we hope we can be confident that the pill we take will do what it says on the packet and make us better – and as soon as possible. However, the science of education is still at an early stage of development and not a "natural" science obeying the laws of nature. The world of education and educational processes (and the infinite variations of human behaviour that follow) are more complex and uncertain than the certainties of the biological functions of humankind. We clearly don't (yet?) have the tools or methods in social sciences to encompass the complexity, varieties, and vagaries of human behaviour reliably or with the certainties that some medical interventions appear to provide. As we have already noted, bearing in mind Herb Simon's paradigm of science of the artificial (what happens at the interface systems), the best we may hope to do is to observe carefully and thoughtfully what happens in education and conjecture what might affect the observed phenomena.

Of course, as Davis and Sumara (2010) noted, there is nothing new in the claim that education is a complex process. Ongoing work in the field of "implementation science" (see, for instance, Bauer, Damschroder, Hagedorn, Smith, & Kilbourne, 2015; Davis, 2008; Forman et al., 2013) attempts to refine methods that "improve the quality and effectiveness of services" through the systematic application of research findings in routine professional practice. For us this signals a dialectic of paradigms with an uncertain outcome. Although, for example, it has been possible to develop interventions that have been shown to help some children gain skills in reading (see, for instance, Hatcher et al., 2006), we still can't with sufficient certainty be sure that these will make a difference for *all* children (in fact we are fairly certain that with regard to reading, for example, none do work for all children – such are the complexities of reading and reading difficulties), even if we thought that such prescriptive validity and reliability were desirable. (Clearly what we are saying here presupposes a view of education that is inclusive and, therefore, idealised, indeterminate, and simultaneously deeply critical of a curriculum and pedagogy that has as sole focus on prescribed outcomes (Biesta, 2013, 2015b, 2015c)).

Alternatively, and for us preferably, a social and collaborative view of intervention is available. In this formulation attention is focussed more on changing the relationships between participants – but not necessarily excluding the additional involvement of someone external to the organisation – and together engaging in collective activity. In this way, by enabling relationships and perceptions to change, new (second order) ideas that, in turn, stimulate further thought, emerge in consciousness of practices that are then iteratively revealed and developed (see, for instance Virkkunen & Schaupp, 2011). In this mode intervention can be seen as a cooperative self-sustaining activity (that emerges in and is sustained by the social discourses, in, for example, school staff rooms) that, by virtue of being brought into critical consciousness, become self-regenerating. While this may be problematic (Miller (1996), for instance, talked about how the culture and discourse of a staff room can sustain a dominant narrative and disable change), others (Powell & Gibbs, 2018; Strahan, Gibbs, & Reid, 2019, for example) have provided evidence of how demonstrations of mutual respect and support within a school can enable organisational growth. As Yrjö Engeström has also shown (Engeström, 1987, 2007a), it is possible to see how "new" understandings emerge, not from studying and reifying the old patterns of behaviour, but as a result of gaining psychological insights and social movements that lead away from the old by learning about – and experiencing – other possibilities . Crucially, such social activity and psychological reorientations depend on revitalising professional relationships, knowledge, and skills that both explore and establish new interconnections that, in turn, help transform activity, learning, and pragmatic understandings within the organisation (see also Lofthouse & Leat, 2013; Szulevicz & Tanggaard, 2017).

In relation to the organisation of education and the work of teachers specifically, it has, therefore, been argued that there is a need to give greater attention to reconstructing teachers as professionals who are able to be – and are held to be – creative and autonomous agents of change (as has been variously emphasised by Biesta, Priestley, & Robinson, 2015; Edwards, 2015; Pietarinen, Pyhältö, & Soini, 2016; Priestley, Biesta, & Robinson, 2015; Vähäsantanen, 2015). Further, this perspective is more likely to ensure (and depend upon) *active* participation in processes of intervention that are collective and democratic, that are

> open and attentive to one another... *[so that]* people often gain new information, learn different experiences of their collective problems, or find that their initial opinions are founded on prejudice and ignorance, or that they have misunderstood the relation of their own interests to others.
>
> (Young, 2002, p. 26)

In other words, we hope that what happens in schools is grounded in and by experiences that are created and reviewed in dialogue amongst communities, staff, between staff and students and, in due course, amongst students. Everything that happens as a result may be seen as a form of intervention if it promotes learning. This raises the next question.

## What is "learning" and how might we understand it in the context of consultation?

As human beings we discover and learn *how* to walk, talk, and count. We may need to be helped to acquire some of these and other skills (such as reading, writing, swimming) that are not necessarily instinctual but are part of what makes us active social beings. We also learn *about* things, what they are called and what their properties are. Knud Illeris (2007, p. 3) offered a general definition of "learning" as "*any process that in living organisms leads to permanent capacity change and which is not solely due to biological maturation or ageing.*" This, we think, subsumes all the complexities of human learning that *may* be possible but are not always easily achieved (or, sadly, not achieved at all by some) as well as implying the development of the capacity to function appropriately across the range of situations in which we may find ourselves. As a species we have discovered (learned) *how* to make fire, how to forge metal, how to make tools, and *what* we can do consequentially. (And, of course, this leads the problem of differential power: who has the tools (including those that are either material or communicative) that others can't access or use.)

Being able to describe and label things as we see them provides a communicative shorthand but also involves others in a complementary process of seeking and confirming our intended meanings. (Here, as always, we need to be aware of the ethics of our behaviour. The codes of language may also be mis-used – as all tools may – to obfuscate, exclude or otherwise disempower.) Learning is a process that continues hand-in-hand with developing consciousness and problem solving. In that sense, therefore, of course there are many facets to learning and how we may help each other learn. Some of these facets have been formalised in systems of education; some remain informal, socially constructed processes that occur incidentally in social settings. As social beings we (need to and, mostly, do) learn how to behave with others, how to help each other (Levine et al., 2005; Tajfel, 2010).

While we don't wish to underestimate the importance of "organisational learning," "learning organisations," and the organisational context for learning (Engeström, 2007b; Örtenblad, 2001; Wang & Ahmed, 2003), our focus here is on how individuals (but none-the-less social beings and contributing members of organisations) can learn in and from psychological interactions, intervening with each other. We are not here concerned with biological or neurological models of what happens inside our heads when we are learning (for discussion of some of these issues, see Dehaene, 2019). Here we will restrict ourselves to thinking about how we can learn ethically, in dialogic interactions, consultations, with others.

In sum, learning enables and transforms us – often, in our experience and hopes, in unplanned and surprising ways. Our hope is that consultation in educational settings should be seen as an important means of active professional learning that is transformative; but we cannot necessarily predict what the outcome will be other than that participants should recognise that learning is taking place. We agree with others such as Mezirow (1997), Lave and Wenger (1991), Korthagen (2010) that learning is and has to be socially situated. Learning is, for us (as this book attempts to show), a social, dialogic, and community process. The activities of learners in "communities of practice" (that are nothing without communication) lead to changes in knowledge and action that are not primarily related to biology or ageing but are directly linked to their interaction with other people or objects (see Bruner, 2009; Engeström, 2007a; Illeris, 2009; Korthagen, 2010; Lave, 2009; Leat et al., 2006). We also suggest that learning, recognising changes in knowledge, understanding and skill, can arise because the perception of something has changed or (and this is not a mutually exclusive "or") the circumstances in which something is perceived as having potential have themselves changed. (So, for example, in the context of another species, as has been seen in the behaviour of certain birds, a twig is no longer just a twig but becomes a tool that can be used to probe for food.) Learning takes place in a context, but it does not (cannot; should not) always take place for a pre-ordained purpose other than to understand what it takes to become a human being (Biesta, 2013; Macmurray, 1958/2012).

Here again we are trying to be careful with the language that we use. Some researchers and theorists have expressed concern about some concepts of "learning" and how these fit within "education" as it may be perceived in the present political and economic climate. Since consultations in schools often seem to revolve around concerns about how children are or, possibly more frequently, are not thought to be learning (or, more generally, "behaving") as well as they might, it seems important to look at why and how some have problematised "education" and "learning" and the context for concern. Gert Biesta, for instance, has been critical of the way the "language of learning" has, in the narratives of educators, educationalists, and politicians, supplanted the problematisation and conceptualisation of "education" (Biesta, 2016). Biesta has seen such language as symptomatic of the commercialisation and individual-isation of learning, with learners becoming "consumers" of "learning oppor-tunities" provided by educational entrepreneurs. As may already be obvious, we share his concerns about the neoliberal marketisation of education and learning that turn education, schools, and students into commodities.

For Biesta, constructing learners as consumers presumes that they know what they need, what they might seek to purchase. Biesta has also suggested that this "misconstrual" of learners and educators fails to take account of "*the major reason for engaging in education* [which] *is precisely to find out what it is that one actually wants or needs*" (Biesta, 2016, p. 22). That rationale for education matches our own view of why people might wish to enter into consultation: "*to find out* (to discover) *what it is that one actually wants or needs.*" Elsewhere Biesta (2013) has indicated that the dialogic character of education should remain essential if education and learning are to survive as fundamental components of democratic societies. Again, we would agree and hope that consultation being dialogic should also be democratic, mutually respectful, educational but not prescriptive of any specific outcome. But, while it is clear that Biesta sought to confirm a distinct and important role for teachers and educators, as agents of change (a view we also endorse), it seems strange that he has been apparently dismissive of the function of "scaffolding" in the processes of learning (Biesta, 2016, p. 17).

The concept of "scaffolding" that was introduced by David Wood, Jerome Bruner, and Gail Ross followed from Vygotsky's proposition that children learn through their engagement *in dialogue* with a more knowledgeable other (Vygotsky, 1962). This notion describes the role of a more competent other in helping someone learn (make more progress in solving a problem) in their "zone of proximal development." In a professional consultation we suggest that it will be the consultant's initial competence as the "scaffolder" that may make it possible to see how, in the contingencies and open questions that contribute to the dialogue, each participant will subsequently use "conversational repair" strat-egies increasingly successfully to reciprocally "scaffold" their verbal exchanges and, thereby, help to sustain the development of mutual understanding and learning (Hayashi, Raymond, & Sidnell, 2013; Wood, Bruner, & Ross, 1976). We must, however, stress that in constructing the process of consultation in this way we do not want to suggest that the consultant is in any way more expert than the consultee other than perhaps having some greater experience of scaffolding and, as we suggested in the previous chapter creatively building the dialogic processes (for instance making sure all are comfortable, understand and agree with the process) – but not the substance, specific focus or outcome – of consultation. This collaborative approach was demonstrated in a study of the process of consultation by Nolan and Moreland (2014) in which the use of "we" language by psychologists overcame the potential problem of scaffolding conversations without dominating the process. The study showed, for instance, how psychologists might downgrade

> their expert status through the use of mitigating language such as "maybe we could think about ..." or "I don't know but I'm wondering if ..." The EPs used questioning throughout, and built upon the contributions of all the participants. They utilised warmth, genuineness and empathy ... to ensure consultees felt supported and comfortable to collaborate.
>
> (Nolan & Moreland, 2014, p. 68)

Constructing and attempting to understand learning in this way implicates models of thinking and, we suggest, the processes implicit in consultation. In the present context we want to promote learning for those involved in education and, most particularly, create opportunities for learning when teachers, other professionals and parents meet. We seek, as Anne Edwards put it, to consider how we might think about *"building common knowledge at the boundaries between professional practices"* (Edwards, 2011) (see also Daniels et al., 2007; Leadbetter et al., 2007). This, we think, links to the work of Akkerman and Bakker (2011, pp. 132–3) who suggested that:

> The challenge in education and work is to create possibilities for partici- pation and collaboration across a diversity of sites, both within and across institutions... A boundary can be seen as a socio-cultural difference leading to discontinuity in action or interaction.

and that crossing boundaries (and experiencing the associated socio-cultural differences) offers opportunities for learning, and to the work of Burt (1992, 2004, 2015) – that we discussed in Chapters 3 and 4 – who suggested that since

> Opinion and behavior are more homogeneous within than between groups, so people connected across groups are more familiar with alterna- tive ways of thinking and behaving. Brokerage across the structural holes between groups provides a vision of options otherwise unseen, which is the mechanism by which brokerage becomes social capital.
>
> (Burt, 2004, p. 349)

Thus, it seems clear, working dialogically, consultatively, as psychologists (and others) may, in the spaces (interfaces) within and across organisations can help to generate creative thinking.

But, taking another position, we also think we can benefit from a "meta" view about what it means to be a "thinker." Jerome Bruner wrote in considering how one might model "the mind" (note: not "the brain") and what is implicated in trying to make sense of text (or a conversation):

> In interpreting a text, the meaning of part depends on a hypothesis about the meanings of the whole, whose meaning in turn is based upon one's judgement of meanings of the parts that compose it.
>
> (Bruner, 2009, p. 163)

This, we suggest, may help to illustrate how for each participant in a conversation the different possible meanings of individual components (words, phrases, sentences) will, in turn, be conditional on the prevailing professional context, the culture, customs and conventions of the contrasting organisations and, more widely, of aspects of a society at large (Lave, 2019; Vygotsky, 1978). In thinking, therefore, we turn in on ourselves but simultaneously relate and aggregate our thoughts with reference to the broader contexts.

So, in thinking about, for example, the sense of "consultation" in the context of this book (about education) our points of reference are likely to be different from those that might apply in the context of a meeting with a medical professional, for instance. But, although the formal difference in the context of the settings for these "consultations" might superficially be ascribed to perceived status, or even power, in the face-to-face experience of exchanges learning can occur never-the-less. As Mikhail Bahktin said of verbal exchanges:

> The word in language is half someone else's. It becomes "one's own" only when the speaker [*and, by necessary implication, the listener or partner in the exchange*] populates it with his intention, with his own accent, when he appropriates the word, adapting it to his own semantic and expressive intention.
>
> (Bakhtin, 1986, pp. 293–4)

Thus, it is possible to see how meaning, understanding, and learning will arise in the exploratory and provisional nature of a professional dialogue. However, the underlying differences of position and prior expectation that we find in consultations in which the search for meaning and greater understanding of possibilities are mutual responsibilities, exemplify two basic processes necessary for learning identified by Bruner (2009). First there needs to be an external interaction of the learner with the socio-psychological environment; second, internal (intra-personal) reflection and elaboration is necessary. This second process calls into question both the motivation and openness of the learner as well as the content of what is sought in terms of knowledge, understanding and skills which, as Biesta has indicated, may not be known in advance.

These processes are also embedded in the nature of dialogue as described by Rupert Wegerif:

> For each participant in a dialogue *[as in a consultation]* the voice of the other is an outside perspective... The boundary between *[participants]* is not, therefore, a demarcation line, or as an external link between self and other, but an inclusive "space" of dialogue within which self and other mutually construct and reconstruct each other.
>
> (Wegerif, 2008, p. 353)

More recently Wegerif (2022, p. 170) has written about "dialogic open-mindedness":

> Openness to the other is not about agreeing with the other but is about listening to the other and being prepared to learn something from the encounter. This virtue... is not the same as the psychological category of <u>open-mindedness</u> because it is an embodied and dialogic openness, and not only cognitive openness.
>
> (Emphasis in the original)

In the detailed description of his understanding of human learning, Knud Illeris (2009) discussed the dimensions and types of learning as well as the potential barriers to learning that he observed. In his account it is in overcoming some of the barriers to learning that profound and extensive learning, "transformative learning" (Mezirow, 1997), may occur. Illeris described the conditions that might precipitate a transformation of perspective or practices when, for example work-related issues (that many teachers may recognise) become unendurable, such as

> ...the endless changes and reorganisations many people experience... or by the helplessness that can be felt when consequences of the decisions of those in power encroach on one's life situation and possibilities.
>
> (Illeris, 2009, p. 15)

In our experience teachers often seek to consult about a work-related situation when they are confronted with a classroom or other professional problem they have so far been unable to resolve. When the teacher's concerns are about a specific child, if as is often possible, parents can also be involved in the consultation this can provide for a more democratic forum for exploration though with care for the vulnerabilities of both. Given the opportunity of a "safe space" (Gayle et al., 2013; Gibbs et al., 2016) for reflection and learning, the opportunity to explore possibilities (aka consultation), perspectives on (beliefs about) the erstwhile problem can change – or even be transformed; but, to reiterate, the outcome of exploration and learning may not be anticipated or predetermined.

We have little doubt that in the safe space of ongoing and thoughtful dialogue, and in the reverberations of later reflection, participants can learn something new about their own (and others') practice (Akkerman & Meijer, 2011). In the next section we will describe and consider some examples of consultation in practice.

## The effects of consultation with schools and school staff

Practical examples of studies of consultations in the context of professional work in schools in the UK can be found, for instance, in the work of Andy Miller and Gerda Hanko who both explored the interpersonal effects and outcomes of consultations, albeit in slightly different contexts and from differing theoretical and professional orientations. In his close examination of the narratives of teachers who felt they had gained from meetings with an educational psychologist, Miller found that what teachers said they had most valued was the creation of a sense of safety and protection. The provision of a sense of safety that Miller detected in the teachers' narratives clearly provided them with a psychological environment in which it was possible to explore alternative scenarios to those which at the time had appeared to be undermining their professional confidence and capability. Miller found that this arose within teachers' perception of a *"temporary and overlapping system"* that was fostered by a psychologist. This temporary, alternative, system that to some extent and of necessity overlapped with the explicit and implicit cultures of the school, enabled teachers to feel they could, for the purposes of exploring alternative strategies, *"step outside the values and norms of behaviour imposed [on them] through membership of the school system"* (Miller, 1996, p. 106). The creation of this "safe space" for the teachers typically emerged in Miller's view in a *"seemingly paradoxical combination of the fragile and intangible with the authoritative and reassuring"* empathic manner of the psychologist.

While it might be tempting to imagine that the psychologist possessed some form of magical expertise in this respect, this would not be respectful of the beliefs and different expertise of others. For, as Gerda Hanko had found in her work in schools (see Hanko, 1985, 2002, 2003), groups of teachers can be empowered and become skilful in providing themselves with a very similar "micro-climate." In this way it becomes possible for teachers to reflect on their feelings and opportunities (about work-related issues) while avoiding the adverse consequences of giving/receiving advice about predetermined solutions. They may thus support each other emotionally through the process of discovering ways of working with, for example, children whose special needs might call for a range of different approaches. It is clear that Hanko's work to empower groups of teachers to help themselves showed that an external agency is not always essential to the development of professional skill and sensitivity. Further, although teachers in schools don't typically have access to formal, non-managerial "supervision" (unlike psychologists, for instance), peer supervision and coaching can, as Hanko's work demonstrated, provide alternative "safe spaces" within which teachers could help each other examine and explore their classroom practices. There is, we think, therefore scope for seeing both peer-coaching and peer-supervision as means of discovering alternative perspectives on professional practice (see, for instance, Leat, Lofthouse, & Towler, 2012; Lofthouse, Leat, & Towler, 2010). What both Hanko and Miller, and others more recently (Gibbs & Miller, 2014; Hayes & Stringer, 2016; Nolan & Moreland, 2014; Sullivan, Artiles, & Hernandez-Saca, 2015) have pointed to, are ways of helping to enhance teachers' beliefs in their competence and self-efficacy. Teachers can be surprised to discover how much they can do to help children who might otherwise be deemed to be the responsibility of other "specially trained experts."

As we have already noted, over the past two decades there has been a steady but seemingly inexorable rise in the proportion of children defined as having "special educational needs." As we have also noted, there has been a parallel upward trend in the number and proportion of children and young people permanently excluded from schools. It is possible to argue that the data that illustrate that the increasing exclusion of children and young people from mainstream education[1] are a direct consequence of historical cultural traditions as well as successive social, economic, and educational policies that are grounded in those traditions. It has also been argued (Gibbs, 2018a) that these same policies and the practice of school inspections has led to a curriculum that is constrained and dehumanising for both teachers and students. It is, then, perhaps more than ever pertinent to claim a necessary and vital role for educational and psychological consultations that provide a safe and collaborative forum for work with school staff that has as its aim the enhancement (and validation) of teachers' humanity, professional skills, autonomy, and creativity. There are, as we have indicated above, grounds for recognising that properly constituted, mutually respectful dialogues between teachers and psychologists can benefit teachers, schools, and communities. There is a substantial body of evidence that psychological consultation with schools and school staff can be helpful, lead to greater teacher skill, creativity and inclusivity (Cappella et al., 2012; Forman, 1995; Gutkin, 2012; Medway & Updyke, 1985; Ruble, Dalrymple, & McGrew, 2010; Sheridan, Eagle, Cowan, & Mickelson, 2001; Sheridan, Welch, & Orme, 1996). It is with this in mind that in the last section of this chapter we turn to consider what might be the significant features of a professional model of consultation.

## In conclusion

As we have indicated, introducing "consultation" may be seen as a form of intervention. Care is, therefore, needed so that it does not seem to be just another "good idea" introduced by an external "expert." Thus, we emphasise that at the outset there is a need for a clear and agreed inter-organisational agreement about consultation as an intervention and that its introduction comes from a careful analysis of what schools (or a school) may say they "want," feel will benefit them, as well as what they might be perceived to "need." It is, we think, important that there is a shared and agreed understanding at the highest level (and for all concerned) within both the Educational Psychology Service and the schools with whom the service wishes to work, about what Consultation is, who it is intended for, and how school staff can engage in the process. Such agreement needs also to be clear about the ethical issues we have discussed above, including who the primary clients are and what the obligations are for all parties. Without a clear contract that affirms these points, misunderstandings, and misleading expectations about the outcome of consultation may, sadly (as we have learned from experience), sabotage the process.

The opportunity offered by consultation to find new ways of learning and practising is at the heart of the enterprise. We continue to emphasise that teachers are skilled professionals and that respect for the professionalism of teachers (that, as we have commented elsewhere, may be missing in much of the political discourse about teachers and education) is critical in supporting their problem-solving skills and motivation.

Accordingly, it is of critical importance at the outset of their engagement with schools for psychologists to be aware of and skilled in the use of psychological processes that can both enable school staff to explore issues related to their professional concerns and possible vulnerabilities but also support and appreciate the development of professional expertise and understanding amongst the school staff as a whole. For their part school staff will need to be willing to engage openly in the exploration and not expect the psychologist to simply provide the remedy for their concerns. As an intervention consultation can provide an empathetic means for professional learning and a way of exploring how systems and positions that hinder learning can become more amenable to change and development. Although empirically hard to "prove" this assertion, a number of sources provide theory and evidence that warrant the claim (Downer, Locasale-Crouch, Hamre, & Pianta, 2009; Mayworm, Sharkey, Hunnicutt, & Schiedel, 2016; Rogers & Babinski, 2002; Truscott & Truscott, 2004; Watson & Gatti, 2012). Anne Jordan and her colleagues investigated the relationship between teachers' beliefs about the nature of children's "disabilities" and effective inclusionary practices, and highlighted the implications for teachers' professional development (Jordan, Schwartz, & McGhie-Richmond, 2009; Jordan & Stanovich, 2004). As has been suggested elsewhere there is also a distinctive role for educational psychologists in supporting teachers' resilience and professional development (Gibbs & Miller, 2014). We continue to emphasise, therefore, that interpersonal professional dialogue embedded in consultation that explicitly demonstrates the mutual respect of school staff and psychologist can provide the space in which learning, and change can occur.

But we also hope that consultants continue to reflect on the extent to which their approaches involve attending to the space between them and others (including staff in schools, parents, young people, for instance) as well as their ability to be listening to others. For psychologists embarking on the process, they will need to consider what the way of working they propose has to say about the psychology they apply, how they apply it, and how the psychology they draw upon and use may, both in theory and practice position those with whom they work.

In summary, therefore, the necessary conditions that we envisage for psychological consultation in and with schools (with school staff) include first some form of *organisational agreement* between the psychologist (as a representative of the psychological service as a whole) and the school (or the schools in the locality) that provides understanding of what consultation is, what it is aiming to do (provide supportive dialogue to explore professional concerns), and what the possible outcomes of a consultation may be. This agreement will, secondly, help ensure understanding of the *ethical considerations* and of the *mutual moral responsibilities* of, respectively, the psychologist and school staff. Further, the agreement will help to ensure that all staff should be aware of the nature of the process of consultation so that school staff may feel "safe," but also confident that consultation is intended to be helpful in exploring and examining what they can do as a result. We are under no illusions that consultation is "easy." Working with a teacher who is finding her or his professional situation difficult can be an emotional process and just as the school staff need to feel confident that they have professional and organisational support so does the psychologist. Accordingly, it is important, therefore, that psychologists working as consultants with staff in schools have access to regular professional supervision.

In the next and final chapter, we will return to our starting point to summarise and synthesise the understandings and resources that psychologists may bring to dialogic conversations amongst themselves and with fellow educational professionals as being some of those who may find themselves confused, concerned or, in extremis, distressed in their professional work. We hope that in doing so we will help promote and support psychological theories and inclusive practices capable of encompassing without demur the tensions between mutuality and difference, and individuality and communion.

## Note

1  Either because of formal exclusion or because of segregated placement in a special school. The most recent available data from the DfE show that between 2008 and 2018 the proportion of young people attending a special school rose from 1.07% to 1.31% of all school age pupils and the percentage of children and young people permanently excluded from schools rose from 5,740 (0.08%) in 2009/10 to 7,894 (1.0%) in 2019/20.

# 7 Synthesis

## Introduction

This book is dedicated to all those involved in education. With our focus on dialogue as being at the heart of good professional relationships and the development of education, we hope it will first support practitioners in their daily work; but secondly, we hope that it will stimulate and support those who meet to help each other envisage how things could be different in both policy and practice. Ultimately, we hope our narrative about why meetings and dialogic conversations are so important in themselves, why it is important to talk about how to talk and how to listen, why it is important to talk about what education is, will help to revitalise what education in schools can do – and, maybe, *should* do. As we hope is clear from the text our view (and the views of many of those we have cited) is that education should, at least, be about learning how to become human. Given the global context of widespread inequality and poverty our central (meta) intention has been, therefore, to set out some of what we see as forming relational steps toward making the world a better place in which to be and develop; because if we do not first have relationships with each other then we cannot become human. We are with Macmurray (1958/2012, p. 670), therefore, in thinking that:

> For this reason the first priority in education – if by education we mean learning to be human – is learning to live in personal relation to other people. Let us call it learning to live in community. I call this the first priority because failure in this is fundamental failure, which cannot be compensated for by success in other fields; because our ability to enter into fully personal relations with others is the measure of our humanity.

When we look around us and see the gross inequalities and poverty in our own country that is, somewhat ironically, amongst the wealthiest and most technologically advanced, and when we consider that, despite this economic and technical wealth, our education system fails so many by not providing an educational environment that attracts and stimulates them with a desire to learn, we wonder what needs to be different. So, we ask, how can we undivide

DOI: 10.4324/9780429343766-8

society at least for our youngest and most vulnerable citizens? How can we do this as soon as possible? How can we foster relationships that show how in education we can support growth of human beings? We have to agree with John Dewey (1900, p. 3) who wrote:

> What the best and wisest parent wants for his own child, that must the community want for all its children. Any other ideal for our schools is narrow and unlovely; acted upon it destroys our democracy.

As Nel Noddings (2016) emphasised, we must assume that Dewey did not mean to suggest that the "best and wisest" parents would want the same homogenous education for all children but would want, as Dewey was at pains to emphasise elsewhere, education to involve addressing the distinctive needs, interests, and contributions of each child who has to take account of the actions of others since:

> the number of individuals who participate in an interest so that each has to refer his own action to that of others... is equivalent to the breaking down of those barriers of class, race, and national territory which kept men [*sic*] from perceiving the full import of their activity.
>
> (Dewey, 1916/2011, p. 50)

We fear there may still not yet be the political determination to make Dewey's vision real. Being pragmatic, therefore, and acknowledging we do not here have either a political or judicial mandate but do profess to having a moral and ethical remit, we have the temerity to suggest that we can, meanwhile, do our best to prioritise and promote professional relations (teacher–teacher; teacher–child) that are as ethical and as human as possible. As Buber also held, relationships that embody dialogue are at the heart of education and the main bulwark against meaninglessness:

> Trust, trust in the world, because this human being exists – that is the most inward achievement of the relation in education. Because this human exists, meaninglessness, however hard pressed you are by it, cannot be the real truth. Because this human being exists, in the darkness the light lies hidden, in fear salvation, and in the callousness of one's fellow-men the great Love.
>
> (Buber, 2002, p. 98)

It is because of the dialogue we can have, each with each other, showing respect and care, as well as accepting dissonance and difference, signalling that we are not alone and that the future remains a possibility, that we felt it important to write this book and set out how and why dialogic professional relationships are so important in education. But it is not enough to uphold dialogic relationship because of their quality and exploratory power; they are also, at every moment of our existence, the fulcrum for change, since educational moments are located at the interface of the past and the future or as Paul Ricoeur said, between "*the history one suffers and the history one makes*"[1] (Ricoeur, 2020, p. 17).

This idea of the artefact of the interface, the "Sciences of the Artificial," brings us back to the introductory chapter in which we made use of Herb Simon's parable of the ant as a means of illustrating how "behaviour" (in its most general sense of what people think and do) emerges in the interaction of systems. We hope it is by now clear that while that illustration was too simple to provide sufficient acknowledgement of the complexity of human interactions and endeavours in the contexts we have outlined, it is still a useful parable. So, to provide a synthesis of what we have tried to address in each of the chapters it may be helpful to set out the systems that we perceive as affecting what does and could happen in schools. These may be seen as being located as either remote, global, matters; national and local policies; organisational functions; or inter-personal and intra-personal relations.

The global systems include those that determine nutrition, population growth and health, climate change, and international conflict. Clearly these interact with each other and determine the future of the planet. It remains to be seen whether human endeavours to halt the corrosive effects of some of those interactions (economic greed and population growth, for instance) can success-fully avert disaster. We would like to suggest that since there are some major threats (such as climate change) to the future of all societies, seeking to avert such a disaster is a worthwhile and globally shareable aim. Although it might seem a grandiose aim, and perhaps seeming a long way from the objectives of everyday education, there are signs that young (and older) people are motivated by this to effect change. "*If you give me a lever and place to stand, I will move the world*" Archimedes is reputed to have said. If we want to make a difference via education, where shall we stand and what might be the lever?

From the perspective of an observer of Herb Simon's ant-person our indi-vidual and collective societal behaviours (these being the sum and synergies of our thoughts, words, and deeds) are constructed as the resultant of our interactions with these systems. The interaction of these systems may, however, themselves be influenced by national political and economic policies, and inter-national agreements. National (and international) economic and political pol-icies in turn provide the context for local policies and practices – what happens in schools as organisations as well as, ultimately, for practitioners as individuals. This "top down" deterministic perspective, however, might lead us to a conclu-sion that as individuals we are helpless pessimists unable to exert any meaningful control over factors that determine our future. It is our contention that we can take a much more optimistic and pragmatic approach. Formulating a strategy to implement the "pragmatic" approaches is, however, dependent on how we answer questions about our motivation, aims, and ethics and, if we really want to make a difference?

As will be clear from all that has preceded this, we think that at the heart of education are the relationships that support social and educational development;

relationships in which the quality of the interactions is remarkable and memorable. (Anecdotally, it seems very likely that amongst our memories of those who taught us, prominent are those with whom the quality of our relationship stands out (see, for instance, O'Reilly-Scanlon, 2000; Uitto, Lutovac, Jokikokko, & Kaasila, 2018)). It is in our meetings with each other that we may learn how to regain ethical autonomy that is respectful of our differences, understanding our diversity and, simultaneously, being helpful to others. As Zygmunt Bauman (1993, p. 235) remarked:

> … it is by being different that we most resemble each other and that I cannot respect my own difference but by respecting the difference of the other.

But the meeting of one with another in a dialogue, learning from each other, forms, as Hubert Hermans (2013, p. 84) suggested, a reciprocal link – or a bridge – between an individual and society at large since:

> The voices of other individuals, the collective voices of groups, and even the power games of societal institutions enter the self-space of the individual and challenge the self to give an answer. Along these lines, a self emerges in which different voices agree or disagree with each other, lead to unification or opposition, and are involved in relations of power and counterpower. Along these lines, real, remembered, or imagined voices of friends, allies, strangers, or enemies figure as transient or more stabilized positions in and around the self that is able to open or close itself to the globalizing environment.

For this to be educationally practical, to provide an environment and spaces in which such real and virtual, personally and socially positioned interactions can have a meaningful place (a place to stand), there is a need to reimagine and safeguard the curriculum as a locus of creativity, a potential fulcrum for our lever. We think this requires recognition of both the dialogic space between people and the "empty space" between contacts in a social network referred to by Burt (1992, 2004) as "structural holes," and that both can stimulate and catalyse new thinking. As we have said in Chapter 3 the curriculum is, itself, the interface of systems in which relationships may prosper. For that to happen, we suggest, the curriculum, like relationships, needs to be open for exploration, discovery, and transformation, not yoked to predetermined specific objectives. Gert Biesta (2013) and Herb Simon (1996) have separately and differently conceptualised human development and education as essentially involving processes of discovery designed without an ultimate goal. Simon (p. 162) asked:

> How can we evaluate a design unless we have well-defined criteria against which to judge it, and how can the design process itself proceed without such criteria to guide it?… A paradoxical, but perhaps realistic view of

design goals is that their function is to motivate activity which will in turn generate new *[proximal]* goals.

Likewise, Biesta (2013) suggested that education has to be a process (not without risk) of discovering things that we didn't know we were looking for. Education should be, therefore, a process that interrupts our everyday experience. That aim makes it clear that we cannot – should not – try to formulate a defined endpoint for education. However, since as we have argued earlier in the book, this *ideal* may not be most helpful for staff in schools in the present circumstances as there are very real constraints on teacher agency with regard to curriculum and pedagogy. Being pragmatic, therefore, having some proximal goals which, as Simon suggested, become the motivators of the next step of design, could both encourage the achievement of attainable proximal goals and maintain the focus on the aim of becoming human.

In line with this proposal, in writing the book we have tried to practise and delineate some of the transformative features of dialogic relationships that may be enacted to support learning in the most general, non-specific meaning of "learning." Thus, we suggest, through authentic dialogue with a fellow professional one's relationship with another (person, object, issue…), and indeed the curriculum may be changed. As we have said, although the topology of education may not have altered much in the past century (or more), remaining largely monologic and focussed on the transmission of knowledge, there are, however, spaces for alternative practice (see Chapters 3 and 5 for examples of how this may be achieved). But, if it is possible to change the nature of the professional relationships amongst the educational staff and those who support them, to be dialogic and democratic, it becomes possible to change the essence and purpose of education itself. We would certainly wish to suggest that by transforming inter- and intra-professional relations (the meta-curriculum), the relationships between staff and students must also be transformed.

Accordingly, we have mapped out how and why we are socially, practically, necessarily interconnected, not just in education it seems, but almost inextricably in every conceivable way. Since we are so interconnected, it seems to us, that there are, therefore, moral and ethical, social, psychological, and educational implications. We suggest that if we try to ignore or deny the validity of these in education (as in society at large) we are in deep trouble, as indeed we may be at present. Our view of the current predicament, as documented here (in Chapters 1 and 2) and elsewhere (e.g. by Gibbs, 2018a), forms the premise for what we have tried to achieve. The most stark and brutal evidence and implications of this "trouble" is easy to see in the number and characteristics of the children and young people excluded from schools (see Chapter 1). For us, therefore, the clear implication is that "Education," as presently instantiated in schools in the UK is not fit for purpose. In fact the purpose has not changed since formal education was prescribed for all (see, for a brief review Gibbs, 2021, 2022). That it is not now fit for purpose could, we suggest, be simply because it does not include all children and young people in activities that are meaningful and valuable (for them and society at large). We argue that some of the reasons for this lie directly in policies enacted by consecutive central government over the past 50 years and more. As we have pointed out elsewhere (Gibbs, 2018a) this has also resulted in a demoralised and under-supported work force: teachers attempting to deliver a poorly conceptualised and dehumanising curriculum (see Chapter 3). One of our aims, therefore, has been to talk about how teachers may be supported in regaining professional dignity and autonomy. These are critical moral and ethical issues (as discussed in Chapter 4) and unless, and until, these are addressed, teachers and other educational professionals will be stuck in the morass that confuses all at present. We would urge that all staff in schools are supported in exploring how they can rethink and reclaim their purposes as educators. In particular, we suggest that the work of staff who are responsible for coordinating support for children and young people who seem to experience extraordinary difficulties in school would be enhanced by the sort of experiences advocated by Gerda Hanko (Hanko, 1985, 2002, 2003) and by being enabled to engage in dialogues as we too have suggested here (in Chapters 5 and 6).

It is through telling and retelling stories such as that which we have created here that we can reveal, examine, and reframe the nature of education as it is and might be. Retelling stories needs some imagination (but less than may be imagined!); we do not have to keep reinventing the present, never mind the past.

Thus, we contend that our thesis will help to increase the numbers of children and young people (CYP) who are allowed and enabled to be in – and stay in – mainstream schools; help sustain staff in their endeavours; help to preserve or recreate schools where the curriculum is not restricted; and to create opportunities and environments where the citizens of the future can learn how to be with others who are all different in different ways. To reiterate the main theme of our book, central to what we want to endorse is the space for dialogue in which answers may be found even when the questions or issues that are troubling colleagues are unclear. So, for example, why is it that so many children and young people are still not educated entirely in their local mainstream and inclusive school?

Although we have not discussed this in our text, we earnestly believe that changes in the nature, purpose and context of education, and how schools operate could (should) also reduce the proportion of children living in poverty who are excluded from education. For too many around the world poverty and ill-health are barriers to education, education that might help young people become "goodenough" parents, people who do not have to fight to survive, people with respect for and interest in others. Those who are victims of a society in which "equality of opportunity" (or as the UK government of 2022 had it, "levelling up") as it is currently conceptualised does not work. Although the causal mechanisms are complex, there appears to be an association of economic and educational poverty with subsequent law breaking that is contingently associated with further damage to families (Hodge & Wolstenholme, 2016; Kulz, 2019; Parsons & Castle, 1998). The fragmentation of individual lives and of families that result from socio-economic and educational poverty is a fragmentation of society. In saying this we do not want to blame parents. They too are most likely victims of circumstance and an environment that is not their creation. As Farrar and Ahuja (2021, p. 214) commented, reflecting on what happened (and is still happening) as a result of the COVID pandemic, "A divided world is a diseased world." Although Farrar and Ahuja were specifically addressing issues of physical health, we continue to suggest that there are matters relating to "organisational" health that also need to be addressed and, therefore, what they say later (p. 219) in their book also applies to organisational factors, especially in view of the disruption of children and young people's education that has been seen over the past couple of years:

> Protecting the health of our interconnected world insulates us all from the kind of mass disruption we are currently living through, some more painfully than others.

Ensuring we have psychologically and physically healthy educational settings in which young people can be helped to envisage other possibilities and to relearn how to be human means ensuring schools themselves are supported. Support for schools as organisations and their staff may be provided by, for example, applied psychologists; psychologists who believe in and practise inclusive education who can thus help others learn what is possible by working across the network of support and the structural holes (Burt, 1992, 2004) therein.

We also need to think about setting aside self-interest and recognise that our collective best interests in education are not necessarily best served by pure self-interest. As we have shown in the previous chapter, the entrepreneurial climate in which many psychologists (for instance) are now required to generate income is, therefore, an ethical issue. We suggest this provides a possible interim goal on the road to re-humanising education: to ensure that psychological services are centrally financed service and free to schools at the point of delivery. There will be other similar opportunities for educationalists of all professional backgrounds to work out how better to work together, particularly since as Hubert Hermans (2013, p. 85) saw in the potent link between enlightened dialogic selves and society.

> In an era when professional work is increasingly fused with private and personal life circumstances, the coalition of social and personal positions becomes particularly salient to both persons and organizations.

So, here we are, in professional relations with each other, poised at every moment between two monumental systems, the past and the future, or, as Paul Ricoeur (2020, p. 17) suggested more agentically: "*the history one suffers and the history one makes.*" There, in that micro-moment within a dialogue, inextricably ethically motivated, there is the fulcrum we all have where we can place our lever and create a difference that will stimulate further, distal change.

# Note

1 This is Ricoeur's version of Marx's view (in The Eighteenth Brumaire of Louis Bonaparte) that

> Men make their own history, but they do not make it as they please; they do not make it under self-selected circumstances, but under circumstances existing already, given and transmitted from the past. The tradition of all dead generations weighs like a nightmare on the brains of the living.

# References

Achinstein, B. (2002). Conflict amid community: The micropolitics of teacher collaboration. *Teachers College Record*, *104*(3), 421–55.

Agamben, G. (2005). *State of exception* (K.Attell, Trans.). Chicago: Chicago University Press.

Agre, P. E. (2003). Hierarchy and history in Simon's "architecture of complexity". *The Journal of the Learning Sciences*, *12*(3), 413–26.

Ahlstrom-Vij, K. (2019). The epistemic benefits of democracy: A critical assessment. In M. Fricker, P. J. Graham, D. Henderson, & N. J. Pederson (Eds.), *The Routledge handbook of social epistemology* (1st ed., pp. 406–14). New York: Routledge.

Akkerman, S. F., & Bakker, A. (2011). Boundary crossing and boundary objects. *Review of educational research*, *81*(2), 132–69. doi:10.3102/0034654311404435

Akkerman, S. F., & Meijer, P. C. (2011). A dialogical approach to conceptualizing teacher identity. *Teaching and Teacher Education*, *27*(2), 308–19. doi:10.1016/j.tate.2010.08.013

Aldridge, J. (2015). *Participatory research: Working with vulnerable groups in research and practice*. Bristol: Policy Press.

Aldridge, J. M., & Fraser, B. J. (2016). Teachers' views of their school climate and its relationship with teacher self-efficacy and job satisfaction. *Learning Environments Research*, *19*(2), 291–307. doi:10.1007/s10984-015-9198-x

Allen, R., & Bartley, J. (2017). The role of the eleven-plus test papers and appeals in producing social inequalities in access to grammar schools. *National Institute Economic Review*, *240*, R30–41. doi:10.1177/002795011724000112

Andersen, T. (1987). The reflecting team: Dialogue and metadialogue in clinical work. *Family Process*, *26*(4), 415–28. doi:10.1111/j.1545-5300.1987.00415.x

Anderson, E. S. (1999). What is the point of equality? *Ethics*, *109*(2), 287–337. doi:10.1086/233897

Anderson, R. K., Boaler, J., & Dieckmann, J. A. (2018). Achieving elusive teacher change through challenging myths about learning: A blended approach. *Education Sciences*, *8*(3), 98. Retrieved from www.mdpi.com/2227-7102/8/3/98

Appiah, K. A. (2007a). *Cosmopolitanism: Ethics in a world of strangers (issues of our time)*. London: Penguin.

Appiah, K. A. (2007b). *The ethics of identity*. Woodstock: Princeton University Press.

Arendt, H. (1958/1998). *The Human condition* (2nd ed.). Chicago: University of Chicago Press.

Arnardóttir, O. M. (2014). The differences that make a difference: Recent developments on the discrimination grounds and the margin of appreciation under Article 14 of the European convention on human rights. *Human Rights Law Review*, *14*(4), 647–70. doi:10.1093/hrlr/ngu025

Arnett, R. C., & Arneson, P. (1999). *Dialogic civility in a cynical age: Community, hope, and interpersonal relationships.* Albany: SUNY Press.

Arnett, R. C., & Arneson, P. (2014). *Philosophy of communication ethics: Alterity and the other.* Teaneck: Fairleigh Dickinson University Press.

Arnett, R. C., Arneson, P., & Bell, L. M. (2006). Communication ethics: The dialogic turn. *The Review of Communication, 6*(1–2), 62–92. doi:10.1080/15358590600763334

Arnold, C., & Hardy, J. (2017). *British educational psychology: The first 100 years* (C. Arnold & J. Hardy Eds.). Leicester: British Psychology Society Press.

Arnold, M. H., Kerridge, I., & Lipworth, W. (2020). An ethical critique of person-centred healthcare. *European Journal for Person Centered Healthcare, 8*(1), 34–44. doi:10.5750/ejpch.v8i1.1818

Asterhan, C. S., Howe, C., Lefstein, A., Matusov, E., & Reznitskaya, A. (2020). Controversies and consensus in research on dialogic teaching and learning. *Dialogic Pedagogy, 8,* S1–S16.

Au, W. (2012). What curriculum could be: Utopian dreams amidst a dystopian reality. *Kappa Delta Pi Record, 48*(2), 55–8. doi:10.1080/00228958.2012.680385

Avis, J. (2003). Re-thinking trust in a performative culture: The case of education. *Journal of Education Policy, 18*(3), 315–32.

Bakhtin, M. (1984). *Problems of Dostoevsky's poetics* (C. Emerson, Trans.). Minneapolis: University of Minnesota Press.

Bakhtin, M. M. (1986). Speech genres and other late essays (V. W. McGee, Trans.). In C. Emerson & M. Holquist (Eds.), *Speech genres and other late essays* Austin: University of Texas Press.

Ball, S. J. (2003). The teacher's soul and the terrors of performativity. *Journal of Education Policy, 18*(2), 215–28. doi:10.1080/0268093022000043065

Ball, S. J. (2015). Education, governance and the tyranny of numbers. *Journal of Education Policy, 30*(3), 299–301. doi:10.1080/02680939.2015.1013271

Bandura, A. (1997). *Self-efficacy: The exercise of control.* New York: Freeman.

Barrow, W. (2010). Dialogic, participation and the potential for philosophy for children. *Thinking Skills and Creativity, 5*(2), 61–9. doi:10.1016/j.tsc.2010.01.002

Bass, B. M. (1985). *Leadership and performance beyond expectations.* New York: Free Press.

Bass, B. M. (1990). From transactional to transformational leadership: Learning to share the vision. *Organizational Dynamics, 18*(3), 19–31. Retrieved from http://search.ebscohost.com/login.aspx?direct=true&db=bth&AN=9607211357&site=ehost-live

Bateson, G. (1979). *Mind and nature: A necessary unity.* New York: Dutton.

Bauer, M. S., Damschroder, L., Hagedorn, H., Smith, J., & Kilbourne, A. M. (2015). An introduction to implementation science for the non-specialist. *BMC Psychology, 3*(1), 1–12. doi:10.1186/s40359-015-0089-9

Bauman, Z. (1993). *Modernity and ambivalence.* Cambridge: Polity Press.

Bauman, Z. (1995). Making and unmaking of strangers. In P. Beilhartz (Ed.), *The Bauman reader* (pp. 200–17). Oxford: Blackwell.

Baumeister, R. F., & Leary, M. R. (1995). The need to belong: Desire for interpersonal attachments as a fundamental human motivation. *Psychological Bulletin, 117*(3), 497.

Benlian, A. (2014). Are we aligned…enough? The effects of perceptual congruence between service teams and their leaders on Team performance. *Journal of Service Research, 17*(2), 212–28. doi:10.1177/1094670513516673

Bentham, J. (1791/1995). *Panopticon or the inspection house.* In M. Bozovic (Ed) *The Panopticon Writings* (pp. 29–95) London: Verso.

Berkeley, G. (2009). *Principles of human knowledge and three dialogues*. Oxford: Oxford University Press.

Berndt, T. J., & Perry, T. B. (1986). Children's perceptions of friendships as supportive relationships. *Developmental Psychology, 22*(5), 640. doi:10.1037/0012-1649.22.5.640

Bernstein, B. (1973a). *Class, codes and control: Applied studies towards a sociology of language* (Vol. 2). London: Routledge & Keegan Paul.

Bernstein, B. (1973b). *Class, codes and control: Applied studies towards a sociology of language* (Vol. 1). London: Routledge & Keegan Paul.

Bernstein, B. (1996). *Pedagogy, symbolic control, and identity*. London: Taylor & Francis.

Bernstein, B. (1999). Vertical and horizontal discourse: An essay. *British Journal of Sociology of Education, 20*(2), 157–73. doi:10.1080/01425699995380

Biesta, G. (2009). Good education in an age of measurement: On the need to reconnect with the question of purpose in education. *Educational Assessment, Evaluation and Accountability (formerly: Journal of Personnel Evaluation in Education), 21*(1), 33–46. doi:10.1007/s11092-008-9064-9

Biesta, G. (2013). *Beautiful risk of education*. London: Routledge.

Biesta, G. (2015). *Good education in an age of measurement: Ethics, politics, democracy*. Abingdon: Routledge.

Biesta, G. (2016). *Beyond learning: Democratic education for a human future*. Abingdon: Routledge.

Biesta, G., Priestley, M., & Robinson, S. (2015). The role of beliefs in teacher agency. *Teachers and Teaching, 21*(6), 624–40. doi:10.1080/13540602.2015.1044325

Biesta, G., & Tedder, M. (2007). Agency and learning in the lifecourse: Towards an ecological perspective. *Studies in the Education of Adults, 39*(2), 132–49. doi:10.1080/02660830.2007.11661545

Blackwood, L., Hopkins, N., & Reicher, S. (2013). I know who I am, but who do they think I am? Muslim perspectives on encounters with airport authorities. *Ethnic and Racial Studies, 36*(6), 1090–108. doi:10.1080/01419870.2011.645845

Boaler, J. (2008). Promoting 'relational equity' and high mathematics achievement through an innovative mixed-ability approach. *British Educational Research Journal, 34*(2), 167–94. doi:10.1080/01411920701532145

Bobbitt, J. F. (1924). *How to make a curriculum*. Boston: Houghton Mifflin.

Bogotch, I. E. (2002). Educational leadership and social justice: Practice into theory. *Journal of School Leadership, 12*(2), 138–56. doi:10.1177/105268460201200203

Bolden, R. (2011). Distributed leadership in organizations: A review of theory and research. *International Journal of Management Reviews, 13*(3), 251–69. doi:10.1111/j.1468-2370.2011.00306.x

Bondi, J., & Wiles, J. (2007). *Curriculum development: A guide to practice* (7th ed.). London: Prentice-Hall.

Borman, G. D., & Dowling, N. M. (2008). Teacher attrition and retention: A meta-analytic and narrative review of the research. *Review of Educational Research, 78*(3), 367–409.

Bouko, C., & Garcia, D. (2020). Patterns of emotional tweets: The case of Brexit after the referendum results. In G. Bouvier & J. E. Rosenbaum (Eds.), *Twitter, the public sphere, and the chaos of online deliberation* (pp. 175–203). Cham: Springer International Publishing.

Bowlby, J. (1978). Attachment theory and its therapeutic implications. *Adolescent Psychiatry, 6*, 5–33.

Braten, S. (Ed.) (2007). *On being moved: From mirror neurons to empathy* (Vol. 68). Amsterdam/Philadelphia: John Benjamins Publishing Company.

Brazier, D. (1993). The necessary condition is love: Going beyond self in the person-centred approach. In D. Brazier (Ed.), *Beyond Carl Rogers* (pp. 72–91). London: Constable and Company.

Brazier, D. (1993). *Beyond Carl Rogers*. London: Constable and Company.

Brewer, M. B. (1991). The social self: On being the same and different at the same time. *Personality and Social Psychology Bulletin, 17*(5), 475–82.

Brighouse, T. (2015). Co-operation and competition – A commentary. In T. Woodin (Ed.), *Co-operation, learning and co-operative values: Contemporary issues in education* (pp. 195–200). Abingdon: Routledge.

Brighouse, T., & Waters, M. (2022). *About our schools: Improving on previous best.* Carmarthen: Crown House Publishing Ltd.

Brinkmann, S. (2016). Psychology as a normative science. In J. Valsiner, G. Marsico, N. Chaudhary, T. Sato, & V. Dazzani (Eds.), *Psychology as the science of human being: The Yokhama manifesto* (pp. 3–16). London: Springer.

Brouwers, A., & Tomic, W. (2000). A longitudinal study of teacher burnout and perceived self-efficacy in classroom management. *Teaching and Teacher Education, 16*(2), 239–53. doi:10.1016/s0742-051x(99)00057-8

Brown, A. D. (2015). Identities and identity work in organizations. *International Journal of Management Reviews, 17*(1), 20–40.

Brown, J., Gilmour, W. H., & Macdonald, E. B. (2006). Ill health retirement in Scottish teachers: Process, outcomes and re-employment. *International Archives of Occupational and Environmental Health, 79*(5), 433–40. doi:10.1007/s00420-005-0060-9

Brown, M. E., & Treviño, L. K. (2006). Ethical leadership: A review and future directions. *The Leadership Quarterly, 17*(6), 595–616. doi:10.1016/j.leaqua.2006.10.004

Brownell, M. T., & Pajares, F. (1999). Teacher efficacy and perceived success in mainstreaming students with learning and behavior problems. *Teacher Education and Special Education: The Journal of the Teacher Education Division of the Council for Exceptional Children, 22*(3), 154–64. doi:10.1177/088840649902200303

Bruner, J. (1987). Life as narrative. *Social Research, 54*, 11–32. Retrieved from www.jstor.org/stable/40970444

Bruner, J. (2009). Culture, mind and education. In K. Illeris (Ed.), *Contemporary theories of learning: Learning theorists.. in their own words* (pp. 159–68). Abingdon: Routledge.

Buber, M. (1965). *Between man and man* (R. Gregor-Smith, Trans.). London: Routledge.

Buber, M. (2002). *Between man and man*. Abingdon: Routledge.

Burt, R. S. (1992). *Structural holes*. London: Harvard University Press.

Burt, R. S. (2004). Structural holes and good ideas. *American Journal of Sociology, 110*(2), 349–99. doi:10.1086/421787

Burt, R. S. (2015). Reinforced structural holes. *Social Networks, 43*, 149–61. doi:10.1016/j.socnet.2015.04.008

Busch, S. D., & Fernandez, J. (2019). *Influencing high student achievement through school climate: A quantitative approach to organizational health-based leadership.* New York: Routledge.

Butler, J. (2004). *Precarious life: The powers of violence and mourning*. New York: Verso.

Campbell, C. (2016). Developing professional capital in policy and practice: Ontario's teacher learning and leadership program. *Journal of Professional Capital and Community, 1*(3), 219–36. doi:10.1108/JPCC-03-2016-0004

Campbell, D. (1986). Rationality and utility from the standpoint of evolutionary biology. *The Journal of Business, 59*(4), S355–64.

Caplan, G. (1970). *Theory & practice of mental health consultation.* London: Tavistock Publications.

Cappella, E., Hamre, B. K., Kim, H. Y., Henry, D. B., Frazier, S. L., Atkins, M. S., & Schoenwald, S. K. (2012). Teacher consultation and coaching within mental health practice: Classroom and child effects in urban elementary schools. *Journal of Consulting and Clinical Psychology, 80*(4), 597.

Caprara, G. V., Barbaranelli, C., Steca, P., & Malone, P. S. (2006). Teachers' self-efficacy beliefs as determinants of job satisfaction and students' academic achievement: A study at the school level. *Journal of School Psychology, 44*(6), 473–90. doi:10.1016/j.jsp.2006.09.001

Carr, S. (2020). Dampened motivation as a side effect of contemporary educational policy: A self-determination theory perspective. *Oxford Review of Education, 46*(3), 331–45.

Carroll, B., & Levy, L. (2010). Leadership development as identity construction. *Management Communication Quarterly, 24*(2), 211–31. doi:10.1177/0893318909358725

Carroll, M., & Holloway, E. (Eds.). (1998). *Counselling supervision in context.* London: Sage.

Cecchin, G. (1987). Hypothesizing, circularity, and neutrality revisited: An invitation to curiosity. *Family Process, 26*(4), 405–13.

Chartrand, T. L., & Lakin, J. L. (2013). The antecedents and consequences of human behavioral mimicry. *Annual Review of Psychology, 64*, 285–308. doi:10.1146/annurev-psych-113011-143754

Cianciolo, A. T., & Regehr, G. (2019). Learning theory and educational intervention: Producing meaningful evidence of impact through layered analysis. *Academic Medicine, 94*(6), 789–94. doi:10.1097/ACM.0000000000002591

Clark, J., Laing, K., Leat, D., Lofthouse, R., Thomas, U., Tiplady, L., & Woolner, P. (2017). Transformation in interdisciplinary research methodology: The importance of shared experiences in landscapes of practice. *International Journal of Research & Method in Education, 40*(3), 243–56. doi:10.1080/1743727X.2017.1281902

Claxton, G. (2014). School as an epistemic apprenticeship: The case of building learning power/La escuela como aprendizaje epistémico: el caso de construyendo el poder para el aprendizaje. *Infancia y Aprendizaje, 37*(2), 227–47. doi:10.1080/02103702.2014.929863

Claxton, G., & Lucas, B. (2016). The hole in the heart of education (and the role of psychology in addressing it). *The Psychology of Education Review, 40*(1), 4–12. Retrieved from www.researchgate.net/profile/Bill-Lucas/publication/301635707_The_Hole_in_the_Heart_of_Education/links/571f29b908aed056fa227b7a/The-Hole-in-the-Heart-of-Education.pdf

Claytor, A. (2021). Permanent and fixed term exclusions from academies and local authority schools. Personal Communication from DfE Schools Statistics.

Clifton, J. (2012). A discursive approach to leadership: Doing assessments and managing organizational meanings. *The Journal of Business Communication (1973), 49*(2), 148–68. doi:10.1177/0021943612437762

Coburn, C. E. (2006). Framing the problem of reading instruction: Using frame analysis to uncover the microprocesses of policy implementation. *American Educational Research Journal, 43*(3), 343–9. doi:10.3102/00028312043003343

Coburn, C. E., & Russell, J. L. (2008). District policy and teachers' social networks. *Educational Evaluation and Policy Analysis, 30*(3), 203–35.

Cohen, E. G., & Lotan, R. A. (1997). *Working for equity in heterogeneous classrooms: Sociological theory in practice.* New York: Teachers College Press.

Contractor, N.S. (1999). Self-organizing systems research in the social sciences: Reconciling the metaphors and the models. *Management Communication Quarterly, 13*(1), 154–66. doi:10.1177/0893318999131009

Courtney, S. J. (2015). Corporatised leadership in English schools. *Journal of Educational Administration and History, 47*(3), 214–31. doi:10.1080/00220620.2015.1038694

Courtney, S. J. (2016). Post-panopticism and school inspection in England. *British Journal of Sociology of Education, 37*(4), 623–42. doi:10.1080/01425692.2014.965806

Cox, E. (2012). Individual and organizational trust in a reciprocal peer coaching context. *Mentoring & Tutoring: Partnership in Learning, 20*(3), 427–43. doi:10.1080/13611267.2012.701967

Cox, J. A., Bañez, L., Hawley, L. D., & Mostade, J. (2003). Use of the reflecting Team process in the training of group workers. *The Journal for Specialists in Group Work, 28*(2), 89–105. doi:10.1177/0193392203028002002

CPAG. (2019). *Child poverty facts and figures.* Retrieved from https://cpag.org.uk/child-poverty/child-poverty-facts-and-figures

Crang, M., & Thrift, N. (2000). *Thinking space* (Vol. 9). London: Routledge.

Crigger, N. J. (1997). The trouble with caring: A review of eight arguments against an ethic of care. *Journal of Professional Nursing, 13*(4), 217–21. doi.org/10.1016/S8755-7223(97)80091-9

Dadvand, B. (2020). Performative pedagogies of care and the emerging geographies of school exclusion for students with disability. *International Journal of Inclusive Education,* Ahead-of-print, 1–15. doi:10.1080/13603116.2020.1791981

Dadvand, B., & Cuervo, H. (2020). Pedagogies of care in performative schools. *Discourse: Studies in the Cultural Politics of Education, 41*(1), 139–52.

Dahl, R. A. (2020). *On democracy.* New Haven: Yale University Press.

Daniels, H., Leadbetter, J., Warmington, P., Edwards, A., Martin, D., Popova, A., ... Brown, S. (2007). Learning in and for multi-agency working. *Oxford Review of Education, 33*(4), 521–38. doi.org/10.1080/03054980701450811

Davies, A. J., Milton, E., Connolly, M., & Barrance, R. (2018). Headteacher recruitment, retention and professional development in wales: Challenges and opportunities. *Cylchgrawn Addysg Cymru/Wales Journal of Education, 20*(2), 204–24.

Davis, B. (2008). Complexity and education: Vital simultaneities. *Educational Philosophy and Theory, 40*(1), 50–65. doi:10.1111/j.1469-5812.2007.00402.x

Davis, B., & Sumara, D. (2010). 'If things were simple...': Complexity in education. *Journal of Evaluation in Clinical Practice, 16*(4), 856–60. doi:10.1111/j.1365-2753.2010.01499.x

Day, C., & Leithwood, K. (Eds.). (2007). *Successful principal leadership in times of change: An international perspective* (Vol. 5). Dordrecht: Springer.

Deci, E. L., & Ryan, R. M. (1985). *Intrinsic motivation and self-determination in human behavior.* New York: Plenum Publishing Corporation.

Decuypere, M., & Simons, M. (2016). Relational thinking in education: Topology, sociomaterial studies, and figures. *Pedagogy, Culture & Society, 24*(3), 371–86. doi:10.1080/14681366.2016.1166150

Dehaene, S. (2019). How we learn: Building bridges between neuroscience and education. *IBRO Reports, 6,* S2. doi.org/10.1016/j.ibror.2019.07.169

Demir, E. K. (2021). The role of social capital for teacher professional learning and student achievement: A systematic literature review. *Educational Research Review, 33*, 100391. doi.org/10.1016/j.edurev.2021.100391

DeRue, D. S., & Ashford, S. J. (2010). Who will lead and who will follow? A social process of leadership identity construction in organizations. *Academy of Management Review, 35*(4), 627–47.

Descartes, R. (1637/1968). *Discourse on method and the meditations.* London: Penguin UK.

Dewey, J. (1900). *The school and society.* Chicago: University of Chicago Press.

Dewey, J. (1916/2011). *Democracy and education: An introduction to the philosophy of education.* Milton Keynes: Simon & Brown.

Dewey, J. (1937/1987). The challenge of democracy to education. In J. A. Boydston (Ed.), *John Dewey, The later works, Vol 11* (pp. 181–90). Carbondale: Southern Illinois University Press.

Dewey, J. (1954). *The public and its problems.* Denver: Swallow Press.

Dewey, J. (1958 [1929]). *Experience and nature.* New York: Dover Publications.

DfE. (2011). *Permanent and fixed period exclusions from schools and exclusion appeals in England, 2009/10* (SFR 17/2011). London: DfE.

DfE. (2019a). *Permanent and fixed period exclusions in England: 2017 to 2018.* London: Dfe.

DfE. (2019b). *Pupil absence in schools in England: Autumn term.* London: Dfe.

DfE. (2019c). *School workforce in England: November 2018.* London: Dfe.

DfE. (2020a). *Permanent and fixed-period exclusions in England: 2018 to 2019.* London: DfE.

DfE. (2020b). *School workforce in England.* London: DfE.

DfE. (2020c). *Schools, pupils and their characteristics.* London: DfE.

DfE. (2021a). Proposals to drive up training standards for teachers. Retrieved from www.gov.uk/government/news/proposals-to-drive-up-training-standards-for-teachers

DfE. (2021b). *Transparency data: Open academies, free schools, studio schools and UTCs.* London: DfE.

Dibben, M. R., Morris, S. E., & Lean, M. E. (2000). Situational trust and co-operative partnerships between physicians and their patients: A theoretical explanation transferable from business practice. *QJM, 93*(1), 55–61.

Di Fabio, A. (2017). Positive healthy organizations: Promoting well-being, meaningfulness, and sustainability in organizations. *Frontiers in Psychology, 8*(1938). doi.org/10.3389/fpsyg.2017.01938

DiGiovanna, J. (2015). Literally like a different person: Context and concern in personal identity. *The Southern Journal of Philosophy, 53*(4), 387–404. doi:10.1111/sjp.12155

Diller, A. (2018). The ethics of care and education: A new paradigm, its critics, and its educational significance. *Curriculum Inquiry, 18*(3), 325–42. doi.org/10.2307/1179833

Dorling, D. (2015). Income inequality in the UK: Comparisons with five large Western European countries and the USA. *Applied Geography, 61*, 24–34.

Dorling, D. (2018). Peak inequality. *New Statesman,* 30–5. Retrieved from www.dannydorling.org/wp-content/files/dannydorling_publication_id6678.pdf

Dorling, D., & Tomlinson, S. (2016). The creation of inequality: Myths of potential and ability. *Journal of Critical Education Policy Studies, 14*(3), 56–79. Retrieved from www.jceps.com/

Downer, J. T., Locasale-Crouch, J., Hamre, B., & Pianta, R. (2009). Teacher characteristics associated with responsiveness and exposure to consultation and online professional development resources. *Early Education and Development, 20*(3), 431–55.

Dudley-Marling, C. (2020). School choice and inclusive education. In G.W. Noblit (Ed.), *Oxford research encyclopedia of education*. doi.org/10.1093/acrefore/9780190264093.013.1241

Duffy, G., & Gallagher, T. (2014). Sustaining school partnerships: The context of cross-sectoral collaboration between schools in a separate education system in Northern Ireland. *Review of Education, 2*(2), 189–210. doi.org/10.1002/rev3.3034

Duncan, G. (1983). *Democratic theory and practice* (G. Duncan Ed.). Cambridge: Cambridge University Press.

Eddleston, A., & Atkinson, C. (2018). Using professional practice frameworks to evaluate consultation. *Educational Psychology in Practice, 34*(4), 430–49. doi:10.1080/02667363.2018.1509542

Edwards, A. (2007). Relational agency in professional practice: A CHAT analysis. *Actio: An International Journal of Human Activity Theory, 1*, 1–17.

Edwards, A. (2011). Building common knowledge at the boundaries between professional practices: Relational agency and relational expertise in systems of distributed expertise. *International Journal of Educational Research, 50*(1), 33–9. doi.org/10.1016/j.ijer.2011.04.007

Edwards, A. (2015). Recognising and realising teachers' professional agency. *Teachers and Teaching, 21*(6), 779–84. doi:10.1080/13540602.2015.1044333

Edwards, A., Lunt, I., & Stamou, E. (2010). Inter-professional work and expertise: New roles at the boundaries of schools. *British Educational Research Journal, 36*(1), 27–45.

Edwards, R., & Fowler, Z. (2007). Unsettling boundaries in making a space for research. *British Educational Research Journal, 33*(1), 107–23. doi:10.1080/01411920601104565

Ehrich, L. C., Harris, J., Klenowski, V., Smeed, J., & Spina, N. (2015). The centrality of ethical leadership. *Journal of Educational Administration, 53*(2), 197–214. doi:10.1108/JEA-10-2013-0110

Eisner, E. (2014). What can education learn from the arts about the practice of education? *International Journal of Education & the Arts, 5*(4), Retrieved [September 6, 2021] from www.ijea.org/v2025n2024/

Eldor, L., & Shoshani, A. (2016). Caring relationships in school staff: Exploring the link between compassion and teacher work engagement. *Teaching and Teacher Education, 59*, 126–36. doi.org/10.1016/j.tate.2016.06.001

Elias, A., Ben, J., Mansouri, F., & Paradies, Y. (2021). Racism and nationalism during and beyond the COVID-19 pandemic. *Ethnic and Racial Studies, 44*(5), 783–93. doi:10.1080/01419870.2020.1851382

Ellis, V., Mansell, W., & Steadman, S. (2021). A new political economy of teacher development: England's Teaching and Leadership Innovation Fund. *Journal of Education Policy, 36*(5), 605–23. doi:10.1080/02680939.2020.1717001

Emirbayer, M., & Mische, A. (1998). What is agency? *American Journal of Sociology, 103*(4), 962–1023. doi:10.1086/231294

Engeström, Y. (1987). *Learning by expanding*. Cambridge: Cambridge University Press.

Engeström, Y. (1999). Activity theory and individual and social transformation. In Y. Engeström, R. Miettinen, & R.-L. Punamaki (Eds.), *Perspectives on activity theory* (pp. 19–37). Cambridge: Cambridge University Press.

Engeström, Y. (2007a). From communities of practice to mycorrhizae. In J. Hughes, N. Jewson & L. Unwin (Eds.), *Communities of practice: Critical perspectives* (pp. 42–54). Abingdon: Routledge.

Engeström, Y. (2007b). From stabilization knowledge to possibility knowledge in organizational learning. *Management Learning, 38*(3), 271–5. doi:10.1177/1350507607079026

Engeström,Y., Engeström, R., & Kärkkäinen, M. (1995). Polycontextuality and boundary crossing in expert cognition: Learning and problem solving in complex work activities. Learning and Instruction, *5*(4), 319–6. doi:10.1016/0959-4752(95)00021-6

Eraut, M. (2000). Non-formal learning and tacit knowledge in professional work. *British Journal of Educational Psychology, 70*(1), 113–36. doi:10.1348/000709900158001

Farrar, J., & Ahuja, A. (2021). *Spike: The virus vs the people; the inside story.* London: Profile Books.

Figg, J., & Gibbs, S. (1990). I'm an EP – I think! – The development of intra-team support processes. *Educational and Child Psychology, 7*(2), 82–90.

Figg, J., & Stoker, R. (1989). A school consultation service: A strategy of referral management leading to second order change. *Educational and Child Psychology, 6*, 34–42.

Figlio, D. N., & Getzler, L. S. (2006). *Accountability, ability and disability: Gaming the system?* Bingley: Emerald Group Publishing Limited.

Fogel, A., de Koeyer, I., Bellagamba, F., & Bell, H. (2002). The dialogical self in the first two years of life. *Theory & Psychology, 12*(2), 191–205. doi:10.1177/0959354302012002629

Forman, S. G. (1995). Organizational factors and consultation outcome. *Journal of Educational and Psychological Consultation, 6*(2), 191–5. doi.org/10.1207/s1532768xjepc0602_7

Forman, S. G., Shapiro, E. S., Codding, R. S., Gonzales, J. E., Reddy, L. A., Rosenfield, S. A., ... Stoiber, K. C. (2013). Implementation science and school psychology. *School Psychology Quarterly, 28*(2), 77. doi:10.1037/spq0000019

Foucault, M. (1977). *Discipline and punish* (Alan Sheridan, Trans.). New York: Pantheon.

Foucault, M. (1982). The subject and power. *Critical Inquiry, 8*(4), 777–95. doi:10.1086/448181

Foucault, M. (2002). *The order of things: An archaeology of the human sciences.* Abingdon: Routledge.

Fox, A. R. C., & Wilson, E. G. (2015). Networking and the development of professionals: Beginning teachers building social capital. *Teaching and Teacher Education, 47*, 93–107. doi:10.1016/j.tate.2014.12.004

Frank, K. A., Zhao, Y., & Borman, K. (2004). Social capital and the diffusion of innovations within organizations: The case of computer technology in schools. *Sociology of Education, 77*(2), 148–71. doi:10.1177/003804070407700203

Fredriksson, L., & Eriksson, K. (2003). The ethics of the caring conversation. *Nursing Ethics, 10*(2), 138–48. doi:10.1191/0969733003ne588oa

Frowe, I. (2001). Language and educational practice. *Cambridge Journal of Education, 31*(1), 89–101.

Fuller, A., Hodkinson, H., Hodkinson, P., & Unwin, L. (2005). Learning as peripheral participation in communities of practice: A reassessment of key concepts in workplace learning. *British Educational Research Journal, 31*(1), 49–68. doi:10.1080/0141192052000310029

Fuller, K. (2019). "That would be my red line": An analysis of headteachers' resistance of neoliberal education reforms. *Educational Review, 71*(1), 31–50. doi:10.1080/00131911.2019.1522042

Fulton, P. R. (2008). Anatta: Self, non-self, and the therapist. In S. F. Hick & T. Bien (Eds.), *Mindfulness and the therapeutic relationship* (pp. 55–71). London: Guilford Press.

García-Moya, I., Brooks, F., & Moreno, C. (2020). Humanizing and conducive to learning: An adolescent students' perspective on the central attributes of positive relationships with teachers. *European Journal of Psychology of Education, 35*(1), 1–20. doi:10.1007/s10212-019-00413-z

Gardner, D. M., & Ryan, A. M. (2020). What's in it for you? Demographics and self-interest perceptions in diversity promotion. *Journal of Applied Psychology, 105*(9), 1062–72. doi:10.1037/apl0000478

Gatto, J.T. (2002). *Dumbing us down: The hidden curriculum of compulsory schooling.* Gabriola Island, BC, Canada: New Society Publishers.

Gayle, B. M., Cortez, D., & Preiss, R. W. (2013). Safe spaces, difficult dialogues, and critical thinking. *International Journal for the Scholarship of Teaching & Learning, 7*(2), 1–8.

Gee, J. P. (1990). *Social linguistics and literacies: Ideology in discourses.* Philadelphia: Falmer Press.

Geijsel, F., Sleegers, P., Leithwood, K., & Jantzi, D. (2003). Transformational leadership effects on teachers' commitment and effort toward school reform. *Journal of Educational Administration, 41*(3), 228–56. doi: 10.1108/09578230310474403

Gergen, K. J. (1991). *The emergence of the relational self.* New York: Basic Books.

Gergen, K. J. (2009). *Relational being: Beyond self and community.* Oxford: Oxford University Press.

Gibbs, S. (2018a). *Immoral education: The assault on teachers' identity, autonomy and efficacy.* Abingdon: Routledge.

Gibbs, S. (2018b). Inclusion and teachers' beliefs in their efficacy. In L. Rycroft-Smith & J. L. Dutaut (Eds.), *Flip the system UK: A teachers' manifesto* (pp. 127–38). Abingdon: Routledge.

Gibbs, S. (2021). It may take a while… but do we know where we want to get to with education? 1. A brief partial history of education. *Debate, 180,* 8–12.

Gibbs, S. (2022). It could take some time… but do we know where we want to go with education? 2. A philosophical perspective on aspects of education in Britain. *Debate, 181,* 12–8.

Gibbs, S., Atkinson, C., Woods, K., Bond, C., Hill, V., Howe, J., & Morris, S. (2016). Supervision for school psychologists in training: Developing a framework from empirical findings. *School Psychology International, 37*(4), 410–31. doi:10.1177/0143034316653443

Gibbs, S., Beckmann, J. F., Elliott, J., Metsäpelto, R.-L., Vehkakoski, T., & Aro, M. (2020). What's in a name: The effect of category labels on teachers' beliefs. *European Journal of Special Needs Education, 35*(1), 115–27.

Gibbs, S., & Elliott, J. (2015). The differential effects of labelling: How do 'dyslexia' and 'reading difficulties' affect teachers' beliefs. *European Journal of Special Needs Education, 30*(3), 323–37.

Gibbs, S., & Miller, A. (2014). Teachers' resilience and well-being: A role for educational psychology. *Teachers and Teaching, 20,* 609–21. doi:10.1080/13540602.2013.844408

Gibbs, S., & Papps, I. (2017). Identifying the costs and benefits of educational psychology: A preliminary exploration in two local authorities. *Educational Psychology in Practice, 33*(1), 81–92. doi:10.1080/02667363.2016.1233489

Gibbs, S., & Powell, B. (2012). Teacher efficacy and pupil behaviour: The structure of teachers' individual and collective efficacy beliefs and their relationship with numbers of children excluded from school. *British Journal of Educational Psychology, 82*(4), 564–84. doi:10.1111/j.2044-8279.2011.02046.x

Giles, J. (1993). The no-self theory: Hume, Buddhism, and personal identity. *Philosophy East and West, 43*(2), 175–200. doi:10.2307/1399612

Glaeser, E. L., Ponzetto, G. A., & Shleifer, A. (2007). Why does democracy need education? *Journal of Economic Growth, 12*(2), 77–99. doi:10.1007/s10887-007-9015-1

Glaesser, J., & Cooper, B. (2012). Educational achievement in selective and comprehensive local education authorities: A configurational analysis. *British Journal of Sociology of Education, 33*(2), 223–44. doi:10.1080/01425692.2011.649833

Goddard, C., & Bedi, G. (2010). Intimate partner violence and child abuse: A child-centred perspective. *Child Abuse Review: Journal of the British Association for the Study and Prevention of Child Abuse and Neglect, 19*(1), 5–20.

Goddard, R., & Goddard, Y. L. (2001). A multilevel analysis of the relationship between teacher and collective efficacy in urban schools. *Teaching and Teacher Education, 17*(7), 807–18. doi:10.1016/s0742-051x(01)00032-4

Goffman, E. (1967/2005). *Interaction ritual: Essays on face-to-face interaction.* New Brunswick: Transaction Publishers.

Good, T. L., & Lavigne, A. L. (2015). Rating teachers cheaper, faster, and better: Not so fast. *Journal of Teacher Education, 66*(3), 288–93. doi:10.1177/0022487115574292

Gorard, S., & Siddiqui, N. (2018). Grammar schools in England: A new analysis of social segregation and academic outcomes. *British Journal of Sociology of Education, 39*(7), 909–24. doi:10.1080/01425692.2018.1443432

Greany, T., & Waterhouse, J. (2016). Rebels against the system. *International Journal of Educational Management, 30*(7), 1188–206. doi:10.1108/IJEM-11-2015-0148

Green, F., Parsons, S., Sullivan, A., & Wiggins, R. (2017). Dreaming big? Self-valuations, aspirations, networks and the private-school earnings premium. *Cambridge Journal of Economics, 42*(3), 757–78. doi:10.1093/cje/bex023

Greenfield, L. (2012). Nationalism. In G. Ritzer (Ed.), *The Wiley-Blackwell encyclopedia of globalization.* Oxford: Blackwell.

Grossen, M. (2010). Interaction analysis and psychology: A dialogical perspective. *Integrative Psychological and Behavioral Science, 44*(1), 1–22. doi:10.1007/s12124-009-9108-9

Grossen, M., & Salazar Orvig, A. (2011). Dialogism and dialogicality in the study of the self. *Culture & Psychology, 17*(4), 491–509.

Grossman, P., Wineburg, S., & Woolworth, S. (2001). Toward a theory of teacher community. *Teachers College Record, 103*(6), 942–1012.

Grych, J., & Swan, S. (2012). Toward a more comprehensive understanding of interpersonal violence: Introduction to the special issue on interconnections among different types of violence. *Psychology of Violence, 2*(2), 105–10. doi:10.1037/a0027616

Gülerce, A. (2014). Selfing as, with, and without othering: Dialogical (im)possibilities with dialogical self theory. *Culture & Psychology, 20*(2), 244–55. doi:10.1177/1354067x14526897

Gunter, H. M., & Forrester, G. (2009). School leadership and education policy-making in England. *Policy Studies, 30*(5), 495–511. doi:10.1080/01442870902899947

Gutkin, T. B. (2012). Ecological psychology: Replacing the medical model paradigm for school-based psychological and psychoeducational services. *Journal of Educational and Psychological Consultation, 22*(1–2), 1–20. doi:10.1080/10474412.2011.649652

Haack, S. (2010). The differences that make a difference. William James on the importance of individuals. *European Journal of Pragmatism and American Philosophy, 2*(II-1), 1–12

Haney, C., Banks, C., & Zimbardo, P. (1972). *Interpersonal dynamics in a simulated prison.* Retrieved from https://apps.dtic.mil/dtic/tr/fulltext/u2/751041.pdf

Hanko, G. (1985). *Special needs in ordinary classrooms.* Oxford: Blackwell.

Hanko, G. (2002). Making psychodynamic insights accessible to teachers as an integral part of their professional task. *Psychodynamic Practice, 8*(3), 375–89. doi:10.1080/1353333021000018980

Hanko, G. (2003). Towards an inclusive school culture – but what happened to Elton's 'affective curriculum'? *British Journal of Special Education, 30*(3), 125–31. doi:10.1111/1467-8527.00297

Hansen, D. T. (2016). *The teacher and the world: A study of cosmopolitanism as education.* Abingdon: Routledge.

Harding, S., Morris, R., Gunnell, D., Ford, T., Hollingworth, W., Tilling, K., ... Kidger, J. (2019). Is teachers' mental health and wellbeing associated with students' mental health and wellbeing? A cross sectional study. *Journal of Affective Disorders, 242,* 180–7. doi:10.1016/j.jad.2018.08.080

Hargreaves, A. (2004). Inclusive and exclusive educational change: Emotional responses of teachers and implications for leadership. *School Leadership & Management, 24*(3), 287–309.

Hargreaves, A., & Fink, D. (2012). *Sustainable leadership.* San Francisco: Jossey-Bass.

Hargreaves, A., & Skelton, J. (2012). Politics and systems of coaching and mentoring. In S. J. Fletcher & C. A. Mullen (Eds.), *The Sage handbook of mentoring and coaching in education* (pp. 122–38). London: Sage.

Harris, A. (2004). Editorial: School leadership and school improvement: A simple and complex relationship. *School Leadership & Management, 24*(1), 3–5. doi:10.1080/1363243042000172778

Harris, A., & DeFlaminis, J. (2016). Distributed leadership in practice: Evidence, misconceptions and possibilities. *Management in Education, 30*(4), 141–6. doi:10.1177/0892020616656734

Harris, J., Carrington, S., & Ainscow, M. (2017). *Promoting equity in schools: Collaboration, inquiry and ethical leadership.* Abingdon: Routledge.

Haslam, S. A., & Reicher, S. D. (2012). Contesting the "nature" of conformity: What Milgram and Zimbardo's studies really show. *PLoS Biology, 10*(11), e1001426.

Haslam, S. A., Reicher, S. D., & Platow, M. J. (2020). *The new psychology of leadership: Identity, influence and power* (2nd ed.). Abingdon: Routledge.

Hatcher, P. J., Hulme, C., Miles, J. N., Carroll, J. M., Hatcher, J., Gibbs, S., ... Snowling, M. J. (2006). Efficacy of small group reading intervention for beginning readers with reading-delay: A randomised controlled trial. *Journal of Child Psychology and Psychiatry, 47*(8), 820–7. doi:10.1111/j.1469-7610.2005.01559.x

Hayashi, M., Raymond, G., & Sidnell, J. (2013). *Conversational repair and human understanding.* Cambridge: Cambridge University Press.

Hayden, M. J. (2017). The process matters: Moral constraints on cosmopolitan education. *Journal of Philosophy of Education, 51*(1), 248–66. doi:10.1111/1467-9752.12210

Hayes, M., & Stringer, P. (2016). Introducing Farouk's process consultation group approach in Irish primary schools. *Educational Psychology in Practice, 32*(2), 145–62. doi:10.1080/02667363.2015.1129939

Hedegaard-Soerensen, L., & Grumloese, S. P. (2020). Exclusion: The downside of neoliberal education policy. *International Journal of Inclusive Education, 24*(6), 631–44. doi:10.1080/13603116.2018.1478002

Hermans, H. J. M. (2013). The dialogical self in education: Introduction. *Journal of Constructivist Psychology, 26*(2), 81–9. doi:10.1080/10720537.2013.759018

Hermans, H. J. M. (2015). Dialogical self in a complex world: The need for bridging theories. *Europe's Journal of Psychology, 11*(1), 1–4. doi:10.5964/ejop.v11i1.917

Hermans, H. J. M., Kempen, H. J., & Van Loon, R. J. (1992). The dialogical self: Beyond individualism and rationalism. *American Psychologist, 47*(1), 23. Retrieved from https://bit.ly/3pv2YPh

Hirsch, E. D. (1996). *The schools we need: And why we don't have them.* New York: Doubleday.

Hodge, N., & Wolstenholme, C. (2016). 'I didn't stand a chance': How parents experience the exclusions appeal tribunal. *International Journal of Inclusive Education, 20*(12), 1297–309. doi:10.1080/13603116.2016.1168875

Hofman, R. H., & Dijkstra, B. J. (2010). Effective teacher professionalization in networks? *Teaching and Teacher Education, 26*(4), 1031–40. doi:10.1016/j.tate.2009.10.046

Hogg, M. A. (2016). Social identity theory. In S. McKeown, R. Haji, & N. Ferguson (Eds.), *Understanding peace and conflict through social identity theory: Contemporary global perspectives* (pp. 3–17). Cham: Springer International Publishing.

Hogg, M. A., & Terry, D. I. (2000). Social identity and self-categorization processes in organizational contexts. *Academy of Management Review, 25*(1), 121–40.

Holdstock, L. (1993). Can we afford not to revision the person-centred concept of self. In D. Brazier (Ed.), *Beyond Carl Rogers* (pp. 229–52). London: Constable.

Holmberg, I., & Akerblom, S. (2008). "Primus Inter Pares": Leadership and culture in Sweden. In J. S. Chhokar, F. C. Brodbeck, & R. J. House (Eds.), *Culture and leadership across the world* (pp. 33–74). Abingdon: Lawrence Erlbaum Associates.

Hook, D. (2008). Absolute other: Lacan's 'big other' as adjunct to critical social psychological analysis? *Social and Personality Psychology Compass, 2*(1), 51–73. doi:10.1111/j.1751-9004.2007.00067.x

Horn, I. S. (2007). Fast kids, slow kids, lazy kids: Framing the mismatch problem in mathematics teachers' conversations. *Journal of the Learning Sciences, 16*(1), 37–79. doi:10.1080/10508400709336942

Horn, I. S., Garner, B., Kane, B. D., & Brasel, J. (2016). A taxonomy of instructional learning opportunities in teachers' workgroup conversations. *Journal of Teacher Education, 68*(1), 41–54. doi:10.1177/0022487116676315

Horn, I. S., Garner, B., Kane, B. D., & Brasel, J. (2017). A taxonomy of instructional learning opportunities in teachers' workgroup conversations. *Journal of Teacher Education, 68*(1), 41–54.

Horn, I. S., & Little, J. W. (2010). Attending to problems of practice: Routines and resources for professional learning in teachers' workplace interactions. *American Educational Research Journal, 47*(1), 181–217. doi:10.3102/0002831209345158

Hoy, W. K., & Woolfolk, A. E. (1993). Teachers' sense of efficacy and the organizational health of schools. *The Elementary School Journal, 93*(4), 355–72. Retrieved from www.jstor.org/stable/1002017

Hrdy, S. B. (2011). *Mothers and others.* Cambridge, MA: Harvard University Press.

Huang, S., Yin, H., & Lv, L. (2019). Job characteristics and teacher well-being: The mediation of teacher self-monitoring and teacher self-efficacy. *Educational Psychology, 39*(3), 313–31. doi:10.1080/01443410.2018.1543855

Illeris, K. (2007). *How we learn: Learning and non-learning in school and beyond.* London: Routledge.

Illeris, K. (2009). A comprehensive understanding of human learning. In K. Illeris (Ed.), *Contemporary theories of learning: Learning theorists… in their own words* (pp. 7–20). Abingdon: Oxford.

Janaway, C. (1989). *Self and world in Schopenhauer's philosophy.* Oxford: Oxford University Press.

Jeffrey, B., & Woods, P. (1998). *Testing teachers: The effect of school inspections on primary teachers.* London: Routledge.

Jerrim, J., & Sims, S. (2019). Why do so few low- and middle-income children attend a grammar school? New evidence from the Millennium Cohort Study. *British Educational Research Journal, 45*(3), 425–57. doi:10.1002/berj.3502

Jha, N. K. (2020). School choice and marginalization: The case of school district competition and political institutions in the US. *Journal of Applied Educational and Policy Research, 5*(1), 110–48.

Jian, G. (2021). From empathic leader to empathic leadership practice: An extension to relational leadership theory. *Human Relations*, 0018726721998450. doi:10.1177/0018726721998450

Jordan, A., Schwartz, E., & McGhie-Richmond, D. (2009). Preparing teachers for inclusive classrooms. *Teaching and Teacher Education, 25*(4), 535–42. doi:10.1016/j.tate.2009.02.010

Jordan, A., & Stanovich, P. J. (2004). Inclusion as professional development. *Exceptionality Education Canada, 14*(2&3), 169–88.

Kagitcibasi, C. (2005). Autonomy and relatedness in cultural context. *Journal of Cross-cultural Psychology, 36*(4), 403–22. doi:10.1177/0022022105275959

Kahneman, D. (2011). *Thinking, fast and slow.* London: Allen Lane.

Källström, Å., Hellfeldt, K., & Nylander, P.-Å. (2019). Parental imprisonment, child victimization and adult problems. *European Journal of Criminology, 16*(6), 671–88. doi:10.1177/1477370818775286

Keddie, A. (2016). Children of the market: Performativity, neoliberal responsibilisation and the construction of student identities. *Oxford Review of Education, 42*(1), 108–22. doi:10.1080/03054985.2016.1142865

Kelly, A. V. (2009). *The curriculum: Theory and practice* (6th ed.). London: Sage.

Kennedy, D. (1999). Philosophy for children and the reconstruction of philosophy. *Metaphilosophy, 30*(4), 338–59. doi:10.1111/1467-9973.00142

Kennedy, D. (2004). The role of a facilitator in a community of philosophical inquiry. *Metaphilosophy, 35*(5), 744–65.

Kennedy, M. (2005). *Inside teaching: Classroom conditions that frustrate reform.* Cambridge: Harvard University Press.

Kidger, J., Brockman, R., Tilling, K., Campbell, R., Ford, T., Araya, R., ... Gunnell, D. (2016). Teachers' wellbeing and depressive symptoms, and associated risk factors: A large cross sectional study in English secondary schools. *Journal of Affective Disorders, 192*, 76–82. doi:10.1016/j.jad.2015.11.054

Kirschenbaum, H., & Henderson, V. L. (Eds.). (1989). *Carl Rogers: Dialogues: Conversations with Martin Buber, Paul Tillich, BF Skinner, Gregory Bateson, Michael Polanyi, Rollo May, and others.* Boston: Houghton, Mifflin and Company.

Kokkinaki, T. S., Vasdekis, V. G. S., Koufaki, Z. E., & Trevarthen, C. B. (2017). Coordination of emotions in mother–infant dialogues. *Infant and Child Development, 26*(2), e1973. doi:10.1002/icd.1973

Korthagen, F. A. (2010). Situated learning theory and the pedagogy of teacher education: Towards an integrative view of teacher behavior and teacher learning. *Teaching and Teacher Education, 26*(1), 98–106. doi:10.1016/j.tate.2009.05.001

Kulz, C. (2019). Mapping folk devils old and new through permanent exclusion from London schools. *Race Ethnicity and Education, 22*(1), 93–109. doi:10.1080/13613324.2018.1497961

Kutz, C. (2000). Acting together. *Philosophy and Phenomenological Research, 61*(1), 1–31. doi:10.2307/2653401

Kwon, K.-A., Ford, T. G., Salvatore, A. L., Randall, K., Jeon, L., Malek-Lasater, A., ... Han, M. (2020). Neglected elements of a high-quality early childhood workforce: Whole teacher well-being and working conditions. *Early Childhood Education Journal, 50,* 157–68. doi:10.1007/s10643-020-01124-7

Lama, D. (2000). The true source of political success. In S. Kaza & K. Kraft (Eds.), *Dharma rain: Sources of Buddhist environmentalism* (pp. 165–9). London: Shambhala.

Lave, J. (2009). The practice of learning. In K. Illeris (Ed.), *Contemporary theories of learning: Learning theorists… in their own words* (pp. 200–8). Abingdon: Routledge.

Lave, J. (2019). *Learning and everyday life.* Cambridge: Cambridge University Press.

Lave, J., & Wenger, E. (1991). *Situated learning: Legitimate peripheral participation.* Cambridge: Cambridge University Press.

Leadbetter, J., Daniels, H., Edwards, A., Martin, D., Middleton, D., Popova, A., ... Brown, S. (2007). Professional learning within multi-agency children's services: Researching into practice. *Educational Research, 49*(1), 83–98. doi:10.1080/00131880701200815

Leat, D., Lofthouse, R., & Taverner, S. (2006). The road taken: Professional pathways in innovative curriculum development. *Teachers and Teaching, 12*(6), 657–74. doi:10.1080/13540600601029686

Leat, D., Lofthouse, R., & Towler, C. (2012). Improving coaching by and for school teachers. In S. J. Fletcher & C. A. Mullen (Eds.), *The Sage handbook of mentoring and coaching in education* (pp. 43–58). London: Sage.

Leat, D., & Nichols, A. (2000). Observing pupils' mental strategies: Signposts for scaffolding. *International Research in Geographical and Environmental Education, 9*(1), 19–35.

Legrand, D., & Ruby, P. (2009). What is self-specific? Theoretical investigation and critical review of neuroimaging results. *Psychological Review, 116*(1), 252. doi:10.1037/a0014172

Leithwood, K., & Sun, J. (2012). The nature and effects of transformational school leadership. *Educational Administration Quarterly, 48*(3), 387–423. doi:10.1177/0013161X11436268

Levin, B., & Riffel, A. (2019). *Schools and the changing world.* London: Routledge.

Levinas, E. (1985). *Ethics and infinity: Conversations with Philippe Nemo* (R. A. Cohen, Trans.). Pittsburgh: Duquesne University Press.

Levinas, E. (1987). *Time and the other* (R. A. Cohen, Trans.). Pittsburgh: Duquesne University Press.

Levinas, E., & Nemo, P. (1985). *Ethics and infinity.* R. A. Cohen, Translator. Pittsburg: Duquesne University Press.

Levine, M., Prosser, A., Evans, D., & Reicher, S. (2005). Identity and emergency intervention: How social group membership and inclusiveness of group boundaries shape helping behavior. *Personality and Social Psychology Bulletin, 31*(4), 443–53. doi:10.1177/0146167204271651

Lewicki, R. J., & Bunker, B. B. (1995). Trust in relationships: A model of development and decline. In B. B. Bunker & J. Z. Rubin (Eds.), *Conflict, cooperation, and justice: Essays inspired by the work of Morton Deutsch* (pp. 133–73). Hoboken: Jossey-Bass/Wiley.

Li, S. C., & Choi, T. H. (2014). Does social capital matter? A quantitative approach to examining technology infusion in schools. *Journal of Computer Assisted Learning, 30*(1), 1–16. doi:10.1111/jcal.12010

Linell, P. (2009). *Rethinking language, mind, and world dialogically: Interactional and contextual theories of human sense-making.* Charlotte: Information Age Publishing Inc.

Lingis, A. (1994). *The community of those who have nothing in common.* Indianapolis: Indiana University Press.

Lipman, M., Sharp, A. M., & Oscanyan, F. S. (1980). *Philosophy in the classroom.* Philadelphia: Temple University Press.

Little, J. (1990). The persistence of privacy: Autonomy and initiative in teachers. *Teachers College Record, 10*(4), 509–36.

Little, J. W. (2002). Professional community and the problem of high school reform. *International Journal of Educational Research, 37*(8), 693–714. doi:10.1016/S0883-0355(03)00066-1

Littleton, K., & Mercer, N. (2013). *Interthinking: Putting talk to work.* Abingdon: Routledge.

Lofthouse, R., & Hall, E. (2014). Developing practices in teachers' professional dialogue in England: Using coaching dimensions as an epistemic tool. *Professional Development in Education, 40*(5), 758–78. doi:10.1080/19415257.2014.886283

Lofthouse, R., & Leat, D. (2013). An activity theory perspective on peer coaching. *International Journal of Mentoring and Coaching in Education, 2*(1), 8–20. doi:10.1108/20466851311323050

Lofthouse, R., Leat, D., & Towler, C. (2010). *Coaching for teaching and learning: A practical guide for schools.* Reading: CfBT Education Trust.

Louis, K. S., & Kruse, S. D. (1995). *Professionalism and community: Perspectives on reforming urban schools.* Thousand Oaks: Corwin Press.

Lumby, J. (2009). Performativity and identity: Mechanisms of exclusion. *Journal of Education Policy, 24*(3), 353–69. doi:10.1080/02680930802669284

Lupton, R., & Hempel-Jorgensen, A. (2012). The importance of teaching: Pedagogical constraints and possibilities in working-class schools. *Journal of Education Policy, 27*(5), 601–20. doi:10.1080/02680939.2012.710016

Lyotard, J.-F. (1984). *The postmodern condition: A report on knowledge* (Vol. 10). Manchester: Manchester University Press.

MacBeath, J. (2009). Recruitment and retention of senior school leaders: Meeting the challenge. *European Educational Research Journal, 8*(3), 407–17. doi:10.2304/eerj.2009.8.3.407

Macmurray, J. (1957/1991). *The self as agent.* Atlantic Highlands: Humanities Press.

Macmurray, J. (1958/2012). Learning to be human. *Oxford Review of Education, 38*(6), 661–74. doi:10.1080/03054985.2012.745958

Macmurray, J. (1961). *Persons in relation.* London: Faber & Faber.

Maele, D.V., & Houtte, M.V. (2011). Collegial trust and the organizational context of the teacher workplace: The role of a homogeneous teachability culture. *American Journal of Education, 117*(4), 437–64. doi:10.1086/660754

Mandel, D. R. (2005). Threats to democracy: A judgment and decision-making perspective. *Analyses of Social Issues and Public Policy, 5*(1), 209–22.

Marková, I. (2003). Constitution of the self: Intersubjectivity and dialogicality. *Culture & Psychology, 9*(3), 249–59. doi:10.1177/1354067X030093006

Marková, I. (2016). *The dialogical mind: Common sense and ethics.* Cambridge: Cambridge University Press.

Marková, I., Linell, P., Grossen, M., & Salazar Orvig, A. (2007). *Dialogue in focus groups: Exploring socially shared knowledge.* London: Equinox publishing.

Markus, H. R., & Kitayama, S. (1991). Culture and the self: Implications for cognition, emotion, and motivation. *Psychological Review, 98*(2), 224–53. doi:10.1037/0033-295X.98.2.224

Massey, D. (1993). Power-geometry and a progressive sense of place. In J. Bird, T. Curtis, T. Putnam, & L. Tinker (Eds.), *Mapping the futures: Local cultures, global change* (pp. 59–69). London: Routledge.

Matusov, E. (2011). Irreconcilable differences in Vygotsky's and Bakhtin's approaches to the social and the individual: An educational perspective. *Culture & Psychology, 17*(1), 99–119.

Mayworm, A. M., Sharkey, J. D., Hunnicutt, K. L., & Schiedel, K. C. (2016). Teacher consultation to enhance implementation of school-based restorative justice. *Journal of Educational and Psychological Consultation, 26*(4), 385–412. doi:10.1080/10474412.2016.1196364

McKernan, J. (2007). *Curriculum and imagination: Process theory, pedagogy and action research.* Abingdon: Routledge.

McLean, L., Abry, T., Taylor, M., Jimenez, M., & Granger, K. (2017). Teachers' mental health and perceptions of school climate across the transition from training to teaching. *Teaching and Teacher Education, 65*, 230–40. http://doi.org/10.1016/j.tate.2017.03.018

McNamee, S., & Hosking, D. M. (2012). *Research and social change: A relational constructionist approach.* New York: Routledge.

Medway, F. J., & Updyke, J. F. (1985). Meta-analysis of consultation outcome studies. *American Journal of Community Psychology, 13*(5), 489–505.

Meglino, B. M., & Korsgaard, A. (2004). Considering rational self-interest as a disposition: Organizational implications of other orientation. *Journal of Applied Psychology, 89*(6), 946.

Meier, C., & Lemmer, E. (2019). Parents as consumers: A case study of parent satisfaction with the quality of schooling. *Educational Review, 71*(5), 617–30. doi:10.1080/00131911.2018.1465395

Mezirow, J. (1997). Transformative learning: Theory to practice. *New Directions for Adult and Continuing Education, 1997*(74), 5–12.

Michael, J. (2014). Towards a consensus about the role of empathy in interpersonal understanding. *Topoi, 33*(1), 157–72. Retrieved from http://au.academia.edu/John Michael

Michaels, C. A., & Ferrara, D. L. (2009). Promoting post-school success for all: The role of collaboration in person-centered transition planning. *Journal of Educational and Psychological Consultation, 16*(4), 287–313. doi:10.1207/s1532768Xjepc1604_4

Midgley, G. (1992). The sacred and profane in critical systems thinking. *Systems Practice, 5*(1), 5–16.

Mifsud, M. L., & Johnson, S. D. (2000). Dialogic, dialectic, and rhetoric: Exploring human dialogue across the discipline. *Southern Communication Journal, 65*(2–3), 91–104. doi:10.1080/10417940009373160

Mikulincer, M. (2013). *Human learned helplessness: A coping perspective.* New York: Springer Science & Business Media.

Milgram, S. (1973). The perils of obedience. *Harper's, 247*(1483), 62–77.

Miller, A. (1996). *Pupil behaviour and teacher culture.* London: Cassell.

Miller, D. T. (1999). The norm of self-interest. *American Psychologist, 54*(12), 1053. doi:10.1037/0003-066X.54.12.1053

Minkle, B., Bashir, A. S., & Sutulov, C. (2008). Peer consultation for mediators: The use of a holding environment to support mediator reflection, inquiry, and self-knowing. *Negotiation Journal*, *24*(3), 303–23. doi:10.1111/j.1571-9979.2008.00186.x

Mitra, R. (2013). From transformational leadership to leadership trans-formations: A critical dialogic perspective. *Communication Theory*, *23*(4), 395–416. doi:10.1111/comt.12022

Monbiot, G. (2021, August 27). Pegasus spyware is just the latest tool autocrats are using to stay in power. *The Guardian*. Retrieved from www.theguardian.com/commentisf ree/2021/jul/27/pegasus-spyware-autocrats-arsenal-spying

Morgan, G. (1998). *Images of organization*. Thousand Oaks: Sage.

Murphy, D., Duggan, M., & Joseph, S. (2012). Relationship-based social work and its compatibility with the person-centred approach: Principled versus instrumental perspectives. *The British Journal of Social Work*, *43*(4), 703–19. doi:10.1093/bjsw/bcs003

Murray, J., Farrington, D. P., Sekol, I., & Olsen, R. F. (2009). Effects of parental imprisonment on child antisocial behaviour and mental health: A systematic review. *Campbell Systematic Reviews*, *5*(1), 1–105. doi:10.4073/csr.2009.4

NAO. (2019). *Support for pupils with special educational needs and disabilities in England*. (HC 2636). London: NAO.

Nelson, H. L. (1992). Against caring. *Journal of Clinical Ethics*, *3*(1), 8–15.

Nespor, J. (1997). *Tangled up in school: Politics, space, bodies, and signs in the educational process*. New York: Routledge.

Newson, J. (1979). The growth of shared understandings between infant and caregiver. In M. Bullowa (Ed.), *Before Speech: The beginning of interpersonal communication* (pp. 207–22). Cambridge: Cambridge University Press.

Nicolaidou, M., & Ainscow, M. (2005). Understanding failing schools: Perspectives from the inside. *School Effectiveness and School Improvement*, *16*(3), 229–48. doi:10.1080/09243450500113647

Niemiec, C. P., & Ryan, R. M. (2009). Autonomy, competence, and relatedness in the classroom: Applying self-determination theory to educational practice. *Theory and Research in Education*, *7*(2), 133–44.

Nijhof, A., Wilderom, C., & Oost, M. (2012). Professional and institutional morality: Building ethics programmes on the dual loyalty of academic professionals. *Ethics and Education*, *7*(1), 91–109.

Ninković, S. R., & Knežević Florić, O. Č. (2016). Transformational school leadership and teacher self-efficacy as predictors of perceived collective teacher efficacy. *Educational Management Administration & Leadership*, *46*(1), 49–64. doi:10.1177/1741143216665842

Noddings, N. (1984). *Caring: A feminine approach to ethics and moral education*. Berkeley: University of California Press.

Noddings, N. (1990). A response. *Hypatia*, *5*(1), 120–6. doi:10.1111/j.1527-2001.1990.tb00396.x

Noddings, N. (2002). *Educating moral people: A caring alternative to character education*. Williston, VT: Teachers College Press.

Noddings, N. (2016). *Philosophy of education* (4th ed.). Boulder: Westview Press.

Nolan, A., & Moreland, N. (2014). The process of psychological consultation. *Educational Psychology in Practice*, *30*(1), 63–77. doi:10.1080/02667363.2013.873019

Nussbaum, M. C. (2003). Capabilities as fundamental entitlements: Sen and social justice. *Feminist Economics*, *9*, 33–59. doi:10.1080/1354570022000077926

Nussbaum, M. C. (2011). *Creating capabilities*. London: Harvard University Press.

Nussbaum, M. C. (2016). *Not for profit: Why democracy needs the humanities*. Woodstock: Princeton University Press.

Nussbaum, M. C. (2018). *The monarchy of fear: A philosopher looks at our political crisis*. Oxford: Oxford University Press.

OECD. (2020). *Pisa 2018 results*. Paris: OECD.

Ofsted. (2019). *The education inspection framework*. Manchester: Office for Standards in Education, Children's Services and Skills.

Oliverio, S. (2016). Hyphenated subjects, beyond the 'dialectal' Bildung. In A. Surian (Ed.), *Open spaces for interactions and learning diversities* (pp. 37–49). Rotterdam: Sense Publishers.

ONS. (2019). *Total wealth in Great Britain:April 2016 to March 2018*. London: ONS.

O'Reilly-Scanlon, K. (2000). *She's still on my mind: Teachers' memories, memory-work and self-study*. (DPhil in Educational Studies). McGill University.

Örtenblad, A. (2001). On differences between organizational learning and learning organization. *The learning organization, 8*(3), 125–33.

Overmier, J. B. (2002). On learned helplessness. *Integrative Physiological & Behavioral Science, 37*(1), 4–8. doi:10.1007/bf02688801

Ozga, J. (2009). Governing education through data in England: From regulation to self-evaluation. *Journal of Education Policy, 24*(2), 149–62. doi:10.1080/02680 930902733121

Pagán-Castaño, E., Sánchez-García, J., Garrigos-Simon, F. J., & Guijarro-García, M. (2021). The influence of management on teacher well-being and the development of sustainable schools. *Sustainability, 13*(5). Retrieved from www.mdpi.com/2071-1050/13/5/2909

Page, D. (2017a). Conceptualising the surveillance of teachers. *British Journal of Sociology of Education, 38*(7), 991–1006.

Page, D. (2017b). The surveillance of teachers and the simulation of teaching. *Journal of Education Policy, 32*(1), 1–13.

Pantaleo, S. (2007). Interthinking: Young children using language to think collectively during interactive read-alouds. *Early Childhood Education Journal, 34*(6), 439–47. doi:10.1007/s10643-007-0154-y

Papousek, M. (1995). Origins of reciprocity and mutuality in prelinguistic parent–infant "dialogues". In I. Markova, C. G. Graumann, C. F. Grauman, & K. Foppa (Eds.), *Mutualities in dialogue* (pp. 58–81). Cambridge: Cambridge University Press.

Parding, K., McGrath-Champ, S., & Stacey, M. (2017). Teachers, school choice and competition: Lock-in effects within and between sectors. *Policy Futures in Education, 15*(1), 113–28. doi:10.1177/1478210316688355

Parfit, D. (1984). *Reasons and persons*. Oxford: Oxford University Press.

Parsons, C., & Castle, F. (1998). The cost of school exclusion in England. *International Journal of Inclusive Education, 2*(4), 277–94. doi:10.1080/1360311980020402

Pattie, C., Hartman, T., & Johnston, R. (2019). A close-run thing? Accounting for changing overall turnout in UK general elections. *Representation, 55*(1), 101–16. doi:10.1080/00344893.2018.1555676

Patton, A., & Robin, J. (2012). *Work that matters – The teacher's guide to project-based learning*. London: Paul Hamlyn Foundation.

Peetz, T. (2015). Reforming school leadership: From primus inter pares to managers? In T. Klenk & E. Pavolinin (Eds.), *Restructuring welfare governance: Marketisation, managerialism and welfare state professionalism* (pp. 200–15). Cheltenham: Edward Elgar Publishing.

Pelletier, L. G., Séguin-Lévesque, C., & Legault, L. (2002). Pressure from above and pressure from below as determinants of teachers' motivation and teaching behaviors. *Journal of Educational Psychology, 94*(1), 186.

Penuel, W., Riel, M., Krause, A., & Frank, K. (2009). Analyzing teachers. *Teachers College Record, 111*(1), 124–63.

Perryman, J. (2006). Panoptic performativity and school inspection regimes: Disciplinary mechanisms and life under special measures. *Journal of Education Policy, 21*(2), 147–61. doi:10.1080/02680930500500138

Perryman, J. (2007). Inspection and emotion. *Cambridge Journal of Education, 37*(2), 173–90. doi:10.1080/03057640701372418

Philbrick-Linzmeyer, L. (2011). *In pursuit of equity: What happens when I share authority with students.* San Diego: High Tech High Graduate School of Education.

Pickett, K., & Wilkinson, R. (2009). *The spirit level: Why more equal societies almost always do better.* London: Allen Lane.

Pickett, K., & Wilkinson, R. (2015). Income inequality and health: A causal review. *Social Science & Medicine, 128*, 316–26. doi:10.1016/j.socscimed.2014.12.031

Pietarinen, J., Pyhältö, K., & Soini, T. (2016). Teacher's professional agency – A relational approach to teacher learning. *Learning: Research and Practice, 2*(2), 112–29. doi:10.1080/23735082.2016.1181196

Powell, B., & Gibbs, S. (2018). Behaviour and Learning: The Development of Staff Efficacy in One School. *International Journal of Whole Schooling, 14*(2), 63–82.

Powley, E. H., Fry, R. E., Barrett, F. J., & Bright, D. S. (2004). Dialogic democracy meets command and control: Transformation through the appreciative inquiry summit. *Academy of Management Perspectives, 18*(3), 67–80. doi:10.5465/ame.2004.14776170

Price, H. E. (2011). Principal–teacher interactions: How affective relationships shape principal and teacher attitudes. *Educational Administration Quarterly, 48*(1), 39–85. doi:10.1177/0013161X11417126

Priestley, M., Alvunger, D., Philippou, S., & Soini, T. (2021). *Curriculum making in Europe: Policy and practice within and across diverse contexts.* Bingley: Emerald Publishing Limited.

Priestley, M., Biesta, G., & Robinson, S. (2013). Teachers as agents of change: Teacher agency and emerging models of curriculum. In M. Priestley & G. Biesta (Eds.), *Reinventing the curriculum: New trends in curriculum policy and practice* (pp. 187–206). Bingley: Emerald.

Priestley, M., Biesta, G., & Robinson, S. (2015). *Teacher agency: An ecological approach.* London: Bloomsbury.

Raattkainen, P. (2005). On the philosophical relevance of Godel's incompleteness theorems. *Revue internationale de philosophie, 234*(4), 513–34.

Rata, E. (2016). A pedagogy of conceptual progression and the case for academic knowledge. *British Educational Research Journal, 42*(1), 168–84. doi:10.1002/berj.3195

Rawls, J. (1999). *A theory of justice.* Cambridge: Cambridge University Press.

Reay, D. (1998). Micro-politics in the 1990s: Staff relationships in secondary schooling. *Journal of Education Policy, 13*(2), 179–96. doi:10.1080/0268093980130202

Reback, R., Rockoff, J., & Schwartz, H. L. (2014). Under pressure: Job security, resource allocation, and productivity in schools under no child left behind. *American Economic Journal: Economic Policy, 6*(3), 207–41. doi:10.1257/pol.6.3.207

Reeves, J., & Forde, C. (2004). The social dynamics of changing practice. *Cambridge Journal of Education, 34*(1), 85–102.

Reicher, S. (2004). The context of social identity: Domination, resistance, and change. *Political Psychology, 25*(6), 921–45. doi:10.1111/j.1467-9221.2004.00403.x

Remer-Bollow, U., Bernhagen, P., & Rose, R. (2019). Partisan consequences of low turnout at elections to the European Parliament. *Electoral Studies, 59*, 87–98. doi:10.1016/j.electstud.2019.02.003

Renshaw, P. D. (2004). Dialogic learning teaching and instruction. In P. D. Renshaw & J. van den Linden (Eds.), *Dialogic learning* (pp. 1–15). Dordrecht: Kluwer Academic Publishers.

Ricoeur, P. (1992). *Oneself as another. 1990*. Chicago: The University of Chicago Press.

Ricoeur, P. (2020). *Philosophy, ethics, & politics*. Cambridge: Polity Press.

Rogers, C. R. (1995a). *On becoming a person: A therapist's view of psychotherapy*. Boston: Houghton Mifflin Harcourt.

Rogers, C. R. (1995b). *A way of being*. Boston: Houghton Mifflin Harcourt.

Rogers, D. L., & Babinski, L. M. (2002). *From isolation to conversation: Supporting new teachers' development*. New York: Suny Press.

Rogers, M., & Tannock, R. (2018). Are classrooms meeting the basic psychological needs of children with ADHD symptoms? A self-determination theory perspective. *Journal of Attention Disorders, 22*(14), 1354–60. doi:10.1177/1087054713508926

Rosenau, J. N. (1968). The concept of intervention. *Journal of International Affairs, 22*, 165–76. Retrieved from www.jstor.org/stable/24356536

Rosenau, J. N. (1969). Intervention as a scientific concept. *Journal of Conflict Resolution, 13*(2), 149–71. doi:10.1177/002200276901300201

Roth, G., Assor, A., Kanat-Maymon, Y., & Kaplan, H. (2007). Autonomous motivation for teaching: How self-determined teaching may lead to self-determined learning. *Journal of Educational Psychology, 99*(4), 761.

Roth, W.-M., & Lee, Y.-J. (2007). "Vygotsky's neglected legacy": Cultural-historical activity theory. *Review of Educational Research, 77*(2), 186–232.

Rousseau, D. M., Sitkin, S. B., Burt, R. S., & Camerer, C. (1998). Not so different after all: A cross-discipline view of trust. *Academy of Management Review, 23*(3), 393–404. doi:10.5465/amr.1998.926617

Ruble, L. A., Dalrymple, N. J., & McGrew, J. H. (2010). The effects of consultation on individualized education program outcomes for young children with autism: The collaborative model for promoting competence and success. *Journal of Early Intervention, 32*(4), 286–301. doi:10.1177/1053815110382973

Ryan, R. M., & Deci, E. L. (2000). Self-determination theory and the facilitation of intrinsic motivation, social development, and well-being. *American Psychologist, 55*(1), 68.

Sachs, J. (2001). Teacher professional identity: Competing discourses, competing outcomes. *Journal of Education Policy, 16*(2), 149–61. doi:10.1080/02680930116819

Sahlberg, P. (2015). *Finnish lessons 2.0: What can the world learn from educational change in Finland?* New York: Teachers College Press.

Salgado, J., & Clegg, J. W. (2011). Dialogism and the psyche: Bakhtin and contemporary psychology. *Culture & Psychology, 17*(4), 421–40.

Salgado, J., & Hermans, H. J. (2005). The return of subjectivity: From a multiplicity of selves to the dialogical self. *E-Journal of Applied Psychology: Clinical Section, 1*(1), 3–13.

Sampson, E. E. (1985). The decentralization of identity: Toward a revised concept of personal and social order. *American Psychologist, 40*(11), 1203–11. doi:10.1037/0003-066X.40.11.1203

Sampson, E. E. (2008). *Celebrating the other: A dialogic account of human nature.* Chagrin Falls: Taos Institute Publications.

Sannino, A. (2008). Sustaining a non-dominant activity in school: Only a utopia? *Journal of Educational Change, 9*(4), 329–38. doi:10.1007/s10833-008-9080-z

Savolainen, H., Engelbrecht, P., Nel, M., & Malinen, O.-P. (2012). Understanding teachers' attitudes and self-efficacy in inclusive education: Implications for pre-service and in-service teacher education. *European Journal of Special Needs Education, 27*(1), 51–68. doi:10.1080/08856257.2011.613603

Schein, E. H. (2003). On dialogue, culture, and organizational learning. *Reflections: The SoL Journal, 4*(4), 27–38. Retrieved from https://skat.ihmc.us/rid=122433 1576109_874999272_13863/Schein_On%20Dialogue%20Culture%20and%20 Org%20Learning.pdf

Schmitter, P. C., & Karl, T. L. (1991). What democracy is... and is not. *Journal of democracy, 2*(3), 75–88.

Schuller, B., Steidl, S., Batliner, A., Burkhardt, F., Devillers, L., Müller, C., & Narayanan, S. (2013). Paralinguistics in speech and language – State-of-the-art and the challenge. *Computer Speech & Language, 27*(1), 4–39. doi:10.1016/j.csl.2012.02.005

Seligman, M. E. (1972). Learned helplessness. *Annual Review of Medicine, 23*(1), 407–12.

Senge, P. (2006). *The fifth discipline* (2nd ed.). London: Random House.

Sheridan, S. M., Eagle, J. W., Cowan, R. J., & Mickelson, W. (2001). The effects of conjoint behavioral consultation results of a 4-year investigation. *Journal of School Psychology, 39*(5), 361–85. doi:10.1016/s0022-4405(01)00079-6

Sheridan, S. M., Welch, M., & Orme, S. F. (1996). Is consultation effective? A review of outcome research. *Remedial and Special Education, 17*(6), 341–54. doi:10.1177/ 074193259601700605

Shields, C. M. (2004). Dialogic leadership for social justice: Overcoming pathologies of silence. *Educational Administration Quarterly, 40*(1), 109–32. doi:10.1177/ 0013161X03258963

Shirley, D., Hargreaves, A., & Washington-Wangia, S. (2020). The sustainability and unsustainability of teachers' and leaders' well-being. *Teaching and Teacher Education, 92*, 1–12. doi:10.1016/j.tate.2019.102987

Shoji, K., Cieslak, R., Smoktunowicz, E., Rogala, A., Benight, C. C., & Luszczynska, A. (2016). Associations between job burnout and self-efficacy: A meta-analysis. *Anxiety, Stress, & Coping, 29*(4), 367–86. doi:10.1080/10615806.2015.1058369

Shotter, J. (2005). Acknowledging unique others: Ethics, "expressive realism," and social constructionism. *Journal of Constructivist Psychology, 18*(2), 103–30. doi:10.1080/ 10720530590914761

Shteynberg, G., Hirsh, J., Bentley, R. A., & Garthoff, J. (2020). Shared worlds and shared minds: A theory of collective learning and a psychology of common knowledge. *Psychological Review, 127*(5), 918–31. doi:10.1037/rev0000200

Sidorkin, A. M. (1999). *Beyond discourse: Education, the self, and dialogue.* New York: Suny Press.

Simkins, T., Coldwell, M., Caillau, I., Finlayson, H., & Morgan, A. (2006). Coaching as an in-school leadership development strategy: Experiences from leading from the middle. *Journal of In-Service Education, 32*(3), 321–40. doi:10.1080/13674580600841901

Simon, H. A. (1996). *The sciences of the artificial.* London: MIT press.

Singer, P. (1972). Famine, affluence, and morality. *Philosophy and Public Affairs, 1*(3), 229–43.

Singer, P. (1993). *Practical ethics* (2nd ed.). Cambridge: Cambridge University Press.

Skeie, G. (2002). The concept of plurality and its meaning for religious education. *British Journal of Religious Education, 25*(1), 47–59. doi:10.1080/0141620020250105

Skinner, B., Leavey, G., & Rothi, D. (2021). Managerialism and teacher professional identity: Impact on well-being among teachers in the UK. *Educational Review, 73*(1), 1–16. doi:10.1080/00131911.2018.1556205

Small, N., Raghavan, R., & Pawson, N. (2013). An ecological approach to seeking and utilising the views of young people with intellectual disabilities in transition planning. *Journal of Intellectual Disabilities, 17*(4), 283–300. doi:10.1177/1744629513500779

Smith, P. A., Hoy, W. K., & Sweetland, S. R. (2001). Organizational health of high schools and dimensions of faculty trust. *Journal of School Leadership, 11*(2), 135–51. doi:10.1177/105268460101100204

Smith, R. (2020). Misconceptions and misrepresentation: Challenging UK media reports of recent visits of UN special procedures. *Journal of Human Rights Practice, 12*(3), 781–94. doi:10.1093/jhuman/huaa043

Smullyan, R. (2017). Gödel's incompleteness theorems. In L. Gobel (Ed.), *The Blackwell guide to philosophical logic* (pp. 72–89). Oxford: Blackwell.

Smyth, J., Dow, A., Hattam, R., Reid, A., & Shacklock, G. (2000). *Teachers' work in a globalizing economy*. London: Falmer Press.

Solomon, R., & Flores, F. (2001). *Building trust: In business, politics, relationships, and life*. Oxford: Oxford University Press.

Somer, M., & McCoy, J. (2018). Transformations through polarizations and global threats to democracy. *The ANNALS of the American Academy of Political and Social Science, 681*(1), 8–22. doi:10.1177/0002716218818058

Spillane, J. P., Hopkins, M., & Sweet, T. M. (2015). Intra- and interschool interactions about instruction: Exploring the conditions for social capital development. *American Journal of Education, 122*(1), 71–110. doi:10.1086/683292

Spilt, J. L., Koomen, H. M. Y., & Thijs, J. T. (2011). Teacher wellbeing: The importance of teacher–student relationships. *Educational Psychology Review, 23*(4), 457–77. doi:10.1007/s10648-011-9170-y

Stansfeld, S. A., Rasul, F. R., Head, J., & Singleton, N. (2011). Occupation and mental health in a national UK survey. *Social Psychiatry and Psychiatric Epidemiology, 46*(2), 101–10. doi:10.1007/s00127-009-0173-7

Star, S. L., & Griesemer, J. R. (1989). Institutional ecology, translations' and boundary objects: Amateurs and professionals in Berkeley's Museum of Vertebrate Zoology, 1907-39. *Social Studies of Science, 19*(3), 387–420.

Stengel, B. S., & Weems, L. (2010). Questioning safe space: An introduction. *Studies in Philosophy and Education, 29*(6), 505–7. doi:10.1007/s11217-010-9205-8

Stenhouse, L. (1975). *An introduction to curriculum research and development*. London: Heinemann.

Stewart, J., Zediker, K. E., & Black, L. (2004). Relationships among philosophies of dialogue. In R. Anderson, L. Baxter, & K. Cissna (Eds.), *Dialogue: Theorizing difference in communication studies* (pp. 21–38). Thousand Oaks: Sage.

Strahan, C., Gibbs, S., & Reid, A. (2019). The psychological environment and teachers' collective-efficacy beliefs. *Educational Psychology in Practice, 35*(2), 147–64. doi:10.1080/02667363.2018.1547685

Stringer, P., Stow, L., Hibbert, K., Powell, J., & Louw, E. (1992). Establishing staff consultation groups in schools. *Educational Psychology in Practice, 8*(2), 87–96. doi:10.1080/0266736920080204

Suchman, L. (1993). Working relations of technology production and use. *Computer Supported Cooperative Work, 2*(1), 21–39.

Sugarman, J. (2015). Neoliberalism and psychological ethics. *Journal of Theoretical and Philosophical Psychology, 35*(2), 103. doi:10.1037/a0038960

Sugarman, J., & Thrift, E. (2017). Neoliberalism and the psychology of time. *Journal of Humanistic Psychology*, 0022167817716686.

Sullivan, A. L., Artiles, A. J., & Hernandez-Saca, D. I. (2015). Addressing special education inequity through systemic change: Contributions of ecologically based organizational consultation. *Journal of Educational and Psychological Consultation, 25*(2–3), 129–47. doi:10.1080/10474412.2014.929969

Surian, A. (2016). *Open spaces for interactions and learning diversities.* Rotterdam: Springer.

Szulevicz, T. (2018). Psychologists in (neoliberal) schools – what kind of marriage? *Integrative Psychological and Behavioral Science, 52*(3), 366–76. doi:10.1007/s12124-018-9444-8

Tajfel, H. (1981). *Human groups and social categories: Studies in social psychology.* Cambridge: Cambridge University Press.

Tajfel, H. (2010). *Social identity and intergroup relations.* Cambridge: Cambridge University Press.

Teague, L. (2020). Including 'difficult' students: Counter politics, play and liveability in the primary school classroom. *Discourse: Studies in the Cultural Politics of Education*, 1–13. doi:10.1080/01596306.2020.1835827

Thomas, G., Martin, R., Epitropaki, O., Guillaume, Y., & Lee, A. (2013). Social cognition in leader–follower relationships: Applying insights from relationship science to understanding relationship-based approaches to leadership. *Journal of Organizational Behavior, 34*(S1), S63–81. doi:10.1002/job.1889

Thomson, I. (2016). Rethinking education after Heidegger: Teaching learning as ontological response-ability. *Educational Philosophy and Theory, 48*(8), 846–61. doi:10.1080/00131857.2016.1165018

Tiplady, L. (2018). *Impacting on young people's emotional wellbeing through Forest School: The Breeze Project, pilot year.* Newcastle: Research Centre for Learning and Teaching; Newcastle University.

Todd, S. (2003). *Learning from the other: Levinas, psychoanalysis, and ethical possibilities in education.* Albany: SUNY Press.

Todd, S. (2015). *Toward an imperfect education: Facing humanity, rethinking cosmopolitanism.* New York: Routledge.

Tomlinson, S. (2001). *Education in a post welfare society.* Milton Keynes: Open University Press.

Towers, E. (2022). Why do headteachers stay in disadvantaged primary schools in London? *Leadership and Policy in Schools, 21*(2), 206–21. doi:10.1080/15700763.2020.1759651

Towler, C., Lofthouse, R., & Leat, D. (2011). *Comparing coaches' and senior managers' perceptions of how peer coaching interacts with performance management.* Paper presented at the British Educational Research Association Conference, University of London.

Trevarthen, C. (1979). Communication and cooperation in early infancy: A description of primary intersubjectivity. In M. Bullowa (Ed.), *Before speech: The beginning of interpersonal communication* (pp. 321–48). Cambridge: Cambridge University Press.

Trevarthen, C. (1998). *The concept and foundations of infant intersubjectivity* (S. Braten, Ed.). Cambridge: Cambridge University Press.

Trevarthen, C. (2009). The intersubjective psychobiology of human meaning: Learning of culture depends on interest for co-operative practical work–and affection for the joyful art of good company. *Psychoanalytic Dialogues, 19*(5), 507–18. doi:10.1080/10481880903231894

Trevarthen, C. (2015). Awareness of infants: What do they, and we, seek? *Psychoanalytic Inquiry, 35*(4), 395–416. doi:10.1080/07351690.2015.1022488

Trevarthen, C., & Aitken, K. J. (2001). Infant intersubjectivity: Research, theory, and clinical applications. *Journal of Child Psychology and Psychiatry, 42*(1), 3–48. doi:10.1111/1469-7610.00701

Trujillo, T. (2014). The modern cult of efficiency: Intermediary organizations and the new scientific management. *Educational Policy, 28*(2), 207–32. doi:10.1177/0895904813513148

Truscott, D. M., & Truscott, S. D. (2004). A professional development model for the positive practice of school-based reading consultation. *Psychology in the Schools, 41*(1), 51–65.

Trust, P. R. (2019). *Prison: The facts – Bromley Briefings Summer 2019*. London: Prison Reform Trust.

Tschacher, W., Rees, G. M., & Ramseyer, F. (2014). Nonverbal synchrony and affect in dyadic interactions. *Frontiers in Psychology, 5*(1323). doi:10.3389/fpsyg.2014.01323

Turing, A. M. (1950). Computing machinery and intelligence. *Mind, LIX*(236), 433–60. doi:10.1093/mind/LIX.236.433

Turner, J. C. (2010). Towards a cognitive redefinition of the social group. In H. Tajfel (Ed.), *Social identity and intergroup relations* (pp. 15–40). Cambridge: Cambridge University Press.

Tyler, M. (2019). Reassembling difference? Rethinking inclusion through/as embodied ethics. *Human Relations, 72*(1), 48–68.

Uitto, M., Lutovac, S., Jokikokko, K., & Kaasila, R. (2018). Recalling life-changing teachers: Positive memories of teacher-student relationships and the emotions involved. *International Journal of Educational Research, 87,* 47–56. doi:10.1016/j.ijer.2017.11.004

Vähäsantanen, K. (2015). Professional agency in the stream of change: Understanding educational change and teachers' professional identities. *Teaching and Teacher Education, 47,* 1–12. doi:10.1016/j.tate.2014.11.006

Valcea, S., Hamdani, M. R., Buckley, M. R., & Novicevic, M. M. (2011). Exploring the developmental potential of leader–follower interactions: A constructive-developmental approach. *The Leadership Quarterly, 22*(4), 604–15. doi:10.1016/j.leaqua.2011.05.003

Van der Riet, M. (2008). Participatory research and the philosophy of social science: Beyond the moral imperative. *Qualitative Inquiry, 14*(4), 546–65.

Van Hooser, P. (2013). *Leaders ought to know: 11 ground rules for common sense leadership.* Hoboken: John Wiley & Sons.

Vasterling, V. (2003). Postmodern hermeneutics? Towards a critical hermeneutics. In L. Code (Ed.), *Feminist interpretations of Hans-Georg Gadamer.* University Park: Pennsylvania State University Press.

Verhezen, P. (2010). Giving voice in a culture of silence. From a culture of compliance to a culture of integrity. *Journal of Business Ethics, 96*(2), 187–206. doi:10.1007/s10551-010-0458-5

Viel-Ruma, K., Houchins, D., Jolivette, K., & Benson, G. (2010). Efficacy beliefs of special educators: The relationships among collective efficacy, teacher self-efficacy, and job satisfaction. *Teacher Education and Special Education, 33*(3), 225–33.

Virkkunen, J., & Schaupp, M. (2011). From change to development: Expanding the concept of intervention. *Theory & Psychology, 21*(5), 629–55. doi:10.1177/0959354311417486

Vygotsky, L. S. (1962). *Thought and language.* Cambridge: MIT Press.

Vygotsky, L. S. (1978). *Mind in society: The development of higher psychological processes* (M. Cole, V. John-Steiner, S. Schribner, & E. Souberman, Eds.). London: Harvard University Press.

Wagner, A. C. (1987). Knots' in teachers' thinking. In J. Calderhead (Ed.), *Exploring teachers' thinking,* (pp. 161–78). London: Cassell.

Wagner, P. (2000). Consultation: Developing a comprehensive approach to service delivery. *Educational Psychology in Practice, 16*(1), 9–18. Retrieved from www.ingentaconnect.com/content/routledg/cepp/2000/00000016/00000001/art00002

Walton, G. M., & Brady, S. T. (2017). The many questions of belonging. In A. J. Elliot, C. S. Dweck, & D. S. Yeager (Eds.), *Handbook of competence and motivation: Theory and application* (pp. 272–93). New York: The Guilford Press.

Wang, C. L., & Ahmed, P. K. (2003). Organisational learning: A critical review. *The Learning Organization, 10*(1), 8–17.

Watson, C., & Gatti, S. N. (2012). Professional development through reflective consultation in early intervention. *Infants & Young Children, 25*(2), 109–21.

Webb, P. T. (2005). The anatomy of accountability. *Journal of Education Policy, 20*(2), 189–208.

Webb, R., Vulliamy, G., Sarja, A., Hämäläinen, S., & Poikonen, P. L. (2009). Professional learning communities and teacher well-being? A comparative analysis of primary schools in England and Finland. *Oxford Review of Education, 35*(3), 405–22. doi:10.1080/03054980902935008

Wegerif, R. (2007). *Dialogic education and technology: Expanding the space of learning* (Vol. 7). New York: Springer Science & Business Media.

Wegerif, R. (2008). Dialogic or dialectic? The significance of ontological assumptions in research on educational dialogue. *British Educational Research Journal, 34*(3), 347–61. Retrieved from www.jstor.org/stable/40375495

Wegerif, R. (2022). A dialogic approach to education for democratic values illustrated with an empirical study of the effect of internet-mediated dialogue across cultural differences. In P. Iyer & I. Bhattacharjee (Eds.), *Moral and political discourses in philosophy of education* (pp. 170–80). Abingdon: Routledge.

Williams, K., Papadopoulou, V., & Booth, N. (2012). *Prisoners' childhood and family backgrounds.* (4/12). London: Ministry of Justice.

Wood, D. (1998). *How children think and learn* (2nd ed.). Oxford: Blackwell.

Wood, D., Bruner, J. S., & Ross, G. (1976). The role of tutoring in problem solving. *Journal of Child Psychology and Psychiatry, 17*(2), 89–100. doi:10.1111/j.1469-7610.1976.tb00381.x

Woods, P., & Jeffrey, B. (2002). The reconstruction of primary teachers' identities. *British Journal of Sociology of Education, 23*(1), 89–106. doi:10.1080/01425690120102872

Young, I. M. (2002). *Inclusion and democracy.* Oxford: Oxford University Press.

Young, M. (2013). Overcoming the crisis in curriculum theory: A knowledge-based approach. *Journal of Curriculum Studies*, *45*(2), 101–18. doi:10.1080/00220272.2013.764505

Zancajo, A. (2020). Schools in the marketplace: Analysis of school supply responses in the Chilean education market. *Educational Policy*, *34*(1), 43–64. doi:10.1177/0895904819881781

Zembylas, M., & Barker, H. B. (2007). Teachers' spaces for coping with change in the context of a reform effort. *Journal of Educational Change*, *8*(3), 235–56. doi:10.1007/s10833-007-9025-y

# Index

Lightning Source UK Ltd.
Milton Keynes UK
UKHW021956131222
413893UK00006B/51